Communicate!

Text and Coursework Book for LCA English

ANGELA DOYLE

GILL & MACMILLAN

Gill & Macmillan Ltd
Hume Avenue
Park West
Dublin 12
with associated companies throughout the world
www.gillmacmillan.ie

Acknowledgments

For permission to reproduce copyright material, the author and publishers gratefully acknowledge the following:

Mercier Press Ltd for an extract from *Forty-Four Sycamore* by Bernard Farrell, and for an extract from *The Field* by John B. Keane;

Polygon for 'The Choosing' by Liz Lochhead from *Dreaming Frankenstein*;

'Going Nuts' by Paul McNulty from *Shooting From The Lip – Stories From Mayo's Young Writers*, compiled and edited by Ré Ó Laighléis and published by Mayo County Council, 2001;

Bloomsbury Publishing plc for an extract from *Lies of Silence* by Brian Moore;

David Higham Associates for 'Just Suppose There Was No TV' from *Charlie And The Chocolate Factory* by Roald Dahl, published by Penguin;

The Random House Group Ltd for an extract from *My Left Foot* by Christy Brown, published by Martin Secker & Warburg;

HarperCollins Publishers Ltd for an extract from *Angela's Ashes* by Frank McCourt © Frank McCourt 2002;

Methuen Publishing Ltd for an extract from 'The Germans' episode of *Fawlty Towers* by John Cleese and Connie Booth;

Nigel Gray for 'Adman';

Dover Publications for an extract from *Story Of My Life* by Helen Keller;

Wolfhound Press for an extract from *Pictures In My Head* by Gabriel Byrne;

Gillon Aitken Associates for 'Mother To Son' by Langston Hughes;

Henry Holt & Company, LLC, for 'A Time To Talk' by Robert Frost;

Warner Music Group for the lyrics to 'Fast Car' by Tracy Chapman, 'Ironic' by Alanis Morissette, and 'I Am A Rock' and 'Bridge Over Troubled Water' by Paul Simon;

Liam Ó Muirthile for 'In The Café' ('Sa Chaifé').

Images reproduced courtesy of Camera Press, Kobal, David Sleator/The Irish Times and Novosti (London).

For permission to reproduce material on the accompanying CD, grateful acknowledgment is made to the following:

MVD Music and Video Distribution GMDH for permission to use recorded extracts from *Pictures At An Exhibition* by Mussorgsky on Naxos CD 8.550051 (Slovak Philharmonic Orchestra/Daniel Nazareth);

Estate of Martin Luther King Jnr for speech by Dr Martin Luther King ('I Have A Dream') – live recording from the CD *A Call To Conscience* (Time Warner Audio Books);

National Broadcasting Company for recording of *Three Skeleton Key* from the series 'Escape' (17 March 1950), narrated by Vincent Price, written by George Toudouze.

Milan Records/BMG for recording from 'From *Citizen Kane* to *Taxi Driver*, Elmer Bernstein conducts the Royal Philharmonic Orchestra, Bernard Herrmann Film Scores' 7 3138 - 356443 - 2 1.

The publishers have made every effort to trace copyright holders, but if they have inadvertently overlooked any they will be pleased to make the necessary arrangements at the first opportunity.

■ CONTENTS ■ ■ ■ ■ ■ ■ ■ ■

■ Module 4: Critical Literacy and Composition   230

*To all Leaving Certificate Applied
students who have passed
through Pobalscoil
Chiarain, Kells,
since 1996.*

■ CD Track Listing

Unit 1

Introduction to Communication

One of the most basic needs of human beings is the need to communicate with others. In his autobiography *My Left Foot*, Christy Brown vividly brings home to us the importance of communication. Christy was born in 1932 and suffered from cerebral palsy – he was unable to control his muscular movements with the result that his body was either very tensed or very relaxed, his arms and legs twisting and moving in spite of him. He could not control his facial muscles and so was unable to talk. Doctors told his parents that he was a hopeless case, that he was mentally as well as physically defective. His mother refused to give up on him; she was convinced that inside the twisted body there was a mind that was normal. She would spend hours talking to him, reading to him and showing him pictures. The following extract describes the moment when Christy, aged five, proves his mother right.

1   I was lonely, imprisoned in a world of my own, unable to communicate with others, cut off, separated from them as though a glass wall stood between my existence and theirs, thrusting me beyond the sphere of their lives and activities. I longed to run about and play with the rest, but I was unable to break loose from my bondage.

2   Then, suddenly, it happened! In a moment everything was changed, my future life moulded into a definite shape, my mother's faith in me rewarded and her secret fear changed into open triumph.

3   It happened so quickly, so simply after all the years of waiting and uncertainty that

1

I can see and feel the whole scene as if it happened last week. It was the afternoon of a cold, grey December day. The streets outside glistened with snow; the white sparkling flakes stuck and melted on the window-panes and hung on the boughs of the trees like molten silver. The wind howled dismally, whipping up little whirling columns of snow that rose and fell at every fresh gust. And over all, the dull, murky sky stretched like a dark canopy, a vast infinity of greyness.

4 Inside, all the family were gathered around the big kitchen fire that lit up the little room with a warm glow and made giant shadows dance on the walls and ceiling.

5 In a corner Mona and Paddy were sitting huddled together, a few torn school primers before them. They were writing down little sums onto an old chipped slate, using a bright piece of yellow chalk. I was close to them, propped up by a few pillows against the wall, watching.

6 It was the chalk that attracted me so much. It was a long, slender stick of vivid yellow. I had never seen anything like it before, and it showed up so well against the black surface of the slate that I was fascinated by it as much as if it had been a stick of gold.

7 Suddenly I wanted desperately to do what my sister was doing. Then – without thinking or knowing exactly what I was doing, I reached out and took the stick of chalk out of my sister's hand – *with my left foot.*

8 I do not know why I used my left foot to do this. It is a puzzle to many people as well as to myself, for, although I had displayed a curious interest in my toes at an early age, I had never attempted before this to use either of my feet in any way. They could have been as useless to me as were my hands. That day, however, my left foot, apparently of its own volition, reached out and very impolitely took the chalk out of my sister's hand.

9 I held it tightly between my toes, and, acting on an impulse, made a wild sort of scribble with it on the slate. Next moment I stopped, a bit dazed, surprised, looking down at the stick of yellow chalk stuck between my toes, not knowing what to do with it next, hardly knowing how it got there. Then I looked up and became aware that everyone had stopped talking and was staring at me silently. Nobody stirred. Mona, her black curls framing her chubby little face, stared at me with great big eyes and open mouth. Across the open hearth, his face lit by flames, sat my father, leaning forward, hands outspread on his knees, his shoulders tense. I felt the sweat break out on my forehead.

10 My mother came in from the pantry with a steaming pot in her hand. She stopped midway between the table and the fire, feeling the tension flow through the room. She followed their stare and saw me, in the corner. Her eyes looked from my face down to my foot, with the chalk gripped between my toes. She put down the pot.

11 Then she crossed over to me and knelt down beside me, as she had done so many times before.
'I'll show you what to do with it, Chris,' she said, very slowly and in a queer, jerky way, her face flushed as if with some inner excitement.

12 Taking another piece of chalk from Mona, she hesitated, then very deliberately drew, on the floor in front of me, *the single letter 'A'.*
'Copy that,' she said, looking steadily at me. 'Copy it, Christy.'
I couldn't.

13 I looked about me, looked around at the faces that were turned towards me, tense, excited faces that were at that moment frozen, immobile, eager, waiting for a miracle in their midst.

14   The stillness was profound. The room was full of flame and shadow that danced before my eyes and lulled my taut nerves into a sort of waking sleep. I could hear the sound of the water-tap dripping in the pantry, the loud ticking of the clock on the mantelshelf, and the soft hiss and crackle of the logs on the open hearth.

15   I tried again. I put out my foot and made a wild jerking stab with the chalk which produced a very crooked line and nothing more. Mother held the slate steady for me. 'Try again, Chris,' she whispered in my ear. 'Again.'

16   I did, I stiffened my body and put my left foot out again, for the third time. I drew one side of the letter. I drew half the other side. Then the stick of chalk broke and I was left with a stump. I wanted to fling it away and give up. Then I felt my mother's hand on my shoulder. I tried once more. Out went my foot. I shook, I sweated and strained every muscle. My hands were so tightly clenched that my fingernails bit into the flesh. I set my teeth so hard that I nearly pierced my lower lip. Everything in the room swam till the faces around me were mere patches of white. But – I drew it – the letter 'A'. There it was on the floor before me. Shaky, with awkward, wobbly sides and a very uneven centre line. But it was the letter 'A'. I looked up. I saw my mother's face for a moment, tears on her cheeks. Then my father stooped down and hoisted me on to his shoulder.

17   I had done it! It had started – the thing that was to give my mind its chance of expressing itself. True, I couldn't speak with my lips, but now I would speak through something more lasting than spoken words – written words.

18   That one letter, scrawled on the floor with a broken bit of yellow chalk gripped between my toes, was my road to a new world, my key to mental freedom. It was to provide a source of relaxation to the tense, taut thing that was me which panted for expression behind a twisted mouth.

Extract from *My Left Foot* by Christy Brown

FOR DISCUSSION

1. How does Christy describe for us the kind of life he had up to the age of five? (Paragraph 1)

2. What do you think of his description of the scene in paragraphs 3, 4, 5 and 6? Can you remember events that took place when you were five? Why, in your opinion, does he remember that evening so clearly?

3. How does he describe the tension in the room as his family watch and wait? (Look at paragraphs 9 to 14.)

4. How do you think his mother was feeling when she told him to copy the letter 'A'?

5. Christy made several attempts to copy the letter. How important, do you think, was his mother to him as he made these attempts? Could he have done it without her?

6. When he finally succeeded, how did his mother react? Can you try to describe her emotions or feelings?

7. At the end of the extract Christy says that this one letter, scrawled on the floor, was his road to 'a new world'. What, do you think, does he mean by this? (Look at the last two paragraphs.)

What exactly do we mean by COMMUNICATION, and why do we need to study it? After all, we have been communicating quite successfully since the day we were born.

As newborn babies, we managed to communicate to those caring for us if we were hungry, cold or unhappy. We could also communicate feelings of happiness and wellbeing. Our parents had to be able to read the signs and respond to our needs long before we could *tell* them what was wrong. This ability to communicate so efficiently was essential for our very survival; and all this before we learned how to speak!

Communication is as much a part of our daily lives as are sleeping and eating. Communication is:
• talking to one another
• listening to the radio
• sending text messages
Make a list of other examples.

1. ___watching T.V_____
   ___writing letters to others_____

2. _____
   _____

3. _____
   _____

4. _____

_____

5. _____

_____

Because communicating is an activity that comes naturally to us, there is a danger that we simply take it for granted. We need to examine how effective we are at communicating, both at work and in our personal lives. Good communication is a skill that we can improve on once we understand a little bit about it and how it works. Give some reasons why it is important for us to improve our communication skills.

1. *We could improve our chances at job interviews.*

2. _____

_____

3. _____

_____

4. _____

_____

5. _____

_____

In the modern world there is a great deal of emphasis on communication; we hear the word used many times each day in different situations; we hear phrases such as 'lack of communication' or 'failure to communicate'.

Relationships are said to fail because the people involved stop communicating – you just have to look at the problem page of any magazine to see examples of this. In 'soaps' misunderstandings often occur because the characters 'get their wires crossed' in some way.

Think of your favourite soap and identify characters whose relationship has broken down due to lack of communication.

Disputes in the workplace between management and workers often lead to strikes. Very often one side accuses the other of not listening to their side of the story.

So, what exactly do we mean by COMMUNICATION? Since you woke up this morning you have been communicating – you have been SENDING MESSAGES. List some examples of how you have communicated with others today:

1. _____

_____

2. _____

_____

3. _____

_____

4. _____

_____

5. _____

_____

Also, other people have been communicating with you – you have been RECEIVING MESSAGES. List some examples of messages you have received today:

1. _____

_____

2. _____

_____

3. _____

_____

4. _____

_____

5. _____

_____

■ Communication is a Two-Way Process

For communication to take place we need a SENDER and a RECEIVER.

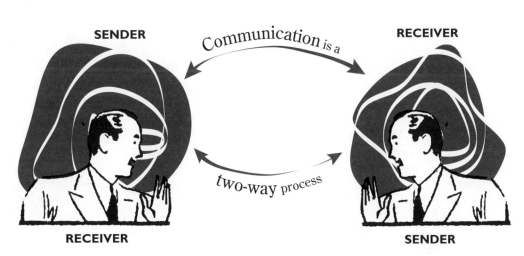

COMMUNICATION

The SENDER is	*The RECEIVER is*
the person who sends a message	the person who gets the message
the teacher who gives an instruction	the pupil who listens to the teacher
the newsreader or DJ on the radio	the radio audience
the sports writer in the daily newspaper	the newspaper reader

Give some more examples:

SENDER

1. _____

_____

2. _____

_____

3. _____

_____

4. _____

_____

5. _____

_____

RECEIVER

_____

_____

_____

_____

_____

_____

_____

_____

_____

_____

The roles of SENDER and RECEIVER are always changing. In most communications, the sender is also a receiver and the receiver is a sender. For example, if we are having a conversation with a friend, we are both SPEAKING (sending messages) and LISTENING (receiving messages). The roles are constantly changing – a bit like a game of tennis. Look again at your lists. How many of your examples involved two-way communication?

Now we need to look at the different ways in which we communicate – the physical means of sending a message. How many can you list?

8

1. Speaking

2. _____

3. _____

4. _____

5. _____

6. _____

7. _____

8. _____

9. _____

10. _____

You have listed the different channels of communication. The CHANNEL is the means by which a message is sent. For example, a television channel is the band of frequencies used to transmit programmes.

Group the channels of communication into two sections – WRITTEN and VERBAL. Add more channels as they come to mind.

WRITTEN

Writing a letter

_____

_____

_____

_____

_____

VERBAL

Talking face to face

_____

_____

_____

_____

_____

■ *Barriers to Communication*

If you try to send a message but nobody receives it communication has not happened. Does the phrase 'I might as well be talking to the wall' ring a bell? What does this phrase mean?

Anything that prevents a message from being received, or makes a message difficult to understand, is called NOISE. For example, if you put an urgent message for your boss on a crowded, untidy desk, he will probably not notice it – this is noise.

What other factors can stop a message from being received? Remember, noise may be the fault of the sender, the receiver or the channel.

1. Receiver not listening

2. An uncomfortable chair at a meeting

3. Bad phone line

4. _____

5. _____

6. _____

7. _____

8. _____

9. _____

10. _____

■ *Message Received and Understood*

When the receiver gets the message he usually responds in some way – list some of the things he might do.

1. Send back some information

2. Ask for an explanation of some points

3. _____

4. _____

5. _____

6. _____

7. _____

8. _____

9. _____

10. _____

This response to a message is called FEEDBACK. For example, when your boss at work explains to you how a particular machine works, he might ask if you understand what he has said. He is looking for feedback. We should always look for feedback, otherwise we have no way of knowing that our message has been received. Remember, **communication is a two-way process.**

■ Recap on key terms

Explain each of the following terms and give an example of each one:

SENDER _____

_____

RECEIVER _____

_____

MESSAGE _____

_____

CHANNEL _____

_____

NOISE/BARRIER _____

_____

FEEDBACK _____

_____

We have now looked at all the elements of communication. Write your own definition of communication in the space below:

_____

_____

_____

★ EXERCISES

1. Collect examples of good and bad communication for discussion in class. You may use as many different channels as you wish: letters, advertisements, posters, photographs, audiotapes, videotapes and newspaper articles.

   In class examine some of the examples of good (effective) communication and bad (ineffective) communication. In pairs, discuss what made these examples effective or ineffective. In the case of the ineffective examples make suggestions as to how they could be improved.

Example 1: *Effective Communication*

Describe the communication.

_____

_____

_____

Why did it work?

_____

_____

_____

Example 2: *Ineffective Communication*

Describe the communication.

_____

_____

_____

Why did it not work?

_____

_____

_____

How would you improve it?

_____

_____

_____

Share your findings with the rest of the class.

2. How effective is the communication system in your school? A good communication system is essential for the efficient running of any organisation. No matter how large or

small your school or centre is, it would be plunged into chaos if the communication system broke down.

Below is a list of different groups of people, both *inside* and *outside* the school, that your school principal has to communicate with. Complete the list by filling in the methods of communication used in each case.

INTERNAL (inside the school)	METHODS USED
1. Students	(a) Timetable
	(b) _____
	(c) _____
2. Teaching staff	(a) _____
	(b) _____
	(c) _____

EXTERNAL (outside the school)	
1. Parents	(a) Letter
	(b) _____
	(c) _____
2. Department of Education	(a) _____
	(b) _____
	(c) _____
3. The local community	(a) _____
	(b) _____
	(c) _____

With a partner, look in detail at the communication between the **principal** and **students** in your school. Discuss the following:

(i) Are the methods of communication used effective?

(ii) Can you suggest improvements?

(iii) Can you give an example of a communication breakdown in your school? What were the consequences?

Do not be afraid to criticise what you see as a lack of communication. Share your thoughts with the class.

3. With a partner work on one communication exercise from the list below. Before starting this exercise you need to ask yourself the following questions:
   - *Who* do I need to communicate with?
   - What *information* do I need to communicate?
   - Which *channel* will I use?
   - Do I need *feedback*? How will I receive feedback?
   - What *noise* might interfere with my message? How can I avoid this?
   (i) Your sister has asked you to help her with the design and wording of the invitations for her wedding.
   (ii) You need to write an announcement to be read over the school intercom regarding a sporting event.
   (iii) You are organising a charity concert in the town and you need to send a notice to the local radio station.
   (iv) You need to write a letter to a visitor who is visiting your class next week. You need to give him all the information he needs, including directions.
   (v) You are trying to sell a second-hand car. Write out the advertisement you would place in the local paper.
   At the end of fifteen minutes each group presents their finished product to the class. These should be displayed so that the class can examine each one carefully, noting the good points and suggesting improvements.

■ A World Without Communication

When she was two years old Helen Keller became ill and was left blind and deaf. For the next five years she grew up in a world of darkness, unable to communicate with anyone. This story tells of her first meeting with Anne Sullivan, the person who would change her whole life by teaching her how to communicate.

■ *Helen Keller and Anne Sullivan*

1 The most important day I remember in all my life is the one on which my teacher, Anne Mansfield Sullivan, came to me. I am filled with wonder when I consider the immeasurable contrasts between the two lives which it connects. It was the third of March, 1887, three months before I was seven years old.

2 On the afternoon of that eventful day, I stood on the porch, dumb and expectant. I guessed vaguely from my mother's signs and from the hurrying to and fro in the house that something unusual was about to happen, so I went to the door and waited on the steps. The afternoon sun penetrated the mass of honeysuckle that covered the porch, and fell on my upturned face. My fingers lingered almost unconsciously on the

familiar leaves and blossoms which had just come forth to greet the sweet Southern spring. Anger and bitterness had preyed upon me continually for weeks and a deep languor had succeeded this passionate struggle.

3   Have you ever been at sea in a dense fog, when it seemed as if a tangible white darkness shut you in, and the great ship, tense and anxious, groped her way toward the shore with plummet and sounding-line, and you waited with beating heart for something to happen? I was like that ship before my education began, only I was without compass or sounding-line, and had no way of knowing how near the harbour was. 'Light! Give me light!' was the wordless cry of my soul, and the light of love shone on me in that very hour.

4   I felt approaching footsteps. I stretched out my hand as I supposed it was my mother. Someone took it, and I was caught up and held close in the arms of her who had come to reveal all things to me, and, more than all things else, to love me.

5   The morning after my teacher came she led me into her room and gave me a doll. The little blind children at Perkins Institution had sent it and Laura Bridgman had dressed it; but I did not know this until afterward. When I played with it a little while, Miss Sullivan slowly spelled into my hand the word 'd-o-l-l'. I was at once interested in this finger play and tried to imitate it. When I finally succeeded in making the letters correctly I was flushed with childish pleasure and pride. Running downstairs to my mother I held up my hand and made the letters for doll. I did not know that I was spelling a word or even that words existed; I was simply making my fingers go in monkey-like imitation. In the days that followed I learned to spell in this uncomprehending way a great many words, among them pin, hat, cup, and a few verbs like sit, stand and walk. But my teacher had been with me several weeks before I understood that everything has a name.

6   One day, while I was playing with my new doll, Miss Sullivan put my big rag doll into my lap also, spelled 'd-o-l-l' and tried to make me understand that 'd-o-l-l' applied to both. Earlier in the day we had had a tussle over the words 'm-u-g' and 'w-a-t-e-r'. Miss Sullivan had tried to impress it upon me that 'm-u-g' is mug and that 'w-a-t-e-r' is water, but I persisted in confounding the two. In despair she had dropped the subject for the time, only to renew it at the first opportunity. I became impatient at her repeated attempts and, seizing the new doll, I dashed it upon the floor. I was keenly delighted when I felt the fragments of the broken doll at my feet. Neither sorrow nor regret followed my passionate outburst. I had not loved the doll. In the still, dark world in which I lived there was no strong sentiment or tenderness. I felt my teacher sweep the fragments to one side of the hearth, and I had a sense of satisfaction that the cause of my discomfort was removed. She brought me my hat, and I knew I was going out into the warm sunshine. This thought, if a wordless sensation can be called a thought, made me hop and skip with pleasure.

7   We walked down the path to the well-house, attracted by the fragrance of the honeysuckle with which it was covered. Someone was drawing water and my teacher placed my hand under the spout. As the cool stream gushed over one hand she spelled into the other the word water, first slowly and then rapidly. I stood still, my whole attention fixed upon the motions of her fingers. Suddenly I felt a misty consciousness as of something forgotten – a thrill of returning thought; and somehow the mystery of language was revealed to me. I knew then that 'w-a-t-e-r' meant the wonderful cool

something that was flowing over my hand. That living word awakened my soul, gave it light, hope, joy, set it free! There were barriers still, it is true, but barriers that could in time be swept away.

I left the well-house eager to learn. Everything had a name, and each name gave birth to a new thought. As we returned to the house, every object that I touched seemed to quiver with life. That was because I saw everything with the strange, new sight that had come to me. On entering the door I remembered the doll I had broken. I felt my way to the hearth and picked up the pieces. I tried vainly to put them together. Then my eyes filled with tears; for the first time I felt repentance and sorrow.

8   I learned a great many new words that day. I do not remember what they all were; but I do know that mother, father, sister, teacher were among them – words that were to make the world blossom for me, 'like Aaron's rod, with flowers'. It would have been difficult to find a happier child than I was as I lay in my crib at the close of that eventful day and lived over the joys it had brought me, and for the first time longed for a new day to come.

(Helen went on to graduate from University. She devoted her life to teaching and giving hope to the deaf blind, as her teacher had done.)

FOR DISCUSSION

1. Helen was a young child of seven, without sight or hearing. She explored the world around her through her other senses such as smell and touch. Find examples of this in paragraphs 2, 6 and 7.

2. In paragraph 3 Helen gives us a very powerful description of how she felt in her dark world, almost completely cut off from the outside world, unable to communicate. To what does she compare herself? Do you think it is a good comparison?

3. In paragraph 4 Helen meets her teacher for the first time. How would you describe Anne Sullivan? What qualities do you think she had?

4. In paragraph 6 Helen becomes frustrated and breaks her doll. What caused this feeling of frustration? How did Anne Sullivan cope with the situation?

5. At the end of paragraph 6 Helen writes 'I knew I was going out into the warm sunshine. This thought, *if a wordless sensation can be called a thought*, made me hop and skip with pleasure.'

   Helen did not have language. Therefore, she could not formulate thoughts – the never-ending stream of ideas and reflections that go through our minds constantly. This is communication in its most basic form and it is called Intrapersonal Communication – it goes on within us all the time and we cannot stop it.

   How did Helen describe the 'thoughts' she was capable of before she learned words?

6. Try to imagine what it must have been like for Helen in her 'still, dark world'. What emotions did she feel?

■ Body Language or Non-Verbal Communication

So far, we have concentrated on VERBAL and WRITTEN forms of communication. There is a third form of communication, which is very powerful – NON-VERBAL COMMUNICATION, or communication without words.

We are constantly sending messages to others through our body language. Our body language can either reinforce or contradict what we are saying; body language is a powerful way of sending messages about our attitudes and feelings. We need to be aware of our own body language, both in the workplace and in our personal lives. An understanding of body language can also help us to understand better what others are thinking and feeling.

Some types of non-verbal communication are learned in a formal way, for example the sign language used by people whose hearing and speech are impaired.

In certain situations signals can replace speech when speech is impossible. The floor manager in a television studio, for example, will use hand signals to count down the seconds before going on air. Can you think of other workers or groups who might use signals?

1. Divers

2. _____

3. _____

4. _____

5. _____

In this section we are mainly interested in the study of body language that has *not* been learned in a formal way, but which we use all the time. While you are studying this section get into the habit of thinking about your own body language and the signals you are sending out. Observe the body language of those around you and try to DECODE what they are really feeling and thinking. Before we start, see how many examples of body language you can come up with by just looking around the room.

BODY LANGUAGE   *MEANING*

1. _____   _____

2. _____   _____

3. _____   _____

4. _____   _____

5. _____   _____

Think about your own ability to 'read' the body language of others. If you can answer 'yes' to all of the following questions you are probably quite good at decoding body language!

1. Do you know when someone is not being honest with you?
2. Can you tell when someone is in a bad mood by just looking at them?
3. Can you tell when someone is attracted to you?
4. Can you tell when someone is losing interest in you?
5. Are your first impressions of people usually correct?
6. Are you good at picking the right moment to ask for a favour?

Can you describe a situation where you did not read the body language correctly and 'put your foot in it'?

We can look at non-verbal communication or body language under the following headings:

• Gestures
• Appearance
• Posture
• Facial expressions
• Eye contact
• Touch
• Personal space

■ Gestures

Below is a list of common gestures. Beside each one write in the meaning.

GESTURES   MEANING

Thumb up   _____

Shrug shoulders   _____

Point   _____

Extend hand   _____

Raise hand _____

Shake hand _____

Shake fist _____

What gestures would we use to communicate the following?

MEANING	GESTURE
I'm hungry	_____
Goodbye	_____
I'm bored	_____
I can't wait for . . .	_____
You played brilliantly	_____
That will not work	_____

When we are speaking we tend to use gestures. If you study your teachers you will notice that they use their hands a lot to emphasise what they are saying.

■ *Appearance*

Appearance includes our clothes, hairstyle, jewellery, tattoos, height and weight.

The clothes we wear send out signals to others. They are a projection of our personality; they make a statement about how we see ourselves. People in the public eye, such as politicians, know they are judged on appearance, and many will consult with 'image consultants' to find out which colours and styles suit them best. They may not be able to do anything about their height and weight, but they can learn how to present themselves in the most flattering way possible. Politicians will be trying to project themselves as intelligent, self-confident and serious.

★ EXERCISE

Think of your favourite pop star and describe his or her appearance. What kind of image is he or she trying to project?

However, it is not just public figures who are aware of the importance of appearance. Study the following advertisement for an evening class. What group of people is the advertisement aimed at?

> ## A NEW IMAGE BY 'COLOUR ME BEAUTIFUL' CONSULTANT
>
> *Colour Me Beautiful is for people who know they don't look as great as they could and want to make the best of themselves.*
>
> *Some want a dramatic new look, while others want to take their image changes one step at a time.*
>
> *This course deals with style, colour, make-up – the whole current look.*

 # FOR DISCUSSION

1. If our politicians were to dress in casual clothes such as shorts, tracksuits and baseball caps, would we find it difficult to take them seriously? Why/why not?
2. Women in business sometimes 'power dress'. What do you understand by this term? Why do you think some women dress in this way?
3. What does the wearing of animal fur tell us about a person? Is it fashionable to wear fur at the moment? Why/why not?
4. What do you understand by the terms 'fashion statement' and 'fashion victim'?
5. Think about the clothes you wear outside of school. What factors influence you when you are buying clothes?

    (a) I want to be different from (or the same as) everybody else

    (b) _____

    (c) _____

    (d) _____

    (e) _____

6. What kind of signals do you think your clothes send out?

(a) I have a mind of my own (or I don't want to stand out from the crowd)

(b) _____

(c) _____

(d) _____

(e) _____

7. We must also remember that the clothes we wear will vary with the context or occasion – clothes that are suitable for a twenty-first birthday party may not be suitable for a job interview! The clothes we wear should respect the people we are with. Give some examples.

(a) _____

(b) _____

(c) _____

(d) _____

(e) _____

8. Many organisations such as banks, airlines and shops require their employees to wear uniforms. Why do you think they do this?

9. Set out the main arguments for and against the wearing of school uniforms.

10. If you were asked to design a uniform for the pupils of your school, what things would you take into account?

(a) Cost

(b) _____

(c) _____

(d) _____

(e) _____

11. In pairs, come up with a design for a new uniform. Imagine that you are trying to convince the Board of Management to choose your design; write out the arguments you would use to persuade them.

12. In courtrooms, judges and barristers wear wigs and gowns. Why do you think they do this?

13. Our hairstyles can be changed very easily, often with dramatic effect. We tend to associate certain hairstyles with certain attitudes. Can you give some examples?

STYLE	ATTITUDE
(a) shaven head	_____
(b) _____	_____
(c) _____	_____
(d) _____	_____
(e) _____	_____

■ *Body Adornments*

In addition to our clothes we use *accessories* and *body adornments* to complete the picture.

For example, look around at the bags which students bring to school. Can you identify the 'images' which students are trying to project?

Glasses are an accessory which bring mixed responses. Designer spectacles have become a fashion accessory – we are constantly being reminded of this by advertisements. Some people like them as they feel they make them look intelligent and serious; others will spend a fortune and go through a lot of discomfort in order to wear contact lenses.

FOR DISCUSSION

Is it fair to make assumptions about people based on their appearance? For example, body piercings and tattoos seem to send out very powerful messages. People who wear them tend to be 'labelled' or stereotyped by those in authority as rebels and troublemakers.

■ *Posture*

Posture refers to the way we sit, stand and walk. Through our posture we can communicate how we are feeling about ourselves, and how we feel towards others.

Two volunteers, please! Student A will play the role of a person who is full of confidence, while Student B will play the role of a person with low self-esteem.

The volunteers are asked to leave the room. They will re-enter the room, one at a time, walk to a chair and sit down. Describe the body language carefully.

STUDENT A

1. _____
2. _____
3. _____
4. _____
5. _____

STUDENT B

_____
_____
_____
_____
_____

If you were meeting these people for the first time, what impressions would you form?

STUDENT A

_____

_____

_____

_____

_____

_____

_____

STUDENT B

_____

_____

_____

_____

_____

_____

_____

■ *Facial Expression*

In our everyday language we use phrases like 'trying to keep a straight face' or 'she put on a brave face'. The human face is capable of a great number of different expressions. If we are trying to hide our true feelings in a situation, it is our facial expression that will usually let us down. It is almost impossible to hide feelings of hurt or surprise, for example, and our facial expressions will usually give quite accurate information about how we are feeling.

At this point it would be very useful if a volunteer from the class could 'make faces'. The volunteer should write down for the teacher what emotion he is going to show. The rest of the class will try and identify the emotion correctly.

✱ EXERCISES

1. Think of all the parts of the face that are able to move independently, such as the mouth, forehead, eyes, eyebrows, eyelids. Bear in mind other factors such as skin colour (pale or flushed), sweat, etc.

   Remember, in our everyday speech, we use phrases that describe body language very well:
   • 'his eyes were popping out of his head'
   • 'he gritted his teeth'
   • 'his jaw dropped'
   • 'his mouth dropped open'
   • 'he was purple with rage'
   • 'he could not look me straight in the face'

   Sketch the human face to show each of the following emotions or feelings:

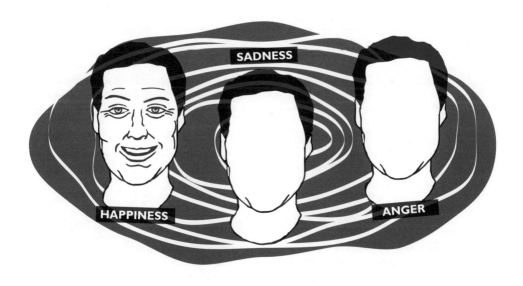

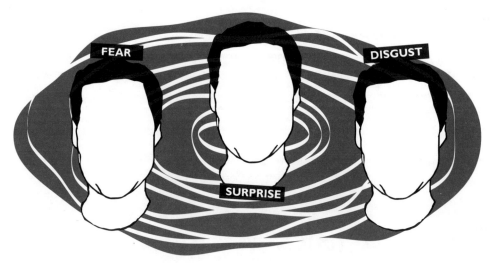

2. Collect pictures of people, individuals or groups, from newspapers or magazines. Choose your pictures carefully, including as many different facial expressions as possible. Identify the emotions or feelings revealed in the pictures.

3. Record some television advertisements that rely on facial expression and other forms of body language to get their message across. View these in class and discuss their effectiveness.

4. Examine a short clip of a programme such as *Mr. Bean*, and identify examples of non-verbal communication used by the characters. How do the characters manage to communicate while using only limited dialogue?

(a) Facial expression

(b) _____

(c) _____

(d) _____

(e) _____

Could you identify the feelings or emotions being communicated?

(a) _____

(b) _____

(c) _____

(d) _____

(e) _____

5. Watch part of a drama or film with the sound turned down. You probably will be able to answer the following questions without too much difficulty!
   (a) What is the general storyline?
   (b) What is the relationship between the characters?

(c) Can you identify the feelings being communicated?

(d) Which character is the stronger or more dominant one? How do you know?

(e) Which character do you prefer? Why?

6. Get into the habit of studying non-verbal communication when watching TV. In your final examination you will be shown an audio-visual clip, and questions are usually asked about body language.

■ *Eye Contact*

Eye contact can be very powerful, either used by itself or to reinforce the spoken word. How often have you exchanged 'a knowing glance' with a friend – no words are spoken but you both know exactly what is meant? We have all seen examples of people who can establish order with just a look.

When we are watching the news on television, the newscaster seems to be looking directly at us. We feel that we are being spoken to personally and directly. If the autocue breaks down and the newscaster has to look down at the text, eye contact has been broken and we lose that feeling of being spoken to personally. It is the same in ordinary conversation. We depend on eye contact to keep the other person's attention. Eye contact also gives us feedback as to how the other person is thinking or feeling. If we do not look at the person who is speaking to us, they might accuse us of not listening.

If we do not maintain good eye contact in an interview situation, we tend to come across as 'shifty' or dishonest. Can you explain why this is so?

On the other hand, in certain situations we might find it easier to talk to people if they are not looking directly at us. Give some examples of this.

1. If we are owning up to something we did wrong.

2. _____

_____

3. _____

_____

4. _____

_____

5. _____

_____

✪ EXERCISES

1. List five groups of people for whom eye contact is very important and explain why this is so.

    (a) People collecting for charity - if they 'catch our eye' we give something!

    (b) _____

    (c) _____

    (d) _____

    (e) _____

2. Suggest reasons why some groups of people deliberately wear dark glasses:
    • Security staff
    • Visually impaired people
    • Traffic police

■ *Our Personal Space*

Our personal space is very important to us and we do not like it to be invaded. We all have a 'bubble' of privacy around ourselves. If our private space is invaded our natural reaction is simply to move away. However, in some situations this will not be possible. We feel uncomfortable if we are packed into a small space with strangers. Think about how people behave in a crowded lift: there is no conversation, eye contact is avoided, everybody seems to stand facing the door with their eyes firmly fixed on the floor indicator!

We also tend to 'stake out' our territory or space if we are in a public area such as a train or a restaurant. We do this by placing some of our belongings on the seat beside us. We are sending out a message that we do not want anybody to sit next to us. In the same way we may have a favourite chair in our home that the rest of the family acknowledges as ours. In school, students tend to lay claim to particular desks and can be quite annoyed if their seat is taken. In the work situation, a new employee has to be careful until he or she finds out who owns different pieces of territory!

✪ EXERCISES

The next time you find yourself in a waiting-room, observe how people use the space. Look at how people select the chairs as they enter the room. You will find that, unless people know each other, they will go to great lengths to keep their private bubble intact.

Also, the next time you find yourself in a queue, observe how people relate to each other. Everybody tends to respect the private space of the person next to them.

Observe the behaviour of people on holiday. How do they 'mark' their territory on the beach or beside the pool? Why do other people respect these markers?

Finally – it's not what we say, but the way that we say it! 'You played great football today' can mean two completely different things – depending on *how* it is is said. It can mean exactly what it says and can be taken as a compliment, or it can mean exactly the opposite if it is said in a **sarcastic** tone of voice. In pairs, come up with some more examples of sarcastic comments that are often used.

■ Work To Do

1. You are a sales person in a large shop. Make a list of ten ways in which you might upset or annoy a customer before you even speak to them.

    (a) Slow to attend to them, although you are not busy.

    (b) _____

    (c) _____

    (d) _____

    (e) _____

    (f) _____

    (g) _____

    (h) _____

    (i) _____

    (j) _____

2. Act out a short scene set in a hotel dining-room. A customer is complaining bitterly about the food and the service and the waiter is not at all sympathetic. Your improvisation should include both verbal and non-verbal communication.
3. Look at a recording of a scene from your favourite 'soap' or situation comedy. Concentrate on one character and make a list of the different types of body language used by him or her during the scene. Remember to include gestures, appearance, posture, facial expressions, eye contact, touch and personal space.
4. Read the following short story: it describes the power of non-verbal communication.

■ *Going Nuts* by *Paul McNulty*

1   Mary stared at the scruffy looking man sitting directly opposite her in the damp, dilapidated waiting room. She focused on his hands. If ever anything irritated her it was people who chewed their nails. And the dirt of his hands! He could have scrubbed himself up a bit before coming out in public. The thought of all those germs coursing through one's bloodstream made Mary squirm in her seat.

2   A crackle broke the early morning silence: 'Would passengers waiting for the 9.30 train to Cork please note that, due to flooding on the line, the train will be delayed until 10.15. Iarnród Éireann apologises for any inconvenience caused.'

3   Mary sighed, crossed her legs and unfolded her newspaper. She skimmed through it, flitting from page to page, then sighed deeply again. The 'Fun at the Weekend' supplement, with the much-hyped interview with her favourite film director, was missing. She returned to the counter to get the supplement and, to her utter disgust, she broke all promises of eating low-fat foods by succumbing to the irresistible charms of a jumbo-sized bag of peanuts. Coming back to the table, she resumed her seat and started to peruse the supplement. Again, the crackling sound broke the peaceful morning air: 'We regret that the 9.30 train to Cork has encountered further difficulties and it will now arrive at the station at approximately 11.15. Iarnród Éireann regrets any inconvenience caused.'

Paul McNulty

4   Mary looked towards the heavens – it seemed like it was going to be one of those days! The packet of peanuts was now looking more and more tempting to her. However, the thought of all those extra calories and the resultant effect on her body put an end to the cravings and she returned once more to the 'Woody Uncovered' interview.

5   In the middle of a paragraph, describing his latest relationship with some young, blond, fame-seeking starlet, Mary heard a faint rustling sound coming from the table in front of her. She peered over the top of her newspaper and nearly fell off the chair with shock when she saw the scruffy man gobbling down the peanuts which lay on the table directly between them. Mary decided she'd let it go this time but, barely had a minute passed when, once more, she saw his busy little hands working their way towards the packet of nuts. This time, Mary decided to use the staring technique. She summoned all the venom she could muster and directed the coldest, steeliest of gazes at this brazen stranger. She could see the result almost instantaneously as a bemused, awkward look came over his face. Mary smiled a smug, satisfied smile and returned once more to reading the interview. There was another rustling sound from behind the newspaper and, this time, the red haze of fury clouded Mary's vision as, ignoring all hygienic consequences, she reached out angrily and snatched a handful of nuts. That should give him the hint, thought Mary, as she re-adjusted herself in her increasingly uncomfortable seat.

6   No sooner had she settled down than the rustling sound was heard again. At this stage Mary was incensed at the sheer impertinence of this cheeky upstart and for the next half-hour, they traded psychological blows, helping themselves in turn to more and more until only five lonely nuts remained at the bottom of the bag.

7   Their eyes locked on these few miserable nuts. The man's hand reached out – and pushed the packet towards Mary. He smiled, tidied up his belongings and walked across the station, boarding a train which had just pulled in at a nearby platform.

8   Mary smiled an empty smile back at him and continued to read her paper until the train to Cork arrived in the station about an hour later. Then, gathering her bits and bobs, she stood and headed towards the train. Suddenly, she stopped and turned back. Her paper – she had forgotten it. Back at the table, picking up the paper, she spotted the discarded 'Business' section. As she reached for the supplement, there, looking up at her, was the unopened jumbo-sized packet of peanuts she had bought earlier.

(Paul McNulty wrote this story when he was 16 years old as a result of a course in creative writing offered by Mayo County Library, funded by the National Reading Initiative. At that time he was a student at St. Joseph's Secondary School, Foxford, Co. Mayo. His interests include reading, basketball and traditional music. He plays the banjo and has won seven All-Ireland medals. He enjoys writing and says 'writing is pretty cool and you don't have to be a dork to like it'.)

Going Nuts by Paul McNulty, from *Shooting from the Lip – Short Stories from Mayo's New Young Writers*, compiled and edited by Ré Ó Laighléis, was published by Mayo County Council 2001.

FOR DISCUSSION

1. In paragraph 1 Mary makes certain assumptions about the stranger. On what does she base her opinions?

2. Look at Mary's body language in paragraphs 3 and 4. What does it tell us about the way she is feeling?

3. In paragraphs 5, 6, 7 and 8, Mary and the stranger are in constant communication, but there is no dialogue – no words are spoken. What message is Mary trying to get across to the stranger? She uses several methods to try and get her message across. Identify three or four different things she does to try to change the stranger's behaviour.
    Why, do you think, does she not just say something like 'Leave my peanuts alone please!'?

4. How would you describe the stranger's reaction to Mary's behaviour? Why did he choose to remain silent?

5. In paragraph 5, the writer uses verbs such as 'She *peered* over the top of her newspaper', 'she saw the scruffy man *gobbling* down the peanuts', and 'she reached out angrily and *snatched* a handful of nuts'. Why do you think these words were chosen instead of, say, 'looked', 'eating' and 'took'?

6. Comment on the writer's description of Mary's staring technique in paragraph 5. How do you think you would feel if you were stared at like that?

7. In paragraph 6, the writer says that the two exchanged 'psychological blows'. What does he mean by this? Can you describe what the two people were actually doing? Can you give an example of a time when you traded 'psychological blows' with someone?

8. In paragraph 8 Mary discovers her unopened packet of peanuts. How do you think she feels? Add a short paragraph to the end of the story describing her reaction.

9. The story is written from Mary's point of view. We know very little about the thoughts and feelings of the stranger. Look again at paragraph 1 where Mary gives us her impression of the stranger. Could you write a short paragraph from the stranger's point of view, giving us his first impressions of Mary? Your opening could be something like 'He sat down opposite a . . .'

10. Do you think 'Going Nuts' is a good title for the story? Why/why not?

11. The story is set in the waiting room of a busy railway station. What details does the writer include in the story to give us some idea of the surroundings and the atmosphere?

12. Would you agree that 'Going Nuts' is a good short story? If so what, in your opinion, makes it a good story? Think about the following:
    • the opening
    • the characters
    • the descriptions
    • the ending

■ Other Channels of Communication

We must not forget that we also communicate through the visual arts, music, etc. For example, when we look at a painting the artist is communicating with us; when we decorate our house or bedroom, we are expressing our personality.

Music can be a very powerful communication medium. For example, church bells can be rung in joyful celebration to bring in a new millennium, or they can reflect the sombre mood of a funeral procession.

Music is used to suggest the mood or atmosphere in a film, and to build up to moments of high drama. Can you think of some films where you felt the music was particularly effective, and say why you found it so?

1. _____

2. _____

3. _____

4. _____

5. _____

✸ EXERCISE

■ *Pictures at an Exhibition*

This is a fun exercise. You will listen to some music on track number one on the CD and try to decide what the composer is trying to communicate to you.

Mussorgsky was a Russian musician who lived between 1839 and 1881. The death of his friend, the artist Victor Hartmann, upset him greatly. He went to visit an exhibition of Hartmann's paintings and was inspired to write ten pieces of music, each one describing a painting. You are going to listen to three of these pieces and see if you can match the musical pieces to the pictures. You might like to work in pairs for this exercise.

The opening music (1 min 54 s) is known as the **promenade** or walk, and when we listen to this we imagine Mussorgsky walking to the first picture. This music is repeated when the composer walks from picture to picture.

PIECE NUMBER 1. As he stands in front of the first picture, we hear the music he composed to capture the mood of the painting. (1 min 19 s)

This is followed by the promenade again (1 min 7 s) as he moves to the second painting.

TRACKS

1-6

PIECE NUMBER 2. Mussorgsky tries to communicate to us his reaction to what he sees in the second picture. (3 min 45 s)

Again we hear a short snatch of the promenade. (38 s)

PIECE NUMBER 3. Composed in response to the third picture. (2 min 35 s)

The pictures are numbered 1, 2 and 3 but are not in the same order as the pieces of music. Your task is to match the pictures to the pieces of music.

1. The Hut on Fowls' Legs
The picture shows the house of an evil Russian witch called Baba Yaga. The house rests on chickens' legs, so that the witch can fly off whenever she needs to. The music which goes with this picture begins with the house slowly beginning to move; then the pace increases as the witch chases her unfortunate victim. When she catches up with him the house slows down; the witch stalks her victim as a cat stalks a mouse; she finally catches him and the hut speeds off again.

2. The Great Gate of Kiev

Hartmann was an architect as well as an artist, and this picture was his design for a huge Russian Gate leading into the town of Kiev. He designed the dome in the shape of a Russian military helmet; the gate was to be made of granite and decorated with the Russian eagle. It was also to contain a small church. The whole structure was very grand and imposing.

As Mussorgsky stands in front of this picture, he imagines a solemn religious procession slowly coming towards the gate; some of the instruments are used to imitate voices singing a Russian hymn. The procession triumphantly goes through the great gate. As you would expect, this is a very serious, sombre piece of music.

3. The Ballet of the Chickens

Hartmann made this sketch for a ballet, showing the dancers dressed in costumes resembling large eggshells. The chickens are beginning to hatch, and in this piece of music the composer is trying to capture the atmosphere of excitement and the hectic activity, with lots of pecking and cheeping.

When you are listening to the pieces of music think about the following:
• the effects of the different instruments
• the speed and changes of speed
• the volume and sudden changes of volume
• the rhythm

Now, match the pieces of music with the pictures and give reasons for your choices.

PICTURES	MUSIC PIECE NUMBER
1. The Hut on Fowls' Legs	_____
2. The Great Gate of Kiev	_____
3. The Ballet of the Chickens	_____

Picture 1 - Piece Number _____

Picture 2 - Piece Number _____

Picture 3 - Piece Number _____

◼ Written communication

Written communication is very important in both our personal and our working lives. At the end of each unit you will find a selection of words which we use frequently, especially in business. It is important that you improve both your spelling and vocabulary during the two years of the LCA programme. As well as checking that you can spell the words listed at the end of each unit, it would be useful to know that you can use them properly. With the help of your dictionary make sure you have the correct meaning of each word; construct phrases or sentences in which the words are used correctly.

You will use many of these words later on in the module when writing business letters and reports. As your spelling and vocabulary improve your confidence will grow. Remember that in the world of work handwriting is still important – you will not always have the benefit of the spell check on your computer!

◼ *Increase Your Word Power!*

Can you spell and use the following words correctly?

Absence, absent, accept, accessible, accident, accidental, accommodation, account, accountant, accurate, achieved, acknowledge, acknowledgement, actually, address, adjourn, adopt, admission, advertise, advertisement.

# Unit 2

Oral Communication and Listening Skills

Speech is the most common method of *interpersonal communication*. It would be very difficult to get through everyday life without speech.

Speech has a lot of advantages over the written word. Make a list these advantages.

1. Speed, because we get immediate feedback.

2. _____

_____

3. _____

_____

4. _____

_____

5. _____

_____

Why do some speakers hold our attention?

1. *They speak clearly.*

2. _____

_____

3. _____

_____

4. _____

_____

5. _____

_____

◼ Meeting New People and Introducing Yourself

Do the following role-playing exercises.

1. Organise yourselves into groups of three, A, B and C. You are going to role-play situations in which you have to introduce yourself to other people. Student A introduces himself to Student B while Student C observes. The student who is observing should give some feedback to those doing the role-play.

Roles

Student A
Is starting a new school
Is seeking sponsorship for a charity event
Is looking for work experience

Student B
Is the principal of the school
Is a local businessman
Is a local employer

In each situation you must provide FIVE pieces of information about yourself. Do not forget the importance of body language.

It is important that this process is repeated twice, so that each student gets a chance to play each role. Each group should present one exercise to the whole class.

■ *Interacting with Others*

Note: Remember what you have learned in Social Education class about passive, assertive and aggressive behaviour.

Role-play some of the following situations:

1. You have just started your work experience placement. Your boss has explained your duties. Just as he is leaving you realise that you do not understand his instructions about how the photocopier works.
2. You have answered the phone at work. The caller insists that he needs to speak to the boss urgently. When you find the boss he is deep in conversation with one of his managers and you have to interrupt them.
3. Your boss has asked you to work overtime. You have made other arrangements that you do not want to change.
4. You need to ask your boss for time off for a hospital appointment.
5. You have just started a new job. The boss has told you not to use a particular machine. When the manager arrives he tells you to start the machine.
6. You are working in a shop. A customer insists that he gave you a €20 note. You are sure he only gave you a €10 note.

At the end of these exercises make a list of helpful suggestions that you could follow in these situations.

1. Be confident.

2. _____

_____

3. _____

_____

4. _____

_____

5. _____

_____

TAPED PRESENTATION

Being able to speak in a group or in front of an audience can be a great help to us, not just in our everyday lives but also in our careers. Identify situations where we might be called upon to speak in public.

IN OUR PERSONAL LIVES

1. Making a speech at a wedding.

2. _____

3. _____

4. _____

5. _____

IN OUR CAREERS

1. You are selling a new machine and you are demonstrating it to a group of workers.

2. _____

3. _____

4. _____

5. _____

SOAPBOX!

Each student will choose a subject and prepare a *short* presentation of no more than one minute. You may choose a favourite sport or hobby or some issue you feel strongly about. You will deliver a speech to the class, which will be taped – audio or video, whichever is convenient. Taping the presentation gives you a chance to listen to the speech yourself.

When we first hear our own voice on tape we usually get a shock! We never hear our own voice as it really is because of the bone structure of our ears. However, we soon get used to it. Remember that our voice is part of our personality and we should not try to change it. Also, if we have a strong accent we should not try to disguise it, but we should make sure that we can be understood – this usually means just slowing down a bit and speaking clearly.

Preparation is the key to a good presentation. Make sure you know what you are going to say. Practise your speech so that you are not just reading it from your notes.

The class should complete a worksheet, such as the one below, for each presentation, listing three or four good points and at least one point that could be improved on.

Remember, take into account all you have learned about good communication. In addition, look at the following list of common mistakes that people make when speaking to an audience:

1. Speaking too fast – your audience will find it hard to follow what you are saying.
2. Speaking too quietly, muttering, looking down at notes all the time.
3. Mispronouncing words – keep it simple and use words that you are familiar with.
4. Not pronouncing 'th' properly.
5. Using bad grammar.
6. Missing the ends of words.
7. A boring voice – using the same tone all the time.

NAME OF PRESENTER _____

Good Points	*Could Be Improved Upon*
1. _____	1. _____
2. _____	2. _____
3. _____	3. _____
4. _____	4. _____

When observing the speaker, ask yourself the following questions:
1. Did the speaker hold my attention? Why/Why not?
2. Was the speaker really interested in what he was talking about?
3. Did the speaker use humour; did he tell a story about himself?
4. Was the body language effective?
Note: If you have enjoyed your 'Soapbox' experience, you might like to get involved in Public Speaking!

■ Martin Luther King – I Have a Dream

Track number seven on the CD is a recording of one of the most powerful speeches of the last century – the famous 'I Have a Dream' speech made by Martin Luther King in 1963.

King worked hard to end the legal segregation of African-Americans in the southern United States. He was a believer in non-violent methods. This speech was made at a massive march in Washington on 28 August 1963. In 1964 King was awarded the Nobel Prize for Peace. He was assassinated in 1968.

Listen to the entire speech first to get some sense of the atmosphere and mood. When you listen to it a second time, stop the recording at various points to discuss the words used and the way they are delivered.

1. In the opening line of his speech, when he talks about a 'great American', Martin Luther King is talking about Abraham Lincoln. King stood on the steps of the Lincoln Memorial in Washington to deliver his speech. Why do you think he picked this setting? Why was Abraham Lincoln important to African-Americans?
2. Listen to the language he uses to paint pictures in the minds of his listeners. For example, he talks about the 'manacles of segregation' and the 'chains of discrimination'. What do these phrases mean? Why do you think he picked these images?
3. He compares the United States to a bank and he says the African-Americans have come to cash a cheque; in business a cheque is a promise of money; he believes the American Declaration of Independence was a promise of freedom for *all* Americans. The African-American has now come to cash in this promise.
   Do you think this is a good comparison? Why/Why not?

4. We can see King's attitude to violence in the line: 'Let us not seek to satisfy our thirst for freedom by drinking from the cup of bitterness and hatred'.
   What does he mean by this?
5. Name some of the civil rights that he is campaigning for on behalf of his people.
6. Towards the end of the speech, King repeats over and over again the words 'I have a dream'. Do you think this is effective? Why/Why not?
7. He uses repetition again with the words 'Let freedom ring'. In this section he mentions many different regions of the United States. Why, in your opinion, does he do this?
8. Listen to the ending – does he end on a *positive* note or a *negative* note? Why does he do this?
9. In his speech he does not criticise the United States Government, or the white people who are denying civil rights to the African-American. Instead he uses the language of *persuasion*. What do you think is his most powerful argument?
10. King uses some beautiful metaphors in his speech. A metaphor is when we say one thing is not just *like* something else, but actually *is* something else. For example, he talks about 'the bright day of justice' and 'the sunlit path of racial justice'.
    Pick out some metaphors that appealed to you.
11. Comment on *how* King delivered the speech. What factors made the delivery so effective?
12. If you can, *watch* a video recording of this speech and examine how King's body language adds to the impact of his words.

■ Discussions and Debates

It can be both educational and fun to take part in a discussion or debate. Discussions tend to happen quite naturally without planning, where you simply give your opinions on different topics that come up in class. A debate is more formal than a discussion and requires a certain amount of planning and preparation. A debate is a type of contest and has winners and losers.

In planning a debate you will first have to decide on the MOTION – a motion is a statement that makes people think.

You then need two teams – the PROPOSITION who will argue in favour of the motion and the OPPOSITION who will argue against the motion.

You will also need a CHAIRPERSON to keep order, and a TIMEKEEPER.

■ *Suggested Topics*

1. Our culture is alcohol obsessed.
2. Homelessness is a symbol of our society's priorities.
3. Refugees are a benefit to our country.
4. Prisons should be abolished.

5. Our politicians are underpaid.

Now, working in pairs, add your own suggestions.

6. _____

7. _____

8. _____

9. _____

10. _____

Choose one topic from the list and prepare a debate.

PREPARATION

There is a lot of work to be done between deciding on the motion and holding the actual debate.

1. Working in pairs, put your thoughts on paper. Divide your page into two columns, FOR and AGAINST, and write as many arguments as you can think of. Group discussion will produce even more ideas.
2. Do your research. You might have to find out some things that you do not know. For example, if you are arguing that politicians should be paid more you will need to find out what they are being paid at the moment.
3. Decide whether you want to argue for or against the motion and volunteer your services! Two teams of four people are needed.
4. Work on your research and on your speech. Each person on the team should concentrate on a different angle or point. Practise your speech in front of a mirror! Put your key points on cards. Do not learn your speech off by heart.

   Remember everything you have learned about effective communication:
   • vary your tone of voice
   • emphasise important points
   • pause for effect
   • make sure your arguments are strong
   • use gestures
   • use visual aids if necessary, e.g. dramatic pictures
   • use humour
   • keep good eye contact with your audience
   • ask questions that will make your audience think

THE DEBATE

Two teams of four people sit at the top of the room on either side of the chairperson.

Each team member is allowed to speak for one minute. The timekeeper will warn you when you have ten seconds left and will ring the bell again when your time is up.

Listen carefully to the speeches of the other team and try to answer their arguments when it comes to your turn.

When all the team members have spoken it is the turn of the audience to give their views on the topic – the chairperson declares the motion open to the floor.

This is followed by the vote – the chairperson asks for a show of hands for and against the motion and declares a winner.

In more formal debates, a judge or judges will decide the winner.

If you enjoyed the class debate, you might consider challenging another class or a class from another school to a debate.

■ Listening Skills

Listen to track number eight on the CD and answer the following questions:

1. How old are Malta's megalithic tombs?
2. Can you name some of the groups who invaded Malta?
3. When did Malta become an independent republic?
4. Malta consists of three islands – can you name them?
5. What is the capital city of Malta?
6. It is recommended that you visit two places – can you name them?

7. What type of food is usually served in Malta?
8. What is the speed limit on the highways?
9. Where can you get more information on Malta?
10. If you were going on holiday to Malta, at what time of the year would you go? Why?

What is LISTENING? Is it different from HEARING? Listening requires **effort** – hearing does not. Would you agree? Give examples of both.

LISTENING

1. Your boss is leaving instructions for the day.

2. _____

_____

3. _____

_____

4. _____

_____

5. _____

_____

HEARING

1. There is a radio in the background.

2. _____

_____

3. _____

_____

4. _____

_____

5. _____

_____

If we are listening, we are giving our **total attention** to what we are listening to. It would be impossible to be doing something else at the same time that requires concentration; however, we could listen while doing some mechanical task like washing the dishes.

BARRIERS TO LISTENING

1. There might be a lot of noise – machines, traffic, people talking, etc.

   Example: _____

   _____

2. The speaker might not be interesting.

   Example: _____

   _____

3. The message might not be interesting.

   Example: _____

   _____

4. We may be tired or hungry, or we may be worried about something else.

   Example: _____

   _____

We all need to practise ACTIVE LISTENING – this means giving FEEDBACK. For example:
- asking questions if we do not understand
- asking the speaker to repeat what he has said
- taking notes
- repeating what has been said in different words

⭐ EXERCISES

The following exercises demonstrate the difference between passive listening and active listening.

1. *The Name Game*

   If possible the students should form a circle. Each member of the group picks a fictitious name from the hat. The teacher will decide who goes first. The first student introduces himself: for example, 'My name is Peter.' The second student says 'My name is Mary and this is Peter' (indicating the first student). Continue like this around the circle trying to remember all the names.

   When you go on work experience or start a new job, you need to make an effort to remember names. Why is this important?

2. A team of five students (team A) will leave the room. They will be brought back one at a time. When the first student comes in, he or she will listen to the instructions on the CD. He or she will try to remember them and relay them to the second member of the team and so on. The person receiving the instructions may not ask questions; the person giving the instructions may not repeat them. The rest of the class will keep a record of the number of mistakes made.

3. A second team of five students (team B) will leave the room. When the first student comes back he or she will listen to the instructions on the CD. He or she will try to remember them and relay them to the second member of the team and so on. This time the members of the team are allowed to ask questions, to take notes or to have parts of the message repeated. Again, the rest of the class should keep a record of mistakes made.

4. Compare the results; the number of mistakes made by team B should be a lot lower than that of team A.

5. Complete this list of suggestions for *giving instructions* clearly.

   (a) Do not give unnecessary information because it will only confuse the listener.

   (b) _____

   (c) _____

   (d) _____

   (e) _____

6. Complete this list of suggestions for *receiving instructions* correctly.

   (a) Repeat the instructions.

   (b) _____

   (c) _____

(d) _____

(e) _____

7. Can you give instructions clearly?
   For this exercise you need to work in pairs. Each pair should sit back to back. Student A is given a simple line drawing by the teacher. Student A must describe the drawing in such a way that Student B can draw it correctly. Student A is not allowed to name the object – he must only describe features such as lines, angles and distance. Student B may not ask questions. At the end of five minutes compare the drawings and see how successful you were!

8. Divide into pairs but select a partner who is not your best friend. One person talks for one minute about himself, giving details such as his date of birth, the number of people in his family, hobbies, interests and ambitions. The second person does the same. Each pair then joins up with another pair to form a group of four. Each student will introduce his partner to the group – your partner will decide how well you listened!

9. Record a news bulletin from a national radio station. How well can you recall what was said?
   (a) What were the headlines?
   (b) What was the main item of home news?
   (c) What was the main foreign news story?
   (d) What was the main sports story?
   (e) Give the main points of one news story that caught your attention and explain why you found it interesting.

10. Listen to a recording of a radio play or short story and answer the following questions.
   (a) Name and describe two of the main characters.
   (b) Describe the setting, i.e. the time and the place.
   (c) Give a brief outline of the plot.
   (d) Describe the most dramatic moment.
   (e) How did you feel at the end of the story or play? Why did you feel like this?

■ *Increase Your Word Power!*

Can you spell and use the following words correctly?
Advice, advise, alteration, alternative, although, altogether, amend, amendment, anticipate, apologise, apology, appearance, application, apply, appreciate, approve, approval, approximately, argument, arrangement, association, attendance.

Unit 3

Telephone Techniques

■ The Telephone Directory

The Telephone Directory is more than just a list of phone numbers: it also contains lots of information, and if we know our way around it we can save ourselves a lot of time and trouble.

The first 60 pages or so contain useful facts which help us to make the best and most efficient use of our phone. Inside the front cover you will find the table of contents – here are a few simple exercises to help you find your way around!

1. You have just received your phone bill and you are not happy – what number will you ring in order to query the amount?
2. You are dissatisfied with the quality of your telephone line – there is a constant buzzing noise on it. What number will you ring in order to have it repaired?
3. If you are ringing a number outside of Ireland, which two digits do you always dial first?
4. What about Northern Ireland – are the same digits used?
5. How much does it cost per minute to ring London during the day?
6. How much does it cost per minute to ring Paris in the evening?
7. What are the area codes for the following cities?
   • Dublin
   • Cork
   • Galway
   • Limerick
8. You want to make a phone call to New York at 3 o'clock in the afternoon local time in New York. At what time would you make the phone call, Irish time?

The GREEN PAGES of the directory contain a full list of all the Government offices. Find the correct number to ring in each of the following situations:

1. You have started a summer job and a lot of tax has been stopped from your wages. You want to sort out the situation.

   Which department will you call? _____

   What is the correct number? _____

2. You have lost your passport and need to replace it urgently.

   Which department will you call? _____

   What is the correct number? _____

3. You want to apply for a visa to work in the United States.

   Which department will you call? _____

   What is the correct number? _____

4. You are trying to get a grant to set up your own business.

   Which department will you call? _____

   What is the correct number? _____

5. You want to change the date of your driving test.

   Which department will you call? _____

   What is the correct number? _____

6. You have come up with an interesting invention and you want to make sure that nobody can copy it.

   Which department will you call? _____

   What is the correct number? _____

7. You feel you have been unfairly dismissed from your job.

   Which department will you call? _____

   What is the correct number? _____

8. You need a birth certificate.

   Which department will you call? _____

   What is the correct number? _____

The main body of the directory is divided into two sections – Residential Listings and Business Listings. The lists are organised *alphabetically*. In the Residential Listings, all people sharing the same surname are listed together; the surname is shown only once at the beginning of the list.

★ EXERCISES

1. Put these names in alphabetical order:
   Colgan, Bernard
   Clyde, Sandra
   Aherne, Pamela
   Hennessy, Donald
   Hennessy, John
   Munn, Brian
   Put these names in alphabetical order:
   O'Callaghan, J
   O'Callaghan, Fiona
   O'Callaghan, Jim
   O'Callaghan, B
   O'Callaghan, Martin

   The BUSINESS SECTION is also listed *alphabetically*. This makes it different from the Golden Pages where all businesses of the same *type* are listed together. For this reason we call the Golden Pages the Classified Directory – businesses of the same class or type appear together. This is very useful if you are trying to get quotations from several different people for the same job.

2. For what other reasons might you consult the Golden Pages?

   1. _____

   _____

   2. _____

   _____

   3. _____

   _____

   4. _____

   _____

   5. _____

   _____

■ *Work To Do*

Using the Golden Pages find phone numbers for the following:
1. the local newspaper
2. the local radio station
3. the Toyota main dealer nearest to you
4. the local FÁS office
Note: customers may now include their mobile phone number and their e-mail address in the telephone directory.

■ *Using the Telephone at Work*

Remember, we are talking about the telephone here in a business context. Even though mobile phones and e-mails are becoming much more common, the office phone is still very important.

It is essential that the first impression given by a business is a good one; if a prospective customer is not treated well or does not have his questions answered, he will simply ring the next company listed in the Golden Pages.

Working in pairs or small groups, make a list of ten points to remember when using the phone at work. In your discussion groups you should think about the following:

• Without customers none of us would have jobs. The customer is the most important person to your company. How should he/she be treated on the phone?
• Your voice is the voice of your company – can you think of any words which would describe a suitable tone of voice?
• All you have on the telephone is your voice – you have no visual signals, no facial expression and no body language.
• What should you do if you need time to find the information the customer needs?
• How will you make sure that you really understand what the caller wants?
• How will you make sure that the caller really understands what you are saying?
• How will you avoid time wasting?
• How will you bring the call to an end?

1. If you answer an incoming call, always give the company name and your own name. For example, 'Kerrigan's Car Sales, John Smith speaking: how can I help you?'

2. _____

_____

3. _____

_____

4. _____

_____

5. _____

_____

6. _____

_____

7. _____

_____

8. _____

_____

9. _____

_____

10. _____

_____

When you have all agreed on these points, make a poster or a series of posters entitled 'TELEPHONE TECHNIQUES – TEN TIPS'. Use IT or Art in this exercise.

Remember, put a smile in your voice! How can you do this? Two volunteers, please! Student A is in charge of answering the telephone in a busy supermarket. Student B is a customer ringing in with a complaint. Role-play the conversation. The class can decide whether or not Student A managed to keep a smile in his voice!

■ Dealing with Difficult Calls

No matter how efficient and customer-friendly your business is, it is inevitable that at some stage you will be on the receiving end of a difficult call, dealing with an angry customer who is complaining about a product or service supplied by you. The following example is typical of the kind of situation that can arise.

You are the manager of a furniture shop. Mrs Byrne has bought an expensive table and six chairs. She insisted that she wanted them delivered immediately as she was preparing for an important family occasion. Your own delivery lorry was completely booked up, so you decided to hire a van and driver.

Mrs Byrne is on the phone to say that the furniture has been delivered, but the table is badly scratched.

Write out the telephone conversation that you think might follow between yourself and Mrs Byrne. You might find it helpful to do this exercise in pairs.

When writing the conversation, keep the following points in mind:

- Make sure you know exactly what the complaint is; get the story straight.
- Acknowledge that there is a problem; do not get defensive.
- Be sympathetic; be apologetic if it is your fault.
- Give an explanation; but if you are in the wrong, do not try to shift the blame.
- Offer a solution; or maybe a couple of alternative solutions.
- Make sure that you have both agreed on a plan of action before you hang up.
  Remember:
1. Stay calm. If you stay calm, the chances are that the customer will also calm down.
2. Understand the complaint.
3. Offer a solution.

When you are satisfied with your script, role-play the conversation.

Now! Role-play the telephone conversation that might take place between you and the van driver.

★ EXERCISES

You are in charge of answering the telephone at work. Can you think of more appropriate ways of saying the following?

1. He has not come back from lunch yet.
2. What do you want him for?
3. He is too busy to come to the phone.
4. Calm down!
5. Could you speak up?
6. What are you talking about?
7. Who are you?
8. Are you deaf?
9. Do not shout at me!
10. You will have to call back.

Complete the following list – when using the telephone at work:

1. Be polite.

2. Be patient.

3. _____

4. _____

5. _____

6. _____

■ *Answering Machines and Messages*

Sometimes when we are confronted with an answering machine, our first instinct is to hang up! However, if used properly, answering machines can be very efficient and can save a lot of time. Can you list some of the advantages of answering machines?

1. You may not lose business.

2. _____

_____

3. _____

_____

4. _____

_____

5. _____

_____

If you do have to leave a message, it should be short and to the point. You will need to leave the following information:
• *Who* you are.
• *Why* you phoned.
• *Where* you can be contacted.

✸ EXERCISES

1. You have just started up your own electrical repair business and the telephone is often left unattended. You do not want to lose prospective customers. Compose a suitable message to leave on your answering machine.

    Record your message on a tape recorder and play it back to the class. Points to note:
    • Have you tried to keep the customer interested?
    • Have you given enough information?
    • Does the message give the impression that you are in a rush and under pressure?
    • What about the tone of voice, clarity, etc?
2. You have made arrangements for a business meeting with a client, Mr John Flood. You now have to change the arrangement. Leave a suitable message on Mr Flood's answering machine. Invent the details as you need them.

■ *Taking Messages*

It is essential that messages are passed on correctly to the person concerned.

It is important that you get the details straight. LISTEN CAREFULLY: repeat phone numbers, times, dates, etc.

Most offices will have preprinted telephone message slips. Fill in the most important details on the telephone message slip – the headings will already be there for you.

Write clearly. Only write down the most important points – you usually use phrases rather than sentences.

Make sure that the person actually gets the message.

TELEPHONE MESSAGE

DATE _____ TIME _____

FOR _____

FROM _____

MESSAGE _____

_____

_____

_____

_____

RETURN NUMBER _____

RECEIVED BY _____

★ EXERCISE

The following telephone conversation took place between you and a customer, Mr John Murphy.

You: Good morning, Smith's Building Supplies, David speaking: how can I help you?
Mr Murphy: This is John Murphy of Murphy Builders. Is Paul Smith available, please?
You: No, I'm afraid he is out of the office at the moment. I am not expecting him back until late this afternoon. Can I help you?
Mr Murphy: No. I really need to speak to Paul.
You: Can I give him a message?
Mr Murphy: Will you tell him that I want to change the order I gave him on Thursday last? If he rings me when he comes back I will discuss it with him.
You: I will see that he gets the message. May I have your telephone number, please?
Mr Murphy: He can get me at 076 21490.
You: 076 21490. Thank you Mr. Murphy. Goodbye.

Write out the telephone message you would leave for Mr. Smith.

```
TELEPHONE MESSAGE
DATE _____     TIME _____
FOR _____
FROM _____
MESSAGE _____
_____
_____
_____
_____
RETURN NUMBER _____
RECEIVED BY _____
```

■ *Mobile Phones*

Mobile phones are becoming increasingly common, both for personal and business use. It would be useful to do a quick survey of the class to find out what percentage of students own a mobile phone and the average amount spent each week on calls.

Make a list of the advantages and disadvantages of mobile phones. Think about cost, health and safety, features and services offered.

ADVANTAGES

1. People can always contact you.

2. _____

_____

3. _____

_____

4. _____

_____

5. _____

_____

DISADVANTAGES

1. It is difficult to get away from work.

2. _____

_____

3. _____

_____

4. _____

_____

5. _____

_____

MOBILE PHONES AND GOOD MANNERS

Mobile phones can be very useful – nobody will disagree with that; however they can also be a **nuisance**. Make a list of situations where the use of mobile phones can be intrusive and inappropriate.

1. _____

   _____

2. _____

   _____

3. _____

   _____

4. _____

   _____

5. _____

   _____

Text messages have become very common, partly because they cost a lot less than a phone call. However, there are some points that we should remember in relation to text messaging.

Text messaging has brought with it a whole new language and a whole new system of spelling – we need to be very careful that this new language does not spill over into our written English.

DISCUSSION TOPIC

If you are in conversation with somebody and you get a text message, what should you do? Do you ignore it and deal with it later, or do you break off your conversation to read it and answer it immediately? Give reasons for your answer.

■ *Increase Your Word Power!*

Can you spell and use the following words correctly?

Balance, banker, bankrupt, barrister, beginning, behaviour, belief, believe, benefit, boundary, budget, budgeted, business.

Calculate, calculating, calendar, campaign, cancel, capable, capital, career, catalogue, category, categories, census, centenary, centimetre, centre, centred, ceremony, character, cheque, circumstance, colleague, collection, commercial, committee, community, competent, complaint, confident, continue, contract, conscientious, convenient.

# Unit 4

Language Skills and Composition

■ *Capital Letters*

When should we use capital letters? Capitals are used for the following:
1. Names of people, places, days of the week, months of the year, important holidays, brand names, names of cinemas and clubs, titles of newspapers, songs, plays, books and films. All of these nouns are proper nouns.
2. Capitals are always used to begin a sentence.
3. All letters in initials are capital letters.
4. Capitals are used to begin titles which are part of a name, e.g. Doctor Coffey.
5. Capitals are used to begin the first part of direct speech, e.g. the words a person is saying.

# ★ EXERCISE

Rewrite the following correctly.

as soon as christmas is over, people start planning their summer holidays travel agents are very busy for the month of january i had just recovered from a serious illness and doctor browne advised me to take a holiday in the sun the people in sun travel were very helpful, and i arrived home armed with brochures and information

the difficult bit was trying to get everyone in the family to agree on a destination mary wanted to visit the magnificant cities of italy while the children had their hearts set on the costa del sol as i am paying for this holiday i said it should be my decision

after a lot of discussion we opted for two weeks in greece one week to be spent in athens and one week on the island of crete a travel programme which we had seen on rte helped us to make up our minds.

■ *Commas and Full Stops*

Commas are used to break up a long sentence and make it easier to understand. You would usually put a comma wherever you would pause if you were reading the sentence. Where would you put commas in the following sentence?

> We were almost late for our flight as on the way to the airport we were forced to take a long detour because of a serious accident on the M 50.

Commas are also used to separate items that are written in the form of a list: **the tone of voice you use on the telephone is very important – it must be businesslike, friendly, helpful and courteous.**

Note: the word 'and' is usually used instead of a comma before the last word in a list.

Full stops are used to mark the end of a sentence. Sometimes we use either a question mark **?** or an exclamation mark **!** at the end of a sentence.

Write three different sentences, one ending with a full stop, one ending with a question mark and one ending with an exclamation mark.

1. _____

_____

2. _____

_____

3. _____

_____

■ *Sentences*

What exactly is a sentence? A sentence is a statement that is complete – it makes perfect sense – it can stand alone.

Pick out the complete sentences from the following list. In the case of examples that are not sentences, see if you can complete them and make them into sentences.

Note: capital letters and full stops have been left out.

1. just before the police arrived
2. the phone rang
3. your dinner's ready
4. in the middle of the desert
5. yes
6. learning is a lifelong process
7. if Tom arrives
8. because we lost the money
9. the old lady, who was in a state of shock, rang the police station and managed, with a lot of help and encouragement, to tell her story
10. don't sound hurried

■ *Apostrophes*

When should we use apostrophes?

1. An apostrophe is used to show ownership of something, e.g. The boy's bag was ruined. In this case there is only one boy, so the apostrophe comes before the **s**.
   If you are talking about two or more people you put the apostrophe after the **s**, e.g. The boys' bags were ruined.
2. An apostrophe is used to show that a letter (or letters) has been left out, e.g. They're (they are) late for dinner.

✪ EXERCISE

Rewrite the following sentences, using apostrophes correctly.
1. Im too tired to go running.
2. The concert is in St. Johns hall.
3. The girls mobile phone was lost.
4. You didnt do the work you were asked to do.
5. Im expecting someone to call, so I cant leave now.

If you look around you at signs in shops you will find plenty of examples of apostrophes being used incorrectly. Some people feel that every word that ends in 's' deserves an apostrophe!

■ *Colons*

Colons are used to introduce a list:

In order to communicate effectively you must remember the following:
• speak clearly
• maintain good eye contact
• vary your tone of voice.

■ *Semi-Colons*

A semi-colon may be used to break up a sentence into parts, each of which makes sense on its own:

Everything was quiet; you could hear a pin drop.

■ *Paragraphs*

We use paragraphs to break up pages of print; to make it easier on the eye. In a letter or an essay, each paragraph usually has a single idea or point.

■ *Increase Your Word Power!*

Can you spell and use the following words correctly?

Decision, decrease, definite, delivery, department, desirable, development, different, difference, difficult, director, directory, disappeared, disappointed, disapprove, disconnect, discrepancy, dissatisfied.

WORDS THAT CAN BE CONFUSED

accept – except
check – cheque
principle – principal
personal – personnel
emigrate – immigrate
advice – advise
their – there
quiet – quite
site – sight

# Unit 5

Letter Writing

Years ago letter writing was very important. People kept in touch with relatives and friends living long distances away by means of regular letters. Historians are able to find out a great deal about the lives of ordinary people from studying letters that have survived.

As the telephone became cheaper and more available, letter writing became less common. Nowadays, however, the art of letter writing is undergoing a revival, thanks to the Internet and e-mail.

You will be using ICT throughout this unit. Keep copies of your letters in a suitable folder.

■ Personal Letters

If we are writing to family members or friends, we write personal letters. These letters are 'chatty' – the language we use is INFORMAL; the type of language we would use if we were talking to them face to face. Our friends will forgive us for mistakes in spelling, grammar and punctuation, but it is good manners to make personal letters as attractive and easy to read as possible.

■ *Layout of a Personal Letter*

Sender's address

Date

Greeting

Body of letter, divided into paragraphs

Closing

Signature

★ EXERCISES

Why not just make a phone call? Why take the trouble to write a letter? Discuss why you might decide to write a letter instead of making a phone call.

1. A letter can be read over and over again.

2. _____

   _____

3. _____

   _____

4. _____

   _____

5. _____

   _____

Here are some examples of situations in which you might write a personal letter.

1. You have just celebrated your eighteenth birthday and you are writing 'thank you' letters. Write a letter to a friend thanking him/her for their gift.
2. Your cousin is getting married on 18 July and has invited you to the wedding. Unfortunately you have arranged to go abroad to work for the summer and will not be able to attend. You know your cousin will be disappointed. Write a suitable letter.
3. You and a friend want to attend a concert in London on 24 August. Paying for the tickets and the airfares is expensive enough without paying for accommodation as well. You have an aunt and uncle living in London whom you do not know very well. Write a letter asking if you can both stay with them for two nights.
4. Your friend's younger brother has been killed in a tragic accident. You are working in the United States and are unable to attend the funeral. Write a letter of condolence.

In each of these examples you need to think before you start writing. Begin your letter with a clear idea of what you are going to say. In a personal letter you will be trying to get your *feelings* or *emotions* across to the other person. In the first example you will be expressing your delight at the present and, of course, gratitude. Look at the other examples and decide what feelings you will be trying to get across in your letter.

EXAMPLE 2	*EXAMPLE 3*	*EXAMPLE 4*
1. _____	_____	_____
_____	_____	_____
2. _____	_____	_____
_____	_____	_____
3. _____	_____	_____
_____	_____	_____

Now, choose one of the situations above and write a suitable letter. When you are satisfied with the content of your letter design a suitable layout and type it up in ICT class.

■ Business Letters

When writing business letters our approach is very different. The language we use is more FORMAL. We would not write to the bank manager in the same way as we would write to a friend – just as we would not speak to the bank manager in the same way as we would

speak to a friend. If we were asking the bank manager for a loan we would behave in a formal manner. We would telephone to make an appointment; we would make sure we were well dressed and well groomed; we would think about what we were going to say and at the interview we would be formal and businesslike. We hope the bank manager will be influenced by the way we look and speak.

It is the same with a business letter – the person reading it will form an impression of the writer. If we want to make a good impression we need to note the following points:

1. Use good quality paper.
2. Proofread: check spelling, punctuation and grammar.
3. Write neatly or use the computer.
4. If the letter is handwritten, do not cross out or write over words.
5. Get your ideas across simply and clearly.
6. Make sure you include all the necessary information.

■ *Layout of a Business Letter*

The most popular layout for a business letter is the FULLY BLOCKED STYLE. Everything except the sender's address begins at the left-hand margin. Most companies also use OPEN PUNCTUATION. This means that no punctuation marks, such as commas and full stops, are used in the address, the date, the inside name and address, the greeting and the closing.

(1) Your own address (do not include your name here).
(2) Date (always *name* the month to avoid confusion).
(3) Name and address of the person you are writing to.
(4) Greeting (Dear Sir or Dear Mr Smith).
(5) Body of letter, divided into paragraphs.
(6) Closing – if you begin ' Dear Sir' close with 'Yours faithfully'; if you begin ' Dear Mr Smith' close with 'Yours sincerely'.
(7) Name of sender. The sender will sign the letter just above his printed name.

                                                    1 Main Street
                                            (1) Kells
                                                    Co Meath

Date *(2)*

Mr John Byrne
14 Bridge Street *(3)*
Navan
Co Meath

Dear Mr Byrne *(4)*

I wish to apply for the position of apprentice electrician which was advertised in the Meath Chronicle on 4th June last.

I am 17 years of age and have completed the Leaving Certificate Applied course. *(5)*

I am particularly interested in this position as one of my school-based work experience placements involved working with an electrician.

I enclose my Curriculum Vitae and I am available for interview at any time.

Yours sincerely *(6)*

John Smith *(7)*

★ EXERCISE

Write a letter to a local company asking for sponsorship for a charity event which the class is organising. Approach this as if it was a real situation. Decide on the event, the charity and the date. Decide which company you are going to approach.

■ Letters of Complaint

If we have reason to complain about a product or service that we have paid for we should make the complaint at once – if we delay our case will not be as strong. We should also put our complaint in writing. Why do you think this is a good idea?

Points to remember:

1. Always keep a copy of a letter of complaint. Do not send originals of receipts – send photocopies. Why should we follow these guidelines?
2. Do not be rude or abusive in your letter – simply state your case clearly and assume that the company will want to put things right.
3. Make sure you give all the necessary information, e.g. date and place of purchase, serial numbers, the exact nature of the problem, etc.
4. Make a suggestion as to how you would like the problem to be sorted out, e.g. a new item supplied or a full refund of money.

★ EXERCISE

Working in pairs or groups, make a list of five situations in which you might write a letter of complaint. Remember to include both goods and services in your list.

1. _____

   _____

2. _____

   _____

3. _____

   _____

4. _____

   _____

5. _____

   _____

Select one of the situations from the list and write a formal letter of complaint. Invent the details. When you are satisfied with the content type it up in ICT class.

Remember, always proofread your work. Check it carefully for mistakes in spelling, grammar and punctuation.

■ *Replying to a Letter of Complaint*

Imagine that you are working for a company that has received a letter of complaint. How should you deal with it?

1. You must investigate the complaint. This could take some time so you need to ACKNOWLEDGE the letter; reply immediately to the customer and assure them you are dealing with the matter.
2. When you have investigated the complaint you will again write to the customer and explain the outcome.
3. If the complaint is valid you will apologise on behalf of the company and accept responsibility for the situation. You will also explain how you intend to put things right.
4. If the complaint is not a valid one you will have to point this out politely and tactfully to the customer. Remember that the company does not want to lose this customer. You do not want them to feel offended, as they could do your company a lot of harm by complaining about the treatment they got.

■ Letters of Request

During your two years in Leaving Certificate Applied you will find yourself constantly writing letters requesting information that you need for tasks or key assignments. For example, you may be involved in organising a weekend away for your class and you will need information from several different outdoor pursuits centres.

Suggest other situations in which you would be writing a letter of request. You may be working on tasks or doing coursework in other subjects where it would be useful to write away looking for information.

1. A letter to FÁS, requesting information on a particular career.

2. _____

_____

3. _____

_____

4. _____

_____

Choose one situation from the list you have drawn up and write a suitable letter. Find the names and addresses you need in the phone book. When you are satisfied with the content type it up in ICT class. Remember always proofread your work; check it carefully for mistakes in spelling, grammar and punctuation.

■ Curriculum Vitae

Curriculum Vitae means 'the course of one's life'. It is a document that contains a brief account of your education and achievements up to the present time.

Your Career Guidance Counsellor will be helping you to prepare your CV and covering letter. When you are satisfied with the content you can decide on a layout in ICT class.

List the purposes of a CV:

1. To help me find a job.

2. _____

_____

3. _____

_____

4. _____

_____

A CV will usually give the following information:
1. Personal Details: name, address, date of birth and contact phone number.
2. Education: the schools you have attended, with dates, and the results of examinations you have taken.
3. Work Experience: part-time work, holiday work, work experience placements, voluntary or community work.
4. Interests and Hobbies: list at least three of your main interests or hobbies.
5. Special Achievements: in this section you could refer to medals you have won for sport, prizes you have won in school, or positions of responsibility you have held in school, clubs, etc.

6. Referees: give the names, addresses and contact numbers of at least two people who know you well. It is usual to give the Principal of your school and your present or last employer. Make sure you ask their permission first.

7. Signature: always sign and date your CV before presenting it to a prospective employer. Remember that presentation is very important. A prospective employer will get an impression of you from your CV.

Make a list of points you should remember when presenting a CV.

1. Proofread: check spelling, grammar and punctuation.

2. _____

_____

3. _____

_____

4. _____

_____

5. _____

_____

■ *Increase Your Word Power!*

Can you spell and use the following words correctly?
Economic, economise, effective, efficient, either, eliminate, embarrass, emergency, emphasise, employee, equipment, especially, essential, examine, excellent, enterprise, equal, exempt, exemption, exhibition, expense, experience, extremely.

 # Unit 6

Research Skills and
Report Writing

In our everyday lives we are constantly doing research or finding information about a range of different subjects. This might be something very simple, like finding out what programmes are on television this evening. Give some more examples.

1. _____

_____

2. _____

_____

3. _____

_____

4. _____

_____

5. _____

_____

Now, think of the different ways in which we approach this routine type of 'finding out':

1. We might ask someone.

2. _____

_____

3. _____

_____

4. _____

_____

5. _____

_____

In the world of work, research is carried out in a much more organised and structured way, but the basic idea is the same. Give some examples of the different types of *formal* research that are common:

1. Medical research.

2. _____

_____

3. _____

_____

4. _____

_____

5. _____

_____

Now, write your own definition of research.

_____

_____

_____

_____

_____

During the LCA course you will be constantly doing research for tasks and key assignments in your different subject areas. You might do some or all of the following:
1. Visit the local library.
2. Visit a local museum or heritage centre.
3. Use the Internet.
4. Conduct an interview.
5. Write a letter requesting information.
6. Conduct a vox pop.
   All of these are **sources** – they all provide us with information.

■ Carrying Out a Career Investigation

When you are doing a project or task you will use more than one source of information. For example, if you were doing a career investigation your plan of action might look something like this:
1. Talk to your Career Guidance Counsellor.
2. Write to FÁS for information on your chosen career.
3. Write to colleges for details of courses and entry requirements.
4. Interview someone already qualified in that line of work.
5. Read books, magazine articles, leaflets, etc.
6. Watch a television programme or video.
7. Visit a workplace.
8. Invite a visitor to the classroom.
9. Look at the 'Situations Vacant' column in local and national newspapers.
10. Surf the Internet.

Below is a list of topics. Choose one topic and draw up an action plan for researching it. Include as many sources as possible and be specific. State exactly what kind of information you would look for.

TOPICS

1. Food and drinks of Italy
2. Leisure and recreational facilities in my local area
3. Attitudes to smoking among first years in my school
4. Road safety in my county
5. Planning a holiday
   Add some topics that you may be working on yourself.

6. _____

7. _____

8. _____

■ Plan of Action

INFORMATION REQUIRED   SOURCE

1. _____   _____

2. _____   _____

3. _____   _____

4. _____   _____

5. _____   _____

6. _____   _____

7. _____   _____

8. _____   _____

■ Using Your Local Library

using the internet
at your local library

A LOCAL AUTHORITY LIBRARY SERVICE INITIATIVE

In the age of the information superhighway or Internet, it is easy to overlook the local library when doing research. However, the library contains valuable resources and it is worthwhile getting to know your way around it.

If you have not been inside your local library for a while, you may be surprised at what you will find there, apart from books. Visit your local library and find out how many of the following are available:

1. Computers with Internet access
2. Photocopying facilities
3. Audio tapes
4. Videotapes
5. Compact discs
6. Sheet music
7. Newspapers
8. Magazines
9. Pamphlets
10. Leaflets
11. A study area
12. Any other resources?

The most important resource in the library is its COLLECTION of books. The collection is divided into two parts.

1. Books that may be used only in the library. These are REFERENCE BOOKS such as encyclopaedias, dictionaries and atlases. You would not want to read them from cover to

cover; you REFER to them to find one particular piece of information. For example, if you were researching food and drinks of Italy, you might use an atlas to draw a map showing the different regions of Italy.

2. Books that may be borrowed. This includes all the fiction and non-fiction books in the library.

How do I find the book I want? Simple – use the catalogue. Every library has a catalogue, which is really a record of every book in the collection and where you will find it on the shelves. The larger libraries have their catalogue on computer, and it is just a matter of typing in the name of the book you are looking for. The computer will give you the CALL NUMBER of the book and will tell you if it is on the shelf or out on loan. If you do not have the name of a particular book in mind, you can type in the name of the subject area you are interested in and the computer will give you a list of suitable books.

In smaller libraries, which are not computerised, you have to use the card catalogue.

THE AUTHOR CATALOGUE

If you know the name of the book you want and who wrote it you can go straight to the catalogue. The catalogue is usually on cards, one card for each book, and it is organised alphabetically according to the name of the author. For example, if you were looking for a book entitled *Wines of Italy* by Adam Clarke you would go to the drawer marked 'C' and find Clarke, Adam. Mr Clarke may have written more than one book, so you will go through his cards until you find the one you want. The card will have a CALL NUMBER on it. Copy down the call number. The library shelves are all clearly numbered. Go to the appropriate section and the call number will guide you to the book you want.

THE SUBJECT CATALOGUE

If you are just starting your project you may not have the name of a particular book. You may just want to find out if the library has any books on the subject that you are researching. In this case you should go to the subject catalogue, which is also organised alphabetically. Again, if you were researching food and drinks of Italy, it might be worth your while looking in the subject catalogue, not just under 'Italy' but also under 'food' and under 'wines'.

Remember, if you have trouble using the catalogue or finding books the librarian will always be ready to help you and to make suggestions. If the library does not have the book you want, the librarian will probably be able to get it for you from another branch.

When you have found the book you want your research work really begins! In most cases, you will not need to read the entire book; you just need to be able to find the sections that are useful to you and take what you need from them. At the beginning of the book, the table of contents will guide you to those chapters that you need.

Many books will also have an index at the back, which is a list of all the subjects covered in the book. This will be in alphabetical order, and page numbers will be given for each topic listed.

When you find the section of the book that you want, read the section carefully and take notes of the main ideas. It is much better to take notes in your own words rather than copying directly from the book. Notes in your own words reflect *your* ideas.

Remember to take a note of the name of each book you have consulted and its author. Include this information in your finished task or project.

A Vox Pop

'Vox pop' means 'the voice of the people'. A vox pop gets the opinions of ordinary people on some topical issue. You may like to bring a tape recorder with you. If you are conducting a vox pop, keep the following points in mind:

1. Choose an issue that is topical and/or controversial, something that people are discussing and giving out about. The issue might be local, national or global. Brainstorming will usually provide a variety of interesting issues.
2. Make out some questions, but not too many. Make sure that your questions are short and easy to understand. It is best to use questions that have 'yes' or 'no' answers. You may also want to include a 'no opinion' category.
3. Decide how many people you are going to survey.
4. Get a clipboard, pens and copies of your questionnaire and position yourself in a busy part of town or school.
5. When you have completed your research, return to school and look at your results. Your maths teacher will help you to turn your figures into percentages.
6. Write a report on your research. Make your report interesting and colourful by showing the results in graph form. A simple bar chart or pie chart can sometimes communicate a message much more clearly than a page of writing.
7. If you are using a tape recorder, make sure that you have enough tapes and batteries.

   Remember, when approaching members of the public keep the following points in mind:
   • Be polite.
   • Introduce yourself.
   • If people are too busy to stop you must respect this and thank them anyway.

◼ An Interview

An interview can be a very useful way of finding information. Talking to someone who has had experience in the area you are researching will bring the topic alive. The more preparation you put into the interview, the better the results will be.

1. When you have decided who you want to interview, make a phone call or write a letter asking for permission to conduct the interview. Make sure you state the purpose of the interview.

Remember that the person concerned is giving up his/her time to speak to you. You should make yourself available at a time that suits them – do not expect them to suit you.

2. Ask if you may tape the interview. Some people will not feel comfortable if they are being taped and you have to respect their decision. If you do not have permission to use a tape recorder, be prepared for a lot of note-taking!

3. Do as much background research as you can on the person and on the topic of the interview. Then prepare a list of questions. Be careful with personal or sensitive questions such as 'how much do you earn?' Try using a different approach for some questions, e.g. 'do you make a good living from this type of work?'

4. If this is your first interview you may be nervous, and it might be a good idea to role-play the interview with the teacher or a classmate acting as the interviewee.

5. Make sure that you arrive on time.

6. Listen carefully. Sometimes we are so busy concentrating on our next question that we fail to listen properly.

7. Take notes. You cannot write down everything that is said. Use key words and phrases which will help you to remember what was said.

8. Some answers will suggest questions that you have not prepared – be ready for this.

9. If you do not understand something do not be afraid to ask. Ask for the correct spelling of technical words that are new to you.

10. If you are using a tape recorder make sure that it is working properly, that you have enough tape and that the batteries will last.

11. Thank the person for their time and, of course, follow this up with a letter of thanks.

12. It is important to write up your report of the interview as soon as possible, while it is still fresh in your mind.

■ Visits to Places of Interest

Another way of accessing information is by visiting a local museum or heritage centre. Different kinds of research can be carried out on such a visit:

1. You might be interested in the history of your local area, or in one particular historical event.

2. You might be interested in the history of the building itself.

3. You might want to find out how important the centre is to the tourist industry in the area.

4. You might want to look at how effective the centre is in giving information to visitors.

If you are looking at the centre as part of a project on tourism, you could get a lot of information by drawing up a simple questionnaire and asking one of the staff members to help you fill it out.

The questions you ask will depend on the purpose of your research, but you should keep the following points in mind:
1. Who owns or runs the centre?
2. How many people are employed?
3. How many visitors go through the centre each year?
   Your powers of observation will also be of help with some questions:
1. What facilities are available?
2. Are disabled people catered for?
3. Are foreign visitors catered for?
4. How is the information presented to the visitor?
5. Is it value for money?

■ Using the Internet

The Internet supplies information at our fingertips. The Internet began as a U.S. military project in the 1960s. In 1969 the first version of the Internet was developed when four American universities were connected. The World Wide Web is the network of websites on the Internet, which we can access by means of a browser. In 1993 it was estimated that 13 million people were connected to the net. In 2002 this had increased to over 300 million. We have never had as much access to information as we have now on the Internet. In Information and Communication Technology you will be looking at the Internet in some detail. Make a list of some of the uses to which the Internet is put.

1. Advertising

2. _____

3. _____

4. _____

5. _____

6. _____

7. _____

8. _____

Make a list some of the problems that are associated with the Internet.

1. Security problems – is it safe to give credit card numbers?

2. _____

_____

3. _____

_____

4. _____

_____

5. _____

_____

■ Reports

Reports of different kinds have featured in your life already, e.g. school reports.

A report *describes* something. In many school and work situations and in our everyday lives, we will be asked to make an *oral* or a *written* report about an event or a situation. For example, if we witness a road accident we will be asked to make a statement – to *report* what we have seen.

During the course of the LCA programme you will write many reports. For example:

- At the end of each work experience placement you will be expected to present a written report on your experiences.
- You will write reports on visits that you make to various places, and on visits made by outsiders to your classroom.
- You will also submit a series of TASK REPORTS.

In this section we are going to look in some detail at how you might go about writing a task report.

■ What Is a Task?

A very important aspect of the LCA programme is the opportunity it gives you to become involved in projects or tasks across many different subject areas. Tasks are varied, exciting and challenging and give you the chance to study something that you are particularly interested in. The task itself is a *practical* activity. It might involve running a mini-company, putting on a play, organising a sports day or a soccer tournament, developing a product, putting a newsletter together – the list is endless. However, all tasks have one thing in common – you are required to write a report describing what you did. Your report will be read and assessed by an outside examiner, and you will be interviewed by the examiner on the content of your report.

Even though your tasks will all be very different, your task reports will all have the same general layout.

What should a task report include?

- At the beginning of the report you need to explain exactly what you are setting out to do and how you intend doing it.
- You will then describe everything you did from start to finish.
- Finally, you will look at how your task turned out by comparing the results of your work to your aims.

Now we need to introduce a formal structure to this; we need to look at suitable headings, and the information we should include under each heading.

1. The TITLE PAGE is where you start and must be suitable. The title should be specific and should state clearly what the task is about. If you use an illustration make sure it is relevant. The title page should also include your name and examination number.

2. The CONTENTS PAGE appears inside the front cover, however it is the last page you will do. It includes the section headings of your report with the correct page numbers.

3. SECTION HEADINGS
   (a) *Aims:* This is a clear statement of what you set out to do. If you are working as part of a group, you must state the group aim and your own individual aim.
   (b) *Research and planning:* In this section you will explain how you intend to gather the information you need. You will describe the different research methods you intend to use. For example, you might write letters, conduct a survey, read books or conduct interviews. You will describe any tools or equipment you are going to use. You will also produce an ACTION PLAN, where you will outline the order in which you intend doing things. In this section you will use phrases such as 'I will' or 'I intend to' – you will be writing in the future tense.
   (d) *Description of activity/record of investigation:* This is an account of everything you did from start to finish. You will write this in the past tense. You must describe everything you did and you must be able to show that you did the work. For example, if you say that you wrote a letter you should have a copy of that letter in your task.
   (e) *Results and conclusions:* In this section you will be looking at the results of your work. Did you achieve what you set out to achieve in your aims? How do you know if your task was a success? If things went wrong, can you say why they went wrong? What conclusions have you come to, having finished this task? Give your own opinions.
   (f) *Self-Evaluation:* How did you measure up? Look at your work in a critical way. What were you particularly pleased with? What did you find difficult? What new skills did

you learn? What did you find out about yourself? What could you have done better? What changes would you make if you were to do this work again?

(g) *Subject integration:* Describe the different subject areas you used in doing your task and say how you used them. Be specific! If, for example, you used maths in doing your task, say exactly how maths helped you; use statements beginning 'I used maths to calculate' or 'I used maths to construct graphs.'

4. ADDITIONAL INFORMATION: A task may take several weeks or even months to complete. It is very important that you keep a TASK DIARY where you keep a note of everything you did and when you did it: phone calls made, letters written, interviews conducted, etc. This will be a great help when it comes to writing up your report.

Do not throw anything away; it is important that you keep everything to do with your task in a safe place: copies of letters, questionnaires, photographs, your task diary, etc. This is evidence that you have actually done the work.

When you have completed your task report you need to organise all this documentation and present it in a folder with your report. For example, you will need to write short captions for your photographs, explaining what is in each one. You should also include a list of any books or articles that you read; this list is called a bibliography.

Before you present your task report for examination make sure you proofread it carefully; check it for mistakes in spelling, grammar and punctuation. It is a good idea to ask someone else to proofread your work, as they are more likely to spot mistakes. Perhaps class members could proofread each other's reports. If your report is saved on disc, it is easy to correct mistakes, change the layout of pages and add extra material. You will probably do several rough drafts before you are satisfied with the finished product.

Before your interview read through your report again to make sure it is fresh in your mind.

■ *Increase Your Word Power!*

Can you spell and use the following words correctly?
Fabulous, facilitate, facility, faithfully, false, falsify, familiar, famous, fascinate, fashionable, fatal, fault, favour, finalise, finance, flavour, flexible, fluctuate, forecourt, format, former, formerly, forward, foundation, fraud, frequent, fulfil, fulfilled, function.

■ Key Assignments

I have visited with my class one of the following:
A library
Cinema
Theatre
Heritage centre
Interpretative centre
Museum
Art gallery
and presented a report on this experience.

☐ Date _____

OR
I participated in a visitor exercise and I completed a report on the event.

☐ Date _____

I have prepared a CV and covering letter.

OR
A personal letter and a business letter using IT.

☐ Date _____

I have read one of the following:
A short story
A novel (or extract)
A drama (or extract)
A poem or song
and I have written or taped my review of one of the above.

☐ Date _____

I have conducted one of the following:
An interview
A vox pop
A piece of research
and I have presented my findings.

☐ Date _____

■ Past Examination Questions

1. Write out the speech you would make to a school assembly on 'My experience of the Leaving Certificate Applied – Highs and Lows'. (30 marks)

2. Complete a detailed report on one of the following class activities, highlighting your own role in the experience:
   (a) Organising an information night for parents.
   (b) Conducting a survey relevant to English and Communications.
   (c) A visit your class made in connection with English and Communications. (30 marks)

3. (a) Prepare a brief profile of yourself, which you would present to an employer when applying for a work experience placement. (10 marks)
   (b) Write a diary entry based on one day of the work experience. (5 marks)
   (c) Write a letter of thanks to the employer that you would send on completion of work experience. (15 marks)

4. (a) Compose a code of good telephone techniques entitled 'Top Tips for Telephone Users'. (15 marks)
   (b) Write out in dialogue form a telephone call made by you to a Travel Agent enquiring about flights to London. You should include discussion of departure and arrival times as well as cost. (15 marks)

5. Write a detailed report on one of your work experience placements under the following headings:
   (a) Finding the work placement. (5 marks)
   (b) The preparations you made before beginning the work experience. (5 marks)
   (c) How you communicated with the other workers. (5 marks)
   (d) The skills you developed. (7 marks)
   (e) What you learned about yourself. (8 marks)

6. (a) Name a visitor who was invited to your English and Communications class and explain the reason for the visit. (5 marks)
   (b) How did you and your class prepare for the visitor? (5 marks)
   (c) Do you think that having visitors in the classroom is an effective learning method for students? Give reasons for your answer. (5 marks)
   (d) Write a letter to the visitor thanking him/her for the visit and outlining how you and the class benefited from the occasion. (15 marks)

7. Imagine you are being interviewed for a job **or** for a place on a further education course. You are asked the following questions in the interview:
   (a) Why did you choose to take the Leaving Certificate Applied programme? (6 marks)
   (b) Was the Leaving Certificate Applied a good experience for you? Give reasons for your answer. (6 marks)
   (c) What have you learned about the world of work from your Leaving Certificate Applied work experience? (6 marks)
   (d) What do you know about this job **or** this course? (Name a particular job or course in your answer.) (6 marks)
   (e) Why should we consider you for this job **or** for a place on this course? (6 marks)

8. (a) Describe a visit which your English and Communications class made to a particular premises **or** company **or** organisation. Name the place visited in your answer. (7 marks)

   (b) List three ways in which your class prepared for this visit. (8 marks)

   (c) Write a letter to the premises **or** to the company **or** to the organisation requesting permission to visit. In your letter you should give a brief outline of the Leaving Certificate Applied programme and state the purpose of the proposed visit. (15 marks)

9. Read this advertisement carefully and then answer the questions that follow.

   Enthusiastic young person required by busy Telesales company.
   Must have good telephone manner and be able to work as part of a team.
   Telephone 01-2345678 for details.

   (a) What do you think the advertisement means by an 'enthusiastic young person'? (5 marks)

   (b) Write out briefly what you would say when telephoning for details of the position. (8 marks)

   (c) How would you describe a 'good telephone manner'? (7 marks)

   (d) How has the Leaving Certificate Applied programme helped you to work as part of a team? (10 marks)

10. (a) What do you think is the purpose of a Curriculum Vitae (CV)? (5 marks)

    (b) You have applied for a job and have been asked to submit a Curriculum Vitae (CV). What would you enter under each of the following headings?
    (i) Hobbies and Interests (5 marks)
    (ii) Work Experience (5 marks)
    (iii) Referees (5 marks)

    (c) What else should be included in your Curriculum Vitae (CV)? (5 marks)

    (d) How would you present your Curriculum Vitae (CV)? (5 marks)

■ MODULE 2 *Communications and Enterprise* ■

 # Unit I

What is Enterprise?

You will all have your own ideas about the meaning of the word 'enterprise', and what it means to be an 'enterprising person' or 'entrepreneur'. A brainstorming session will produce lots of answers to the question 'what is enterprise?' When the ideas run out, look carefully at the words and phrases on the board. Select items that are similar. Group the different types of enterprise together under headings such as:
• Producing a Product
• Providing a Service
• Selling a Product
Keep the following question in mind:
Does 'enterprise' just mean running a business and making a profit or is there a wider meaning to the word? If we look up the word 'enterprise' in the dictionary, we will find it explained in the following ways:
• a business venture
• invention and energy in practical affairs
• any planned task or work
• a business firm
• a bold undertaking (i.e. adventurous or courageous)
• a risky undertaking
What do words such as *venture, bold* and *risk* suggest?
  We have all been involved in enterprise at one time or another. Whenever we *solve a problem* or come up with a new and better *idea* for getting something done, we are acting in an enterprising way. Whenever we are involved in *organising some event* we are acting in an enterprising way. For example, in many schools each year a group of sixth-year

pupils will form a committee to organise the Graduation Ball. This is a massive undertaking and a huge responsibility. The members of the committee are responsible for:
• collecting large sums of money
• organising a suitable venue
• choosing the menu
• arranging transport
• hiring a band and a DJ

They will be criticised if things go wrong, but their hard work is not always acknowledged if everything goes well. It can be a thankless task, but nevertheless people can always be found who are prepared to take the risk – these people certainly have what it takes to be entrepreneurs.

Identify times when you were acting in an enterprising way.

In your personal life:

1. Finding a summer job.

2. _____

3. _____

4. _____

5. _____

Since you started LCA:

1. Planning and completing a task.

2. _____

3. _____

4. _____

5. _____

As a member of a club:

1. Helping with a fund-raising event.

2. _____

3. _____

4. _____

5. _____

At work:

1. Taking decisions if the boss is away.

2. _____

3. _____

4. _____

5. _____

■ Enterprise in Your Local Area

There are examples of enterprising people all around us – not just the business people in the community, but also people who set up and run clubs, such as youth clubs, GAA clubs and political organisations. There are examples of enterprise all around us in our local area. We have all seen examples of communities working together to help the victims of a tragedy, or fund-raising to provide some badly needed service in the area.

In each case this involves at least one person having the *vision*, the *energy* and the *enthusiasm* to organise events, to *inspire* other people to get involved, and to *persuade* members of the public to support the cause by parting with their money.

In 1985, Bob Geldof organised the massive Live Aid concerts, which raised over £50 million for famine relief in Ethiopia. However, we can find the same enterprising spirit in people in every parish in Ireland.

Name five enterprising people in your own local area who work in a voluntary capacity, and give examples of things they have achieved.

NAME

ACHIEVEMENTS

1. _____   _____
                               _____

2. _____   _____
                               _____

3. _____   _____
                               _____

4. _____   _____
                               _____

5. _____   _____
                               _____

Name five enterprising people from the local business community who use their entrepreneurial skills to make a profit.

1. _____

2. _____

3. _____

4. _____

5. _____

■ Enterprise on a National Scale

Since the foundation of the Irish state the Government has been involved in enterprising activities. As early as the 1920s enterprises were set up to help get the infant state on its feet, and to improve the job opportunities and standard of living of the people. The ESB, for example, was one of the first ventures to be established. The Government quickly realised that unless a supply of electricity was available, industries would never develop and farming would never modernise. The ESB has been a hugely successful enterprise, and almost 100 years later they are still looking for new opportunities to expand and develop.

Identify other examples of the Government acting in an enterprising way.

1. Setting up the National Lottery.

2. _____

_____

3. _____

_____

4. _____

_____

5. _____

_____

In this unit we will be concentrating on enterprise as a business venture – for profit. 'Enterprise' has been explained in the dictionary as 'a risky undertaking' and 'a bold venture'. We must remember that in all enterprise there is an element of *risk* involved; the entrepreneur is taking a chance or a gamble and hoping it will pay off.

■ Case Study of a Successful Enterprise

The case study presented here is an example of 'niche marketing'. This means finding a 'gap' in the market and filling the gap by providing a product or a service that is needed and that nobody else is providing.

◼ *Michael Meegan and Maximum Impact Displays*

Michael set up his own business in 1994 and since then he has watched his company go from strength to strength.

BACKGROUND

Up until 1994 Michael had worked as a sales representative for a large pharmaceutical company. His work involved selling products to chemists all over the country. In 1994 the company he worked for was taken over and twenty employees, including Michael, were made redundant.

Instead of looking at this as a problem, Michael saw it as a challenge and an opportunity to do something different. During his years as a sales representative he had noticed that large companies, anxious to sell their products, supplied chemist shops with materials for window displays and in-store advertising. This promotional material was usually thrown out without ever being used. Why?

The staff in the shop were too busy to get involved; nobody had the responsibility for doing window displays and it was not considered to be a priority. The staff were reluctant to get involved in something they felt was creative or artistic; they had never been trained to do it and so lacked confidence.

Large department stores hire fully qualified, professional window dressers as they realise the importance of the front window in attracting people into their store. Michael felt that the owners of smaller shops were also well aware of the effect of a striking window display. They knew that most of the time they were not making the best use of a very valuable advertising opportunity.

Michael's business idea was very simple – for a fee he would come to the shop and design and fit attractive, eye-catching window and in-store displays. This would remove a huge burden from the shop owner and make maximum use of resources.

Michael had noticed a 'gap' in the market – a gap he could fill by providing this service. Although he did not have any formal training in art or design, he knew he had a natural flair for this kind of work and he had plenty of confidence in his own ability to succeed. His years on the road as a sales representative meant that he had built up a large database of contacts. Part of his redundancy money provided the necessary capital for his business venture. He had always wanted to work for himself; when asked why he replies, 'It is just something that was in me – something I felt I had to do'.

■ *Steps in Setting up the Business*

1. Michael did not do any formal **market research**. He already knew from his working experience that there was a market for this type of service. He did speak to his customers and got a very positive response. Every one of them said they would use his services. Michael says that the fact that he had his customers before he started was a huge advantage, and he feels it took about two years off the 'lead-in time' or preparation time.
2. Michael drew up a **business plan**, which he submitted to the County Enterprise Board. He found the Enterprise Board very helpful and feels he could have used them more. If you qualify they will give you a grant. Michael was given a fifty per cent Capital Grant which he used for props, materials and tools. They will also give you a *mentor* or guide: somebody who is already running a successful business and who will give you advice and encouragement, and guide you in the right direction. This system suits some people, but it did not suit Michael. (He says he is too stubborn to take advice!)
3. Michael **registered the name of the company** in Dublin Castle under the Registration of Business Names Act 1963. This did not cost him anything and means that no other company can use this name. He is registered as a **sole trader** and his business is very much a one-man operation. He feels that in this type of work the personal touch is important. He sometimes takes on part-time workers at very busy times such as the run up to Christmas.
4. All aspects of running the company are controlled by Michael:
    • planning
    • sourcing and ordering materials
    • keeping accounts
    • dealing with customers on the phone
    • advertising
    • dealing with correspondence
    • travelling all over the country doing displays
    • and, of course, the work he loves best – constantly coming up with ideas that are new and exciting

◼ *Advantages of Being Self–Employed*

According to Michael the most important benefit of running his own company is that all the work he does is for himself. He is his own boss, not answerable to anybody. He can choose to some extent when he will or will not work, and he enjoys this flexibility. It means that his golfing handicap continues to improve! The fact that his home is also his office means that he sees a lot of his young family and this is very important to him.

While Michael has been successful and makes a good living he stresses that it is not all about money. Personal satisfaction is also very important, as is the sense of achievement he gets when things are going well.

◼ *Disadvantages of Being Self-Employed*

There is a downside to being self-employed. The number of hours worked can sometimes be very long, especially in the early stages. He might be on the road all day and at night he has to catch up on accounts and correspondence. He always has to suit the customer and is always working towards deadlines. His work is constantly with him. He finds it difficult to shut off even when he is on holiday.

WORDS OF ADVICE FROM MICHAEL

Michael's philosophy has always been that 'you get out what you put in'.
1. If you plan carefully, know your market and work hard you have a very good chance of succeeding.
2. Do not go straight into your own business from school or college – get the experience of working for somebody else first.
3. Tread lightly – take one step at a time.
4. Do not get discouraged if things are not going well – if you believe in what you are doing, stick with it!

Michael sees courage as a very important quality in an entrepreneur. He would be the first to admit that had he not been made redundant he might never have realised his dream of running his own business. At the time he had a young family, a mortgage, and was the breadwinner in the family. He might have found it difficult to give up the security of a good job, but the decision was partly made for him and he welcomed the opportunity with open arms.

Having studied Michael's situation, identify the **qualities** needed to be a successful entrepreneur.

1. Courage

2. _____

_____

3. _____

_____

4. _____

_____

5. _____

_____

Identify the **skills** needed to be a successful entrepreneur.

1. Good communication skills.

2. _____

_____

3. _____

_____

4. _____

_____

5. _____

_____

WORK TO DO

Do some research on the differences between a sole trader, a partnership and a limited company. List the advantages and disadvantages of each one.

■ *Time Is Money*

Michael insists that good organisation is the key to a successful business. If you are not organised you will end up wasting a lot of time and not only will you lose money, you will also lose customers. You have to set up your business in such a way that it will run efficiently.

Maximum Impact Displays is a one-man organisation, so Michael does not have the problem of keeping in touch with various managers and members of staff. While this might be an advantage, it can also have a downside as Michael has to take responsibility for all aspects of the work. However, he does have a kind of informal *support system*: his wife, Bernie, and the older children often lend a hand by taking messages, sorting correspondence and answering letters.

If Michael is to be efficient, he needs to be able to *store* information and *access* or *retrieve* it when he needs it.

1. He needs to keep a database of customers, which must be constantly updated.
2. He also needs a database of suppliers.
3. He has to keep records of contact names and phone numbers.
4. He has to remember his appointments.
5. He has to keep a record of money spent and received.
6. He has to keep an eye on stock levels and order new stock when he needs it.
7. He has to produce accounts and VAT returns for the Inland Revenue.
8. He has to keep track of expenses such as petrol, phone calls and postage.
9. He has to pay his bills and make sure that his customers pay him.

Also, because Michael is on the road so much, ideas are constantly coming to mind while he is driving. We call this *intrapersonal communication*; the stream of thoughts that constantly go through our minds even when we are consciously doing something else. Very often business ideas will begin to form somewhere in Michael's subconscious mind, and if he does not make a note of these ideas he might lose them altogether. Michael says that this is one of the differences between someone who is self-employed and someone who is working from nine to five for someone else. If you are self-employed you never switch off. He may not act on these ideas for several months, but if he has committed his thoughts to paper he will not forget them.

In pairs or small groups, suggest an efficient information system that somebody like Michael could set up. Keep the following points in mind:

1. Michael is on the road a lot – his van is also his office.
2. If he is badly organised he will lose business.

While you are doing this exercise you need to think about all the different types of information that Michael has to keep track of. Suggest a way of dealing with each type and in each case look at the advantages and disadvantages of your suggestion.

INFORMATION	SYSTEM	ADVANTAGES	DISADVANTAGES
Phone numbers	stored in mobile phone	always to hand	could get lost/stolen
Addresses			
Appointments			
Stock Levels			
Money			
Ideas			

Remember, you need to make the system as simple and efficient as possible.

■ *Advertising*

Michael maintains that the best type of advertising is 'word of mouth' — one satisfied customer will recommend him to someone else. In the early days he did advertise in the trade journals (magazines relating to a particular trade), but he found that this was not really necessary and he gave it up.

Suggest other ways in which a small company could advertise.

1. _____

2. _____

3. _____

4. _____

5. _____

■ *Plans for Expansion*

Michael knows that his business is very personalised because his customers expect *him* to come through the door, not someone else. On the couple of occasions that he did send someone else his customers were not too happy – they have become used to Michael and the way he works. He has no immediate plans for expansion, but he is thinking about diversifying as he knows that the market can change quite quickly. He worries that a multinational corporation might take over the small chemist shops and bring in their own ideas. If and when this happens he will have to be ready for the challenge.

Any regrets? When asked this question Michael does not hesitate. 'Absolutely none,' he says.

Maximum Impact Displays is an example of a small, one-man organisation. We also need to look at the structure of a large or medium-sized organisation, with several different departments and 'layers' of management.

The number and type of departments will depend on the size of the company and the nature of the work involved: manufacturing, sales or service. We are going to look at an example of a large manufacturing company.

■ Manufacturing Company

A manufacturing company makes or produces a product. It takes in raw materials, changes them in some way and produces a finished product for sale. In Junior Cycle you looked at a manufacturing company as an example of a system, with INPUTS, PROCESSES and OUTPUTS.

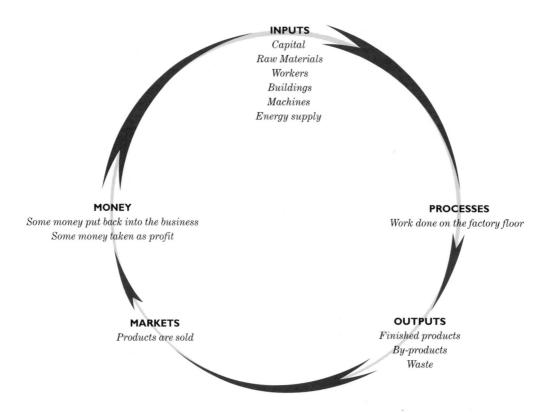

INPUTS
Capital
Raw Materials
Workers
Buildings
Machines
Energy supply

MONEY
Some money put back into the business
Some money taken as profit

PROCESSES
Work done on the factory floor

MARKETS
Products are sold

OUTPUTS
Finished products
By-products
Waste

When we study this flow diagram we can identify *tasks* that need to be done if the system is to function smoothly.

1. Raw materials have to be ordered and stored.
2. These raw materials have to be changed or *processed* in some way.
3. The finished products have to be sold.
4. Bills have to be paid.
5. Money owed to the company has to be collected.
6. Profits have to be calculated and shared out.
7. The cost of all the inputs has to be calculated.
8. Workers have to be hired, trained and looked after.
9. Transport has to be arranged for the raw materials and the finished products.
   Add some more tasks that you can identify.

1. _____

_____

2. _____

_____

The different departments that are set up will reflect the tasks that need to be done. Which tasks are carried out by each of the following departments?

1. Purchasing
2. Production
3. Marketing
4. Finance
5. Human resources
6. Transport

Each department will be under the control of a manager. The structure of the company will look something like the diagram below.

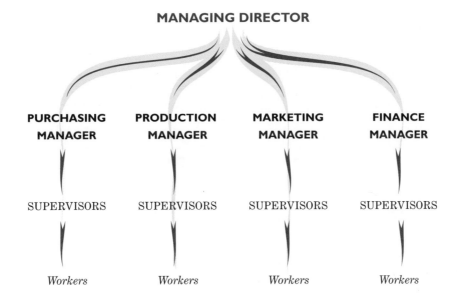

Note: The managing director might be the owner of the company. In a Private Limited Company the managing director will be appointed by the SHAREHOLDERS. As the name suggests, shareholders are people who own a part or a share of the company. The money they pay for their share or shares is used as CAPITAL, to start up or to expand a business.

■ *The Functions of the Management Team*

In pairs or small groups, try and identify four functions of each manager:

MANAGING DIRECTOR

1. To be responsible for the day-to-day running of the business.

2. _____

_____

3. _____

_____

4. _____

_____

PURCHASING MANAGER

1. To get estimates for raw materials.

2. _____

_____

3. _____

_____

4. _____

_____

PRODUCTION MANAGER

1. To make sure machines are in good working order.

2. _____

_____

3. _____

_____

4. _____

_____

MARKETING MANAGER

1. To organise an advertising campaign.

2. _____

_____

3. _____

_____

4. _____

_____

FINANCE MANAGER

1. To make out budgets for each department.

2. _____

_____

3. _____

_____

4. _____

_____

HUMAN RESOURCES MANAGER

1. To provide training for staff.

2. _____

_____

3. _____

_____

4. _____

_____

TRANSPORT MANAGER

1. To keep the fleet of vans or lorries serviced.

2. _____

_____

3. _____

_____

4. _____

_____

FOR DISCUSSION

In this example we have looked at the structure of a company involved in *making a product*.
1. In pairs or small groups, discuss the needs of a company involved in *retailing or sales*, such as a large main car dealership, and draw up a suitable internal structure in diagram form.
2. The needs of a *service industry* will be different. Suggest a suitable departmental division for a large hotel.
3. In a large manufacturing company, in which departments would you find the following personnel?
   (a) a buyer
   (b) an accountant
   (c) a general operative
   (d) a van driver
   (e) a salesperson
4. Draw diagrams to show suitable departmental divisions for each of the following organisations:
   (a) a large second-level school
   (b) a large general hospital
   (c) a daily newspaper
   (d) a transport company, e.g. Bus Eireann
5. It would be useful to do some research on the internal structure of a local business. Perhaps you could use your work experience placement as a basis for your research. Use the following worksheet to help you gather the necessary information.

NAME OF COMPANY _____

TYPE OF BUSINESS

- *Production* ☐
- *Service* ☐
- *Retailing* ☐
- *Other* ☐

NUMBER OF EMPLOYEES ☐

DEPARTMENTS

1. _____
2. _____
3. _____
4. _____
5. _____

When you have gathered your information write a short report on your findings and present it to the class.

FOR DISCUSSION

1. Can you see a relationship between the number of employees and the number of departments?
2. Do you think a large organisation can be run efficiently without departments?
3. Which category does your own mini-company fall into?
   Are you making a product, selling a product or providing a service? Decide on a suitable departmental structure and draw up a *job description* for each manager. A job description should list all the tasks that the manager is responsible for.

4. Brainstorm all the different types of communication you would use if you were running your own business or were part of a large organisation. When you have finished your brainstorming session put the different types of communication into categories, using the following headings:

I. LISTENING TO

   (a) Customers

   (b) _____

   (c) _____

   (d) _____

   (e) _____

2. TALKING TO
   (a) Employees

   (b) _____

   (c) _____

   (d) _____

   (e) _____

3. READING
   (a) Reports

   (b) _____

   (c) _____

   (d) _____

   (e) _____

4. WRITING
   (a) Letters

   (b) _____

   (c) _____

   (d) _____

   (e) _____

5. IT SKILLS
   (a) Sending and receiving e-mail

   (b) _____

   (c) _____

   (d) _____

   (e) _____

In Module 1 you practised all of these skills. You will now have the opportunity of using them in the running of your mini-company!

■ Revision

Can you remember what you learned about **effective communication** in Module 1? Complete the following list.
Effective communication is:

1. Clear

2. _____

3. _____

4. _____

5. _____

Remember the following points:
1. When you are running a business you have to think of both INTERNAL COMMUNI-CATIONS (inside the company) and EXTERNAL COMMUNICATIONS (with the outside world).
2. The type of communications system you set up will depend on the size of the company.
3. Managers need to be able to communicate effectively. Interpersonal skills are very important as it has been estimated that managers spend ninety per cent of their time communicating. A manager is in constant contact with employees, customers, other managers, the managing director, etc.

◼ The Communication System in a Large Company

The communication system in a large organisation is quite complex.

◼ *Internal Communication*

The internal system of communication will be closely related to the departmental structure.

As you can see from the diagram, communication will be downward, upward and horizontal.

Downward communications are messages sent downwards from a point in the structure, e.g. an instruction from the managing director to a department manager. Upward communications are messages sent upwards from a point in the structure, e.g. a report from the finance manager to the Managing Director.

Horizontal communications are messages between two people of the same rank, e.g. the finance manager gets reports on spending and expenses from all other managers.

■ *External Communication*

Every company has to communicate with people and organisations in the outside world: goods have to be ordered and staff recruited, etc.

Complete the following diagram by naming the different groups that a company communicates with.

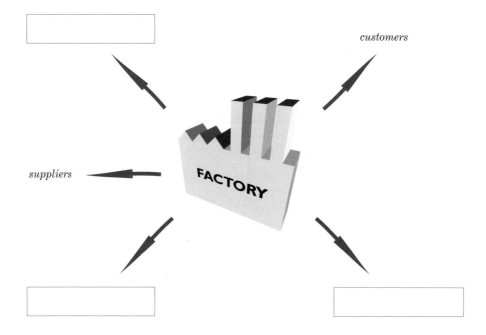

Even though the communication *system* can be quite complicated in a large organisation, the basic *skills* needed to communicate remain very simple.

At every level people must:
- listen
- give instructions clearly and simply
- look for feedback
- write legibly
- understand reports
- use and understand graphs
- interpret body language

Forms of Communication Used in Business

Oral Communication

There are many forms of oral communication used by managers on a daily basis:
• Face-to-face conversations with workers and other managers.
• Telephone conversations with suppliers and customers.
• Formal meetings with colleagues to review progress and to make decisions.

Oral communication can be very efficient as it is fast and the manager gets instant feedback. He can make sure that what he says is understood. The main problem with oral communication is that there is no written record kept of what was said and what decisions were made.

Written Communication

With written communication the message is put in writing. A written communication can take many forms:
• Letter
• Memo
• Notice
• Report
• Fax
• E-mail
• Business Document (e.g. an invoice)

The written word has many advantages over the spoken word. There is a permanent record of what was said, and the document can be referred to again and again if the receiver is confused or forgetful. However, the main disadvantage is that feedback is slow. Also, many managers get so many documents to read that they complain of information overload.

FOR DISCUSSION

1. Imagine that you are the managing director of a large company. What channels of communication would you use in order to communicate the following, and with whom would you communicate?
   (a) Ten per cent of the workforce are to be made redundant.
   (b) An important customer has complained about the quality of his last delivery.
   (c) You want to arrange a meeting with your managers.
   (d) You have an idea for a new product.
   (e) The profits are down by twenty per cent on last year.
2. What do we mean by the term 'communications media'? In what ways can businesses use the media to their advantage?

WORK TO DO

It is important that you know how to use a fax machine. If you have not used one before, make sure you find an opportunity to do so either in your school or centre, or on work experience. Perhaps you could send a fax to your local County Enterprise Board asking if someone would visit your class to give advice on setting up your mini-company.

Identify the communication skills that your class now has, and which ones will be useful in the running of your mini-company.

1. IT skills

2. _____

3. _____

4. _____

5. _____

■ Management Skills

We have looked at the different tasks or jobs which managers are responsible for. We now need to look at the skills that managers need in order to carry out their tasks efficiently.

Obviously, a manager will have to have the practical skills needed to run his own department. For example, a person in charge of finance will most likely be an accountant. As well as these practical skills, probably the two most important managerial skills are the

ability to lead others – **leadership skills**, and the ability to communicate – **interpersonal skills**.

All managers will have a team of people working under them in the different departments. Basically, what a manager is trying to do is to run his department as efficiently as possible, and that means getting the most out of his workers.

The old style of management was AUTOCRATIC, where the managers made all the decisions and controlled their staff largely through fear. The manager often acted like a DICTATOR.

The modern style of management is more DEMOCRATIC. Workers have a say in how the department is run. Research has shown that if workers have a say in making decisions they will tend to work harder. Today's manager is more like a LEADER.

Managers must be able to *motivate* their workers to achieve the targets that are set. One of the most important skills that a manager must have is the ability to *lead* others and to *inspire* people to do as well as they possibly can. In this sense, a business manager is really no different from the manager or captain of a football team. Can you identify a manager from the world of sport who motivates, inspires and leads?

Identify some of the *qualities* that a successful manager or leader might have.

1. Courage – the courage to take risks and to stand up for what he believes in.

2. _____

_____

3. _____

_____

4. _____

_____

5. _____

_____

Identify ways in which a business manager might motivate his team.

1. Giving bonuses based on performance

2. _____

_____

3. _____

_____

4. _____

_____

5. _____

Discuss what it means to be a *motivated worker*. At the end of your discussion write your own definition.

A motivated worker is a worker _____

_____

_____

_____

_____

_____

■ *Increase Your Word Power!*

Can you spell and use the following words correctly?

Gamble, garage, general, generally, generate, generator, generous, genetics, genre, genuine, geriatric, gimmick, glamour, glamorous, global, gourmet, gradient, graphic, grateful, gratefully, guidance.

Unit 2

Preparation

At this stage in the preparation of setting up a mini-company the class needs to decide on a suitable enterprise. Before making a decision, you should spend some time looking at the **strengths** of the group. This can be done by answering the following questions:

What *skills* do *I* have?

What *skills* do we have as a *group*?

What *resources* do *I* have?

What *resources* do we have as a *group*?

■ My Skills

Our skills are things that we can do. We are all good at a wide range of things, and it is only when we go through the exercise of writing them all down that we realise how talented we are! We are always far more ready to admit to things we cannot do than to things we can do. Take a few minutes to think about the skills you have, and note them down under the headings provided.

When you are making your lists, do not just think of your school subjects. Look at all aspects of your life. Your hobbies and interests may be very important. You will also have gained useful skills during work experience, voluntary work, community work or involvement in youth clubs etc.

If you cannot fill in all the blanks yourself ask a friend for help. Very often, other people notice things about us that we do not recognise ourselves.

COMMUNICATION SKILLS

1. I can listen to what others have to say.

2. _____

_____

3. _____

_____

4. _____

_____

5. _____

_____

FINANCIAL SKILLS

1. I can manage my bank account.

2. _____

_____

3. _____

_____

4. _____

_____

5. _____

_____

CREATIVE SKILLS

1. I can take good photographs.

2. _____

_____

3. _____

_____

4. _____

_____

5. _____

_____

PRACTICAL SKILLS

1. I can fix a puncture.

2. _____

_____

3. _____

_____

4. _____

_____

5. _____

_____

PEOPLE SKILLS

1. I can look after children.

2. _____

_____

3. _____

_____

4. _____

_____

5. _____

_____

When everybody in the class has looked at their individual skills and talents, share your results. You are now in a position to look at the combined skills of the class.

Remember, we are more likely to succeed when we are doing something which we are good at and which we really love doing.

Now, in the same way answer the second question, 'What resources do we have?' In small groups, make a list of the resources you have at your disposal. Listed below are a few useful headings.

MY OWN RESOURCES

1. I know somebody who can help with . . .

2. _____

_____

3. _____

_____

4. _____

_____

5. _____

_____

FAMILY/FRIENDS

1. I can borrow . . .

2. _____

_____

3. _____

_____

4. _____

_____

5. _____

_____

MY SCHOOL

1. We have access to computers . . .

2. _____

_____

3. _____

_____

4. _____

_____

5. _____

_____

MY COMMUNITY

1. I can get sponsorship from . . .

2. _____

_____

3. _____

_____

4. _____

_____

5. _____

_____

Once you have completed this analysis of the skills and resources of the group, you will be in a position to come up with ideas for a successful enterprise. Your Vocational Preparation and Guidance teacher will help you to generate ideas.

Before you come to a final decision you will need to carry out some MARKET RESEARCH. You need to find out if anyone out there will be interested in buying what you are trying to sell.

■ *Market Research*

Before spending a lot of money developing a product or service, an entrepreneur needs to know if he is going to be able to sell it. If he is looking for a loan from the bank, the bank manager will insist that the results of a market research survey are available. If he applies to the County Enterprise Board for a grant they will also insist that market research is done.

In the same way, you will need to do market research before you finally decide on what exactly you will be producing or what service you will be offering. You need to be able to answer 'yes' to the following questions before you go into business:
1. Will we be producing what the customers want?
2. Will we be producing it at the right price?
3. Will we be producing a better product than our competitors?

Finding the answers to these questions will involve going out into the marketplace to carry out research. (Note: for the purposes of your mini-company the 'marketplace' will be quite small: your year group, school or the local community. Major companies operate in a much larger geographical area. For example, their marketplace could be the EU, or they might operate in a global market.)

The most common type of research method is the questionnaire. The simplest type of survey to do is a face-to-face survey. Simply set yourself up in some suitable place, such as the local shopping centre. If you know your market is going to be confined to the school, do your research at break-time, when pupils will have time to answer your questions.

It is important that you interview a range of people; in a school-based survey you should interview a certain number from *each* year group, rather than confine yourself to just one. Why?

■ Case Study

An LCA Mini Company, Creative Minds, decided to produce and sell a range of wooden activity toys, suitable for 3–6 year olds. They came up with five different designs. Before going into production, they decided to carry out some market research.

STEP ONE

Creative Minds made a prototype of each design. A prototype is a sample product. It is made for three reasons:
1. To make sure that the design works.
2. To calculate the cost.
3. To see if potential customers like it.

STEP TWO

In order to do some market research the class made out a simple questionnaire as follows:

Q.1 Would you be interested in buying wooden activity toys?

Yes ☐   No ☐

Q.2 Which of these designs would you find most attractive?

(a) Walking Genius   ☐

(b) Acrobat   ☐

(c) Tumbling Clown   ☐

(d) Super Shapes   ☐

(e) Jigsaw   ☐

Q.3 Would you be prepared to pay €5 for one of these toys?

Yes ☐   No ☐

Q.4 Do you know of similar products on sale locally?

Yes ☐   No ☐

STEP THREE

The class then had to decide who they would target with their market research. After discussion, they felt that parents and older brothers and sisters would be most likely to buy the toys.

STEP FOUR

They conducted the market research as follows:
- They surveyed parents who were in school attending a Parent – Teacher meeting.
- They surveyed a sample of students from each year group.

STEP FIVE

When they examined the results, they could see quite clearly that designs (a) and (c) were the most popular, and that there was very little interest in designs (b), (d) or (e). They also knew that people would be happy to pay €5 for each toy.

STEP SIX

The class then had to investigate the competition, in order to find out if similar products could be bought in the local shops. If they were available, they would have to compare them with their own products under the headings of quality, design and price. They found that there were no similar products available locally.

Armed with all this information, Creative Minds decided to produce only designs (a) and (c). They had saved themselves a lot of time, money and heartache by doing market research.

WORK TO DO

Make out suitable market research questionnaires for the following ideas:
- Setting up a school sweet shop
- Selling rolls at lunchtime
- Setting up a car wash

In each case you must identify your target market and decide how many people you are going to survey. Keep the questionnaire as simple as possible. Use 'closed' questions as much as possible (i.e. questions that can be answered by 'yes' or 'no'), otherwise you will end up with too much information, and you will find it difficult to analyse your results. Your maths teacher will help you to analyse the results and put them into graph form.

Now, take some of the enterprise ideas produced by your group and organise some market research. Use your IT skills in the making out of the questionnaire, and your communication skills in carrying out the survey. Present a report on your market research. You should cover all of the following points in your report:

1. the purpose of the research
2. methods used
3. questions asked
4. number of people surveyed
5. locations used by surveyors and why these locations were chosen
6. results of analysis – show these graphically
7. Problems encountered
8. decisions made

When you have finally decided on an idea that you feel will be successful, you need to draw up a BUSINESS PLAN.

■ *A Business Plan*

At this stage you are probably impatient to get on with the real business of producing, selling and making money. However, it is vital that you spend enough time and thought on preparation. If your enterprise idea is thought through carefully it is more likely to succeed than if you just rush in without looking at the pitfalls.

In the real world, setting up in business is a risky undertaking, and you stand to lose a lot of money if things go wrong. A business plan is really a plan of action with a timetable. Working on a business plan will help you to see any problems before they happen. You have to ask yourself the tough questions and you must be brutally honest; do not try to push problems under the carpet or simply hope that they will go away.

If you find that the idea you started off with will probably not work out, drop it immediately and try another one.

Your business plan should include the following sections:

1. THE PRODUCT OR SERVICE

Give a detailed description of the products you are going to make or the service you are going to provide. You must list the strengths and weaknesses of your product or service. Is it safe? Is it legal?

2. YOUR TARGET MARKET

Describe your target market. What size is your target market? Who is going to buy your product? Why will they buy from you? Have you tested your idea in the market?

3. YOUR COMPETITION

Describe the competition you will have. How will you stand up to this competition? How is your product better?

4. MARKETING

Describe your marketing strategy. How will you advertise? Where will you sell? What about delivery? What is your selling price? What about packaging?

5. STRUCTURE

Describe the management structure of your company. How many managers do you need? What tasks will each manager be responsible for? How many workers will you have?

6. PRODUCTION

Describe the skills and resources available. Do you have all the tools you need? Do you know how to use them? Will you be depending on other people to help you? What are the health and safety considerations? How much time do you have each week? How many items can you produce in the time available? Have you costed your raw materials? Do you know how much it costs to produce each item?

7. SALES

Do a sales projection. How many items do you hope to sell and at what price? What profit will you make on each item?

8. FINANCE

Describe your sources of capital. Where are you going to get the money to get started?

WORK TO DO

Using the headings and questions above as a guide, make out a business plan for your mini-company.

■ *Individual Roles in The Mini-Company*

The management structure of the company will have been decided upon at this stage. In order to get the mini-company up and running as quickly as possible, it is important that each individual in the class is aware of the role they will be playing. This means that people will have to be appointed to positions in the company.

Applying for a position in the mini-company and going through a selection procedure can be a great help when you find yourself doing it for real at some future date.

When the positions in the mini-company are advertised, you first of all have to decide which to apply for. In Vocational Preparation and Guidance class, you will have identified the qualities, skills and experience that you have, and this should help you to make up your mind. You may decide to apply for more than one position.

The next step is to submit an application for the position you are interested in.

In Module 1 we looked in some detail at the CV and covering letter. It is important at this stage that you update the CV which you produced last term. Have you achieved anything since then, which you should include? When you are thinking about this question, think about areas such as work experience, results of task work, sporting achievements, voluntary work, etc. It is important that you get into the habit of constantly updating your CV. Also, remember that each job you apply for is different, and you may wish to emphasise different skills and work experience placements depending on the nature of the job you are applying for.

Getting your application right and looking good on paper is the first step towards a career. Carefully check and proofread your CV and letter. There should be no mistakes in spelling, punctuation or grammar. First impressions are important; your IT skills will ensure that your application is clear, concise and neat. Keep your covering letter short and businesslike and make sure you state clearly which position you are interested in.

★ EXERCISES

1. From local and national newspapers, bring in a selection of job advertisements. Using these as a guide draw up advertisements for each of the following positions. Each advertisement should include a job description, and should list the skills and qualities required.
   • Managing Director
   • Purchasing Manager
   • Production Manager
   • Advertising Manager
   • Sales Manager
   • General operatives in the above departments
2. Update your CV. What can you add?
3. Apply for a position in the mini-company. Write a suitable covering letter.

The Interview

Most members of the class will have had several job interviews at this stage for summer work etc. Working in pairs, discuss the following:
1. How did you get the interview?
2. How did you prepare for it?
3. How did you feel going in?
4. What questions did you find difficult to answer?
5. Were you conscious of your body language?
6. How did you feel at the end of the interview?
7. Would you approach your next job interview differently? What would you do?
   Share your thoughts with the class.

We can look at the interview under the following headings:
1. The purpose of the interview
2. Questions to be ready for
3. Preparation
4. Body language
5. Evaluation – how well did I do?

The Purpose of the Interview

Like all communication situations, a job interview is a two-way process. The interviewer and the candidate will use the interview to find out things about each other that will help them to make decisions.

The person conducting the interview is hoping to find the best person for the job. He will have spent money advertising the position; he will have spent time going through applications. He is now spending time – perhaps a whole day – interviewing. When he does make a decision and someone is hired, time and money will probably be spent training that person for the particular job. Because of this investment of time and money, it is important that the right person is hired; no company wants to hire someone who is not suitable or who will leave after a short time.

What does the interviewer need to find out about you, the candidate?
1. Do you have the skills and experience necessary to do the job?
2. Are you an enthusiastic, motivated person?
3. Are you able to work as part of a team?

How is the interviewer going to assess your strengths and weaknesses in these three areas?

Your Skills and Experience

From reading your CV and talking to your referees, the interviewer will already have decided that you probably have the necessary skills and experience, otherwise you would not have been given an interview. At the interview you have to show that you are the most suitable applicant. You need to show that the skills you have fit in with what the employer is looking for. Examine the job description carefully. It is up to you to convince the employer that you can **transfer** skills from one position to another. For example, you may not have worked in a shop before, but you might have worked in a hotel.

What skills can you transfer from one job to the other?

1. Dealing with people.

2. Handling money.

3. _____

_____

4. _____

_____

5. _____

_____

■ *Your Level of Enthusiasm and Motivation*

Here, the interviewer is trying to find out how willing you are to work; are you a self-motivated person or do you need someone constantly telling you what to do? Are you the kind of person who will only do what is in the job description, or are you prepared to pitch in and help with anything if there is a crisis? Are you prepared to go the extra mile to get the job done? Can you solve problems on your own or do you always rely on your supervisor or boss? Are you a determined person who does not give up easily if things go wrong? Can you learn new skills? Can you adapt to change?

Again, it is up to you to convince him that you are the right person for the job. Remember that having done the Leaving Certificate Applied, you are used to working on your own, solving problems and working under pressure.

■ *Your Ability to Work as a Member of a Team*

It will be very important to the interviewer to find out if you can fit in with the people already employed in the company. He will be trying to assess how well you get on with others; your willingness to work with people of different backgrounds and your ability to take orders and criticism.

■ *Questions to Be Ready for*

Interviewers will ask a wide *range* of questions designed to give them answers to the three things they need to know about you. They will also use different *types* of questions.

Open questions, such as 'tell us about yourself', will give you a chance to talk and to expand on your strengths.

Closed questions, such as 'I see you left school a year ago', require just a short yes/no type answer.

Interviewers will usually ask some *hypothetical questions*, to see how you would react in certain situations, e.g. 'What would you do if . . . ?'

As part of your preparation for the interview you should make out a list of questions which you are likely to be asked. Although every interview is different, many of the questions can be predicted, and if you have prepared well there should be no nasty surprises.

SKILLS AND QUALIFICATIONS
1. Why did you choose this career?
2. What were your best subjects at school? Why?
3. What qualities do you think are needed for this job?
4. Do you have plans for further study?
5. Why are you changing careers?
6. What course did you study in school?
7. Have you ever done this type of work before?
8. What do you know about this type of work?
9. What do you think of the last company you worked for?
10. What IT qualifications/experience do you have?
11. Tell me about your present job.
12. Why did you leave your last job?
13. What qualifications do you have that make you suitable for this job?
14. Tell me about the Leaving Certificate Applied. How does it differ from the established Leaving Certificate?
15. What did you like best about the Leaving Certificate Applied?
16. Do you think the Leaving Certificate Applied was a good preparation for the world of work? Why?

ENTHUSIASM AND MOTIVATION
1. Would you be willing to undertake training or further study in your spare time?
2. Where do you see yourself in five years' time?

3. How long do you think you would stay in this job?
4. Which is more important to you – the money or the type of job?
5. Why should we hire you?
6. Tell me about yourself.
7. What achievements are you most proud of?
8. How well do you cope under pressure?
9. Why do you want this job?
10. What are your ambitions?
11. How do you feel about working unsociable hours?
12. How do you feel about wearing a uniform at work?
13. Would you be prepared to travel as part of your job?
14. How would you feel about moving away from home?
15. Give an example of a problem you solved and how you solved it.
16. How would you handle conflict in the workplace?
17. Describe a conflict situation you dealt with.
18. What was your greatest challenge?
19. Can you act on your own initiative?
20. What do you know about our company?
21. Are you a competitive person?
22. What can you contribute to our company?
23. How could you improve yourself?

ABILITY TO GET ON WITH OTHERS

1. How did you get on with your boss/fellow workers in your last job?
2. Do you prefer to work alone or as part of a team?
3. What sort of people do you get on with best?
4. Would you like to be self-employed?
5. How do you deal with criticism?
6. Did you hold any positions of responsibility at school?
7. Tell me about a disappointment you had. How did you deal with it?
8. How do you feel about working with people from other backgrounds?
9. How would you deal with a fellow worker who was not pulling his weight?
10. What did you like/dislike about your last job?
11. What have you learned about yourself from your last job?
12. What was the last book you read? How did it affect you?
13. What was the last movie you saw? How did it affect you?
14. What interests do you have outside of work?
15. Are you interested in sports?
16. How would you describe yourself?
17. How would your friends describe you?
18. Are you creative?

It is vitally important that you think out your answers before the interview, as it can be quite difficult to think 'on your feet'. Remember that the better prepared you are the more confident you will be. While you are trying to make a good impression, you must be honest; your body language is likely to give you away if you are bluffing.

The best approach to some of these questions is to have an example ready of an incident from school or work which shows how you behaved. For example, if you are asked 'How do you cope under pressure?' do not just say that you cope well; give an example of a time when you were under pressure and describe how you handled it.

In your answers, try to avoid meaningless answers such as 'I like a challenge' or 'I am good with people'. Interviewers are fed up listening to these phrases; make your answer more specific. Say why you like a challenge, or what there is about the job that you find challenging or what have you done which shows you are good with people.

Remember that a job interview is a two-way process. It gives you the opportunity to form impressions of the company and the interviewer. You might be given the opportunity to ask some questions about the job or about the company. You should be prepared for this and have some questions ready. It is not a good idea to ask about pay and conditions at this stage. These matters will be discussed when a job offer is made. Also, be careful of asking questions that have already been answered for you during the interview.

FOR DISCUSSION

1. Working in pairs, take some of the more difficult questions from the list and role-play an interview.
2. How would you react if you were asked about your weaknesses?
3. How should you treat questions about your last boss, or the last company you worked for?
4. Suggest four questions that you might want to ask at an interview.

■ *Preparation*

Preparation is vital. Your prospective employer has already found out a great deal about you from your CV and referees. It is important that you also do your homework.

1. Find out as much as possible about the company. Can you answer the following questions about the company:
   - What exactly do they do?
   - What products do they make or what services do they provide?
   - Are they Irish or foreign owned?
   - How long have they been established?
   - How many people are employed?
   - How is it structured?

- Who are the important people?
- What kind of reputation has the company?
- What kind of image do they project?
- Have they expanded recently?
- Are they successful?
- What kind of profit do they make?

   If they have a website, you will be able to get a lot of information there. Libraries will sometimes have information about local companies. If it is a large company they will probably have a Public Relations Department, and you can ring them and ask for information. If it is a local company, the chances are that you, or one of your family, will know someone who is already working there and who would be willing to talk to you.

2. Go over your list of questions and have your answers ready. While you should not learn answers off by heart it is important that you think your answers through. Practise going through your answers with a friend acting as the interviewer. Ask your friend for feedback, not just on your answers, but also on your body language. Have you any annoying mannerisms that you are not aware of? Do you sound enthusiastic? Do you sound enthusiastic only when talking about sports or leisure activities? Are you giving too many yes/no type answers? This type of role-play and feedback can be a great help, especially if you are feeling very nervous.

3. Make sure you know exactly where and when the interview is going to be held. Have your transport arrangements worked out. Leave home earlier than is necessary, in order to allow for delays. There is nothing worse than arriving all hot and bothered with only seconds to spare. You need to be as cool and relaxed as you can. You will be nervous enough without worrying about being late or unable to find the place.

4. Make sure that you have with you any documents you were asked to bring, such as references or certificates. It is also a good idea to bring a copy of your CV so that you can look over it before you go in.

■ *Body Language*

You are bound to be nervous at the thought of an interview. However, if you have prepared well you will be feeling confident. Do not forget that you have already cleared the first hurdle; your application must have made an impression if you have been short-listed for interview. This should boost your confidence and make you feel good about yourself and your chances of getting the job. If you go into the interview feeling positive about yourself and what you have to offer, your nerves will settle after a few minutes.

■ *Appearance*

Your confidence will also be given a boost if you are happy with your appearance. Remember if you look good you will feel good! The best advice regarding what to wear is to choose something that you are comfortable with and that is *appropriate*.

If you are going for a job in the fashion industry or in the entertainment industry, it might be acceptable to dress up to make a statement, but generally it is best to select something which is safe and conservative. Remember that what you wear sends out signals about how you think and feel. At the interview you are trying to project an image of someone who is reliable and trustworthy; someone who is serious about the job and who expects to be taken seriously by the interviewer. You do not want to be worried during the interview about the length of your skirt or the colour of your shirt.

If you are happy with your appearance you will feel confident and you will be able to concentrate on the questions. Remember that a prospective employer may well reject you if you are not suitably dressed.

Other aspects of your appearance are also important. Make out a set of guidelines for each of the following:

	DO	*DO NOT*
Jewellery		
Hair		
Beard		
Perfume/aftershave		
Personal hygiene		
Ties		

Shoes   _____   _____

                 _____   _____

Accessories   _____   _____

                 _____   _____

Make-up   _____   _____

                 _____   _____

Breath   _____

                 _____

◼ *Making an Entrance*

The impression that you create as you enter the room is very important; studies have shown that most interviewers make up their minds about a candidate during the first three or four minutes. When you are invited into the interview room take a deep breath, relax, and enter the room slowly and calmly. Shake hands only if the interviewer offers a handshake. Your handshake should be firm rather than limp, but not a bone-cruncher! Look the interviewer in the eye and smile. The interviewer will introduce himself. Make sure to catch his name. Do not sit down until you are invited to do so.

At this stage you will be at your most nervous. The interviewer will understand this and will make every effort to help you to feel relaxed. In fact if you showed no sign of nerves you might come across as over-confident. He may make a comment about the weather or the traffic, or he might ask if you had any difficulty finding the place. He is only trying to put you at your ease, and he does not expect detailed replies to these comments! When he feels you are ready he will start the actual interview.

Role-play making an entrance; you will need two volunteers. The teacher will take the part of the interviewer, Student A makes an effective entrance and creates a good impression while Student B gives the impression that it would not be a good idea to employ him.

◼ *Posture*

Sit up straight. If you slouch in the chair you will come across as uninterested and inattentive. Do not lean on the interviewer's desk! If you have a bag or a briefcase place it on the floor beside you. Keep your hands on the sides of the chair or on your lap. Try to stay still. Do not fiddle with your hair or your rings. Do not look at your watch. Keep your head up and maintain good eye contact with the interviewer. If you are being interviewed by more than one person, make sure to include everybody in your answers. Good eye contact will show that you are honest and sincere, with nothing to hide. There is a difference, however, between keeping good eye contact and staring; look away from time to time, but do not look at the floor. If you are thinking about the answer to a question, for example, it is perfectly all right to look up.

When the interview is over, get up, shake hands, thank the interviewer by name, smile and leave. Again, it would be helpful if two volunteers would demonstrate the difference between good and bad posture.

EVALUATION – HOW DID I DO?

At this stage of the Leaving Certificate Applied programme you are used to evaluating your work and performance. We cannot learn from our mistakes unless we take time to look back and reflect on how we did and how we could improve. Review your performance as soon as possible, while the experience is still fresh in your mind. Make a note of questions which you feel you handled badly and spend a bit of time trying to improve on your answers, as these questions could come up again in your next interview. Look also at the questions that you know you handled well – make a note of these answers so that you can look over them before your next interview.

Do not forget other aspects of the interview. Can you answer 'yes' to all of the following questions?
• Was I punctual?
• Did I bring any documentation that was required?
• Was I comfortable with my appearance?
• Was I dressed appropriately?
• Did I make a good entrance?
• Did I sound enthusiastic and motivated?
• Did I hold the interviewer's attention?
• Did I show that I knew what was required for the job?
• Was I able to answer questions about the company?
• Did I keep good eye contact?
• Did I sit up straight and look interested?
• Did I listen carefully to the introductions?
• Did I listen carefully to the questions?
• Did I avoid yes/no answers as far as possible?
• Did I respond well to 'open' questions by giving information about myself?
• Did I ask at least one good question when invited?
• Did I make a good exit?

If you have not been successful in your application, it might be possible for you to get some feedback from the interviewer. Some large companies will give feedback about your performance and this can be very helpful. If you do not receive feedback, you may be able to contact the interviewer in a non-threatening way and ask why your application was not successful. Do not give the impression that you are challenging his decision; make it clear that you are simply anxious to improve your chances of being offered a job. This can take a lot of courage on your part, but it can be very helpful.

★ EXERCISES

1. Apply for a position in the mini-company. Study the job description carefully. Make a list of the qualities and skills required for the position.
2. Prepare for your interview. Role-play an interview with a friend and get feedback.
3. Reverse the roles. If possible, record a mock interview on video. When viewing the video analyse the performance of the person being interviewed. After your interview you will be given feedback by the interviewer. With the help of this feedback evaluate your performance.
4. Design a poster entitled 'Interview Tips'.
5. Design a booklet giving LCA students advice on applying for a job. Go through all the stages involved, from answering the advertisement to preparing for the interview. You will have to get your points across in a simple and concise way. Suggest a suitable title for the booklet. This exercise could be used as a Communications Project.

■ Setting up Your Mini-Company
■ *Advice and Support*

Although the group will be totally responsible for the running of the mini-company, you should look for any help and advice you can get from outside. You will find that individuals and organisations are only too willing to offer their time and expertise.

It can be particularly helpful to ask a local, self-employed person to visit the class, talk to you and answer your questions. Do you know anyone who is self-employed? Perhaps a parent, an older brother or sister, or someone you have worked for?

It is important that the class prepares well for such a visit. People who run their own businesses are very busy, and they will not appreciate taking time off to speak to a group who are not interested and motivated. Discuss in advance what you want to find out.

Below are some questions that you might think about and which should trigger further questions.
• Why did you start your own business?
• Was it a difficult decision?
• How did you prepare?
• Where did you go for help and advice?
• Where did you get your capital?
• Did you get grants? Loans?
• What problems did you face in the early stages?

- Did you do market research?
- Did you make out a business plan?
- How many people do you employ?
- What do you enjoy most about running your own business?
- Has your business expanded?
- Have you plans for further expansion?
- What are the disadvantages of running your own business?
- What qualities and skills do you think are needed by a successful entrepreneur?
- How do you advertise your product/service?
- What kind of advertising do you find most effective?
- Have you ever regretted your decision to set up in business for yourself?
  If you prepare well you will get a lot of useful feedback from your visitor.
  When you invite a visitor to the classroom, do not forget the usual courtesies:
- Make sure someone is at the front door to greet the visitor and bring him to the classroom.
- Check in advance to see if your visitor needs anything special, such as a flip-chart, television and video, overhead projector, etc. Make sure that these are available if required and in working order.
- Make sure you have a jug of water available.
- One member of the group should introduce the visitor by giving his/her name and some information on what he/she does.
- Make sure that somebody in the group is prepared to ask the first question. This will avoid awkward silences.
- Offer refreshments at the end of the session.
- Thank your visitor for his/her time, and for sharing his/her experiences with you.
- Always follow up a visit with a letter of thanks.
- Prepare a report on the visit.

You could invite a representative from your local County Enterprise Board to speak to your group. They are always willing to speak to students engaged in enterprise, as they look on you as the next generation of entrepreneurs. There are thirty-five Enterprise Boards throughout the country. They were set up in 1993 by the Government. The Government is convinced that small businesses will always be the backbone of the Irish economy. Ireland should not be dependent on large multinational corporations to provide employment; we need to be self-sufficient and this means supporting and encouraging small local businesses. County Enterprise Boards help businesses that employ up to ten people. They can help in various ways:

- They give financial assistance in the form of grants and low-interest loans.
- They give advice and support to those setting up in business.
- They help with the drawing up of a business plan.
- They run business start-up courses.
- They give computer training.
- They give management training.

- They have a mentoring service, which many people find particularly useful; someone who is just starting out is introduced to an entrepreneur who has 'made it'. The successful entrepreneur will offer advice and encouragement to the beginner.

The County Enterprise Board is also involved in the running of the Young Entrepreneurs Scheme, which is aimed at second-level students. Competitions for the best school-based businesses are held at county, regional and national level. You can find out more about this from the Young Entrepreneurs website at http://www.yes.ie.

It is important that you prepare for the visit of your enterprise advisor by thinking about what information you need. One very important question to ask: 'Can we apply to the County Enterprise Board for a grant for our mini-company?' Prepare a report on the visit.

An official from one of your local banks might be willing to come in and talk to the class. Remember that you are their future customers and they are prepared to invest time and money in you. Invite the Student Officer in your local bank to talk to the class about the financial aspects of running a business: raising the necessary capital, keeping accounts, managing a bank account, etc. Prepare a report on the visit.

Your local Credit Union can also be very helpful. A Credit Union is different from a bank in that it is owned and run by the members for the benefit of the members.

Any profit made is divided out among the members. Invite a member of the Credit Union to speak to the class about the benefits of membership. Prepare a report on the visit.

■ Finance

You have already listed the resources you need for getting started. You have examined the availability of these resources and you know which ones you can get for nothing and which ones you have to buy. Before you splash out on items of equipment, see if you can borrow or hire them. The life of the mini-company is a fairly short one and there is no point in spending a lot of money on items that you may not be able to sell off when you are finished with them. If you do have to buy something, check the second-hand market.

In your business plan you worked out how much start-up cash you needed. You now have to decide where that money is going to come from. The possible sources of capital are:
- Grants – perhaps from your County Enterprise Board.
- Loans – from your local bank or credit union.
- Shares – ask your family and friends to invest in your company.

You may not get enough money from just one of these sources; you may have to use all three.

■ *Selling Shares*

STEP ONE

Decide how many shares you are going to sell, and the value of each share. Remember that you will have to pay back this money to your shareholders when you wind up the company. You will also have to pay your shareholders a share of the profits, this share is called a DIVIDEND, because you pay it out when you divide the profits.

STEP TWO

Who will you offer these shares to? You may decide that your shareholders are the members of the mini-company only, or you may want to offer them to family and friends.

STEP THREE

If you decide to sell the shares to outsiders, you will need to discuss the best ways of approaching people and persuading them to buy shares. Remember, you should not expect people to invest money simply to help you; people should be convinced that they are making a good investment, and they should be confident that they will make a profit.

★ EXERCISES

1. Write a letter to prospective investors, explaining why they should invest in your company.
2. Role-play a conversation between a company member and a member of the public. The company member is trying to convince his listener to invest in the mini-company. What kinds of questions are likely to be asked by the prospective investor? How should these questions be handled?

■ *Increase Your Word Power!*

Can you spell and use the following words correctly? Hacker, Hallowe'en, handicap, handiwork, handle, hangar, hanger, harass, harassment, haulage, haulier, haven't, hazard, hazardous, healthy, heritage, hire, hire purchase, horoscope, hostel, hostile, humour, humorous, hype.

Unit 3

Advertising

At this stage your mini-company is up and running, your finance is sorted out, the management team is in place and production has started.

Your next task is to plan your advertising campaign. Before you begin, you must remember that no amount of advertising or promotion will make up for a shoddy product or service. You must be confident that you are offering a top-quality product, which is value · for money. You should not expect your family and friends to support you just because they know you; you are in a marketplace where you are competing for customers.

The type of image your company projects through its advertising and promotion is very important. These days we are exposed to advertising at every turn. The first aim of an advertisement is to grab our attention. Once we are 'hooked', the next step is to 'reel us in' – to persuade us to buy. The poem 'Adman', by Nigel Gray, describes some of the techniques used by advertisers to get us to part with our money.

Adman
Nigel Gray

I'm the new man
In the ivory tower
The new man
The man with the power
The old village chief
Used to lay down the law
But the medicine man
Had his foot in the door
He taught me the secret

Of how you tick
To use psychology
Like a conjuring trick
So I've found the doorway
Into your brain
When you get a bargain
You lose – I gain
I can get in your bath
I can get in your bed
I can get in your pants
I can get in your head
You're like a man on the cross
You're like a priest at the stake
You're like a fish on a hook
Make no mistake
I can tie you up
I can take you down
I can sit and watch
You wriggle around
'Cos I'm the medicine man
With the media touch
The man with the power that's
Too much

 # FOR DISCUSSION

1. The adman is shown as 'the new man in the ivory tower'. To say that someone is in an ivory tower is to say that they are removed from the rest of us; they are protected from the worries and problems of everyday living. They are superior to us. In these first few lines we get an image of the adman as someone who is looking down on the rest of us. If the adman is the 'new man' in the ivory tower, who or what do you think was there before him?
2. The poet sees the consumer (us) as helpless. Find some of the *similes* he uses where he says that we are like certain things. Which simile do you think works best? Why?
3. The adman understands how we think and feel; he has found the doorway into our brains. How has he done this?
4. One of the points that the poet is trying to get across is that advertising has reached saturation point; we can never escape it. Where does he say this? Read these lines aloud. Why do they stand out?
5. Explain the following lines:
   'When you get a bargain
   You lose – I gain.'

6. In the poem the adman describes himself as 'the man with the power', in fact he uses this line twice. Would you agree that the adman is all-powerful? What kind of power does he have over us?

7. Do you agree with his picture of the consumer? Are we at the mercy of the adman? Do we follow blindly or do we think for ourselves?

8. How does this poem make you feel? Would this poem make you think about the power of advertising?

9. List all the different types of advertising that you have been exposed to since you woke up this morning.

10. List all the different mediums used by advertisers and write a brief description of each one:

MEDIUM

1. posters

2. _____

3. _____

4. _____

5. _____

6. _____

DESCRIPTION

large; colourful; displayed in prominent places, e.g. billboards, bus shelters

■ Techniques Used by Advertisers

When Nigel Gray said that the adman could get inside our heads, he was speaking the truth. Psychologists have studied our behaviour very carefully; they have uncovered our

COMMUNICATION

weaknesses; they know what makes us tick. For example, they know that young mothers are anxious to do the very best for their children. An advertisement aimed at this group might suggest that if you do not use Brand X baby food you are not a good mother. Young mothers are the target market for products such as nappies, baby food and safe cars.

Consumers are grouped into target markets according to age, sex and social class. Groups are STEREOTYPED. For example, if you are a teenager it is presumed you will think, feel and behave in a certain way.

Using a selection of advertisements from television, radio, newspapers and magazines identify other target markets, and their fears and hopes. What product is being aimed at them?

TARGET MARKET	*FEARS AND HOPES*	*PRODUCT*
1. Elderly people	_____	_____
2. _____	_____	_____
	_____	_____
3. _____	_____	_____
	_____	_____
4. _____	_____	_____
	_____	_____
5. _____	_____	_____
	_____	_____

There are many other techniques used by successful advertisers. As you go through the list find examples of advertisements that use the following techniques:
- Suggesting that the product is used by someone rich and famous.
- Linking products with success; if you drive a certain car people will admire and envy you.
- Appealing to our 'good sense' and 'intelligence', so that we feel flattered.
- Making claims about their products that they cannot prove. The classic example of this technique is the washing powder advertisement 'X washes whiter'. This is not even a proper sentence – washes whiter than what?
- Using buzz words such as 'fresh', 'luxury', 'healthy', 'natural' and 'young'. These words give us positive feelings.

- Getting our attention with an interesting story.
- Using clever slogans.
- Using humour.
- Stating that scientists approve of the product.
- Using new words that have been created by the advertising industry, such as 'tangy' and 'chunky'.
- Repeating key words over and over again, usually the brand name of the product.
- Ordering us to do things – 'act now!'
- Using words that sound good. Examples of this would be the use of rhyme or alliteration.

Note: Not all advertising is commercial. Advertising can also be used to try and get us to *change our behaviour.*

Give some examples of this kind of advertising.

1. Road safety advertisements.

2. _____

3. _____

4. _____

5. _____

Would your behaviour be influenced by this type of advertising? Why/Why not?

■ Print Advertising

In spite of the growth of the electronic media, almost fifty per cent of all advertising revenue is still spent on advertising in newspapers and magazines. If you examine large newspaper advertisements, you will notice that they usually consist of four separate parts.

THE CAPTION OR HEADLINE

The caption has to get our attention immediately. It might be in the form of a question, which makes us curious, or it might be a clever slogan.

THE GRAPHIC

This can be a photograph, a drawing or a cartoon. The artist will be trying to link the product with an attractive setting or situation. These pictures usually show happy, smiling people who live in beautiful houses, and who all get on really well together – even first thing in the morning. Their gardens are immaculate and even their pets are well-behaved.

THE LOGO

A logo is a symbol or a picture without words. It is always printed in the same way, and we come to associate the logo with a particular company. The logo is a very important part of the image that a company projects; it becomes the symbol or emblem of an organisation.

THE COPY OR TEXT

The copy or text is really the small print and will give us information about the product. We will only read the copy if we have been attracted by the caption and the illustration. The copy will usually invite us to do something: make a phone call or claim a free gift. The adman has us on the line and is trying to reel us in!

WORK TO DO

1. Collect examples of logos that we associate with different companies. Try to work out why these symbols were chosen and the image each one is trying to get across.
2. Bring in samples of advertisements from newspapers and magazines. Include both colour and black-and-white ads in your selection, and make sure they cover a wide range of products. Working in pairs or small groups, examine at least three advertisements. Use the following questions as a guide:
   (a) What product is being advertised?
   (b) Can you identify the target market?
   (c) List the different advertising techniques used.
   (d) What is it about this ad that first catches your attention?
   (e) Describe the illustration. Do not forget the background and the props.
   (f) What kind of feelings is the picture designed to produce?
   (g) What kind of image is being projected in the advertisement?
   (h) Examine any claims made in the ad. Do you think they are genuine? Why/why not?
   (i) Is there any interesting word play in the ad? Describe the logo used.
   (j) Would you consider this to be a successful advertisement? Why/why not?
3. Compose your own print media advertisement for one of the following, making sure to include a caption, an illustration, a logo and some copy or text:
   • a new hotel and leisure centre about to open
   • a new range of bedroom furniture
   • a package holiday
   • a new shampoo
   • organic meat
   Invent the details as you need them. If drawing is not one of your strong points, just suggest ideas for a suitable illustration.
4. Find out how much it costs to place a full-page colour advertisement in
   (a) a daily paper
   (b) your local paper

5. Teenagers today are big spenders. They earn considerable amounts of money, and have not yet taken on financial responsibility such as mortgages or car loans. They are, therefore, a prime target group for the adman.

Can you identify some products that are aimed almost exclusively at teenagers?

1. _____

2. _____

3. _____

4. _____

5. _____

Can you identify some of the fears and worries of teenagers that the adman might exploit?

1. _____

_____

2. _____

_____

3. _____

_____

4. _____

_____

5. _____

_____

Radio Advertising

In designing an advertisement for radio, the adman is restricted to voices, music and sound effects. In spite of the fact that there is no visual communication, advertising on radio can be very effective. The simplest form of radio advertisement is a 'straight-sell description', i.e. one voice describing a product and saying where it can be purchased. More complex advertisements may have the following components:

- Sound effects (SFX) to set the scene.
- Dialogue, i.e. two or more people having a conversation. In some cases this could be quite dramatic.
- Music used to create a mood or atmosphere.
- A catchy jingle to help us to remember the product.
- A voice-over (VO) to give us information about the product.
- Repetition of important words, particularly the brand-name.

WORK TO DO

1. Record a selection of radio advertisements. Listen to them in class and identify the different components used in the presentations. Try to identify the target audience for each commercial.
2. What is the length of an average radio advertisement?
3. Find out how much it costs to advertise on
   - National radio
   - Local radio
4. Survey three radio stations, two national and one local station, between the hours of 6.00 pm and 8.00 pm. Pick two national stations that are quite different from one another: a serious station and a popular music station. Find the answers to the following questions:
   - How often does the programme break for commercials?
   - What kind of products and services are advertised?
   - Which section of the market is being targeted? How do you know?

   Write a short report on the differences amongst the three stations.
5. Design your own radio advertisement to sell one of the following:
   - a new soft drink
   - a new brand of cat food
   - a face cream
   - a product of your choice

   Use dialogue, drama, SFX, VO and music.

   Try taping your attempt and share it with the class.

■ Television Advertising

Although television is the most expensive form of advertising it accounts for approximately thirty per cent of all advertising revenue. Television has the advantage of using both sound and visual channels of communication. Television advertisements usually have the following features:

1. a visual demonstration of the product
2. an attractive setting
3. dialogue, i.e. a mini-drama where something is happening
4. words superimposed on the screen
5. voice-overs
6. music
7. repetition

Sometimes a shorter version of the ad will appear later in the same commercial break. Advertisers will screen their ads at a time when they know their target audience will be watching. Notice the number of ads for toys that appear during daytime programmes for children.

WORK TO DO

1. Record a selection of television commercials, covering a wide range of products and services. View them in class. Look at each one critically and answer the following questions:
   (a) What product or service is being advertised?
   (b) Break down the advertisement into its different parts. How many parts can you identify?
   (c) What image is the advertiser trying to create? Does he succeed?
   (d) Is the advertisement part of a series of advertisements, with an ongoing story line?
   (e) Can you identify the target audience?
   (f) How does the advertiser appeal to his target audience?
   (g) Does the advertisement appeal equally to males and females?
   (h) What type of mood or atmosphere is set by the music?
   (i) What features of the language used stand out?
   (j) Which part of the advertisement informs us about the product?
   (k) Which part of the advertisement persuades us to buy the product?
   (l) What do you find most attractive about this advertisement?
   (m) Would you regard this advertisement as effective? Why/why not?
2. Survey three commercial television stations (stations which have advertisements) between the hours of 6.00 pm and 8.00 pm.
   (a) How much time is devoted to advertising over this period?
   (b) What is the average length of a television commercial?
   (c) Do the target audiences differ?
   (d) Do the products and services advertised differ?
   (e) Write a short report on your survey.
3. Find out how much it costs to advertise on television.

4. Make a note of the ads screened during the showing of your favourite 'soap' or sitcom. Can you identify the target audience? Can you identify the techniques used to catch and hold your interest?
5. Design a television advertisement for one of the following:
   (a) car tyres
   (b) washing powder
   (c) a credit card
   (d) a product or service of your choice
   Decide on your target market and how you will appeal to them. Describe the setting and the characters. Write the dialogue. Describe the sound effects and the music you would use.
6. Divide the class into three groups. Each group has to design a television advertisement for a different target audience, but for the same product, e.g. a credit card.
   Identify three target markets and assign one to each group. You should end up with three very different commercials, as each group will be emphasising different advantages of credit card ownership.

■ *The Junk Mail Project*

These days we get a lot of advertising mail delivered to our homes; this has become known as 'junk mail'. Collect the junk mail from your home for a period of two weeks. Examine the advertisements carefully to see the techniques of persuasion that are used.

PRODUCT ADVERTISED   TECHNIQUE USED

1. _____   _____

   _____

2. _____   _____

   _____

3. _____   _____

   _____

4. _____   _____

   _____

5. _____   _____

   _____

■ Planning Your Advertising Campaign

When we use the word 'campaign', we are describing a course of action rather than a single event. When you are thinking about your mini-company and the advertising strategy you might use, you have to think like a military commander organising his forces.

- You have to make the best use of your resources.
- You have to make sure that the image you project is attractive.
- You have to appeal to your target market.
- You have to use as many forms of advertising as possible.
- You have to think in terms of different phases of the mini-company. Perhaps the type of advertising you will use before the product comes on the market will not be suitable when production is well under way.

Advertising will be the responsibility of the Marketing Manager and his team.

STEP ONE

Decide on the type of image you want to project. One way of doing this is to examine carefully the image that your competitors have created. Is there any aspect of your product or service that you could emphasise? How does your product or service differ from that of your competitors? Words that can be used to create an image are words like 'reliable', 'speedy', 'guarantee', 'healthy', 'better', and 'efficient'.

STEP TWO

Decide on the company name and logo. Try and be as creative and original as possible. A name and logo should stick in the mind; a name needs to be catchy or amusing; use word-play; change spellings to suit. Have you got a catchy slogan?

STEP THREE

Identify your target audience. Decide how you will appeal to them.

STEP FOUR

List the skills and resources that are available to the advertising team. Do you have a budget? Have you access to computers? Have you access to a photocopier? What artistic talents are available to you? What technical skills are available to you? Who in the group is good at written communication?

STEP FIVE

Decide on the best way to reach your target audience. Think about posters, using the school intercom, flyers, advertising in local shops and on the local radio.

Should you send a press release to your local paper? A press release is different from an advertisement. It is really an article giving information about your enterprise and the

products or services you are offering. If you write an interesting article and include an appropriate picture, you will have a good chance of getting it published.

STEP SIX

Design a range of different advertisements and bring them to a board meeting for approval. Make sure you proofread your advertisements carefully; mistakes can damage the image you are trying to create.

STEP SEVEN

Constantly evaluate your campaign and make changes as necessary. Keep a constant check on posters that you have put up around the school building, for example. Do they need to be protected? Do they need to be replaced?

STEP EIGHT

Discuss other ways in which you might promote your product or service: special opening offers, free samples, etc.

Remember advertising has to be legal, honest and truthful. The Advertising Standards Authority tries to make sure that advertisements are not offensive, and that certain standards are adhered to. It would be useful to contact the Advertising Standards Authority and ask for a copy of their rules.

■ *Increase Your Word Power!*

Can you spell and use the following words correctly?

Ideal, identical, identify, illegal, illegible, immature, immediate, impact, impartial, impatient, important, impossible, impression, improve, incapable, incident, inconvenient, increase, independent, index, indicate, individual, information, install, insurance.

Unit 4

Interpersonal Communication

▮ Teamwork!

Your mini-company will only be successful if the class manages to work together as a team. Teamwork is an important aspect of the LCA, but nowhere is it more important than in the running of the mini-company.

We have seen that the ability to work as part of a team – to be a 'team player' - is a skill that employers look for. Because it is a skill, it is something we can learn.

What are the advantages of teamwork? To answer this question spend twenty minutes on the following activity:

1. Think of a red brick, an ordinary, everyday object. Working alone, each student should write down as many uses for a brick as they can think of. Allow five minutes for this part of the exercise, and during this time do not discuss or share ideas with your colleagues. At the end of five minutes, make a note of the number of ideas you have recorded.

2. Get into small groups. Share your ideas and add more as they come to mind. At the end of five minutes make a note of the number of ideas recorded by the group.

3. Each group should now share its ideas with the whole class. Note the total number of ideas you now have as a class.

COMMUNICATION

NUMBER OF IDEAS GENERATED

ON MY OWN   *SMALL GROUP*   *CLASS*

_____   _____   _____

Would you agree that a team can be far more creative than an individual? If you work as a team, you are more likely to come up with ideas for solving problems than if you work alone. Identify other advantages of working as a team and add them to the list below.

1. Different people will have different skills and talents.

2. _____

_____

3. _____

_____

4. _____

_____

5. _____

_____

What makes a team a successful team? According to the dictionary, the word team means 'a set of people working together for the common good'; in other words, a team is a group of people who have the same aim. For example, a football team will work together with the aim of winning the championship.

A team might be made up of people who have very little in common; they may not even like each other. The only reason they are together is because of their desire to win something, or in the case of business, a desire to run a successful business and make a profit. Members of a successful team are able to put aside their differences for the sake of achieving what they set out to do. They may not get on well together outside of the work situation, but they are able to co-operate for the sake of 'the common good'. Think about your favourite sporting team and what makes them successful:

- A team-player is unselfish, he will share his ideas and achievements with the group; he will not try to take all the glory.
- A team-player is reliable; he will do what he says he will do.

- A team-player will only criticise another member of the team to his face, when he has a chance to defend himself; he will never talk about another member behind his back.
- A team-player will be helpful and supportive to members of the team who may be having problems.
- A team-player will be happy when another member achieves something; when an individual member succeeds the whole team benefits.

What challenges will you meet as a team? You will have to

- plan ahead
- make decisions
- solve problems
- settle arguments
- get things done on time
- keep track of money

If some members of the team do not pull their weight, it places a greater burden on everyone else. Make a list of *specific ways* in which team members can damage or destroy the work of the group:

1. Absenteeism

2. _____

3. _____

4. _____

5. _____

Every team needs a leader who will take overall responsibility for the work of the team. In the mini-company the managing director takes on this role. This does not mean that the individual members of the team have no responsibilities. Everyone in the company has a role to play and the success of the organisation will depend on everyone playing their part and making sure that targets are met.

Good communication plays a vital part in the running of any organisation.

One of the most important ways of encouraging good teamwork is by holding regular meetings.

■ Business Meetings

Time must be set aside for regular meetings of the enterprise team. Although each individual is doing his or her own job, the whole group needs to come together on a regular basis. Meetings are held for the following reasons:

- To organise the running of the company.
- To share information and ideas.
- To deal with production problems.
- To listen to complaints from workers, and to deal with them.
- To make plans for the future.
- To review sales figures.
- To give permission to spend money.
- To give the manager or leader a chance to motivate his team.

■ *How to Organise a Meeting*

PREPARATION

1. You need to decide how often you are going to meet. Do you need frequent, short meetings or is it enough to meet once every two weeks or so? The type of enterprise you are involved in will probably dictate this.
2. Where and when are you going to meet? Perhaps you could hold meetings during English and Communications class.
3. Appoint a CHAIRPERSON. The managing director usually takes on this role. The job of chairperson is a very responsible one; his/her first task is to draw up an AGENDA. This is simply a list of items that need to be dealt with. The most important items should be put near the top of the agenda, to make sure they are discussed.

    During the meeting the chairperson must keep order. He/she must make sure that everyone gets a chance to speak; he must not allow people to interrupt or speak out of turn. He must try to keep everyone focused on the discussion. If there is a disagreement, the chairperson must put the matter to a vote. The chairperson does not have a vote himself, but if there is a tie the chairperson can use his CASTING VOTE.
4. Appoint a SECRETARY to take the MINUTES. The minutes are a brief record of
    - who was present at the meeting
    - the items discussed
    - the decisions made
    - who is going to carry out the decisions

    The minutes secretary does not have to write down everything that is said, but it is vitally important that all *decisions* are recorded, together with the *names* of the people who agreed to carry out these decisions.
5. Make a list of rules of behaviour for the running of the meetings. These rules are called STANDING ORDERS, and if they are not followed meetings will sink into chaos. The chairperson must be able to depend on the support and co-operation of all the members of the group.

HOLDING THE MEETING

1. If the meeting is being held in a classroom, you will need to look at the seating arrangements. Decide what type of seating arrangement is most suitable. When the chairperson opens the meeting, a note will be made of those members who are absent.

(If you know you are going to be absent from a meeting, it is good manners to let the chairperson know.)

2. The minutes secretary will read the minutes of the last meeting. This is a reminder of the decisions made. The chairperson will check that all decisions made were carried out by those who agreed to be responsible for them.

3. The chairperson will then deal with the items on the agenda for today's meeting. People will have a chance to give their opinion. Decisions will be made, very often by majority vote. Each person must accept the result of a vote, even if they do not agree with it.

4. The second-last item on the agenda is usually AOB – ANY OTHER BUSINESS. This gives people a chance to bring up something that is bothering them and which has not been dealt with. The last item of business is usually to decide on the date of the next meeting.

■ *Case Study*
VOTING PROCEDURE

Those of you who are members of sporting organisations or youth clubs will be familiar with the voting procedure. The rules are quite formal, and it is very important that the procedure is followed. The following case study illustrates what is involved.

Shane is the Chairperson of Celtic Crafts. Gavin is the Production Manager and Peter is the Treasurer. The company makes a range of products; the sales figures would suggest that their decorative candles are selling particularly well. In his report to the meeting, Gavin points out that the number of candles that can be made is severely limited by the fact that the production team have only six moulds. He asks for permission to spend twenty euro on moulds. He has worked out what this would mean in terms of production, and feels sure that it would be money well spent.

Peter does not agree. He feels that this type of spending is reckless, and he argues that the company will not be able to sell off the moulds when they are finished with them. Shane gives each of them a chance to explain how they feel, and then he gets the opinions of other members of the team.

After discussing the pros and cons of the situation for five minutes, it is obvious to Shane that the matter will have to be put to a vote. He brings the discussion to an end and asks Gavin to put his proposal to the meeting.

Gavin PROPOSES a MOTION: 'I propose that twenty euro should be spent on buying more moulds.'

The motion is SECONDED by someone who supports it: 'I second the motion.'

Shane asks all those in favour of the motion to raise their hands. He makes a note of the number of people who support the motion.

He then asks all those against the motion to raise their hands. He makes a note of the number of people who are against the motion. (A person may ABSTAIN from voting if they wish.)

Shane announces the result of the vote. Everybody has to abide by this result, no matter how strongly they might feel about it. The decision has been arrived at in a fair and democratic way. The minutes secretary records the result of the vote.

AGENDAS

The chairperson and secretary usually get together to plan the agenda. It is a good idea to put a copy of the agenda on the notice-board the day before the meeting, so that people have time to think about the items that are going to be discussed. An agenda should be short and simple. The following is the agenda for the meeting of the mini-company Mega Bytes.

AGENDA

Meeting of Mega Bytes
On Monday 22 February at 2.30 p.m.
In Room 20

1. Apologies for absence
2. Minutes of last meeting
3. Matters arising out of the minutes will be discussed
4. Results of market research will be discussed
5. Capital – shares or loan?
6. AOB
7. Date of next meeting will be decided.

In order to have successful meetings, it is essential that all the members of the team co-operate as follows:
1. Follow the agenda and make a note of anything you are asked to do. Remember you will be asked to account for yourself at the next meeting!
2. Listen carefully to what other people in the group have to say.
3. Take turns in speaking.
4. Speak clearly.
5. Do not waste time repeating the same points over and over again.
6. Follow the correct voting procedure.

★ EXERCISES

1. Draw up a set of STANDING ORDERS for the running of your enterprise meetings.
2. The chairperson is having difficulty with one group member 'who loves the sound of his own voice'. How do you think he should deal with this situation?

3. Some members of the group never say a word at meetings. How could they be encouraged to speak? Do you think it is important that everyone speaks? Why/why not?
4. Describe a suitable seating arrangement for a meeting, and give reasons for your choice.
5. Department managers are called upon to make reports at enterprise meetings. List three points that should be included in the reports from each of the following departments:
   • Purchasing
   • Production
   • Advertising
   • Sales

■ Business Documents

If an enterprise is to be successful, proper records must be kept. Everything that happens must be *recorded*, otherwise there will be confusion. We have looked at how decisions made at meetings are recorded in the minutes.

1. If your company is ordering materials you will use an ORDER FORM. This will contain your company name, logo, address and telephone number at the top. The body of the form will be divided into columns as follows:

   DATE   QUANTITY   DESCRIPTION OF GOODS

2. When you receive goods you will be asked to sign a DELIVERY NOTE to say you got the goods.
3. An INVOICE is a bill, which shows how much you owe.

★ EXERCISES

1. Set up a simple accounts system for your mini-company. You need to show where your start-up money has come from, your outgoings, and the money you get in from sales.
2. Collect a set of business documents from a local business, perhaps while you are on work experience.
3. Using IT, design a set of business documents for your enterprise. Make sure you include the company logo and letterhead.

■ *Increase Your Word Power!*

Can you spell and use the following words correctly?
January, jewellery, journal, journalism, journalist, judge, junction, junior, justice, juvenile.

■ Key Assignments

I have participated in a visitor exercise with one of the following:
A self-employed person
An enterprise advisor
A bank/credit union representative
And I have presented a report on the exercise.

☐ Date _____

OR
I have participated in an outing with my class in relation to enterprise, e.g. a Trade Fair, and I have presented a report on the exercise.

☐ Date _____

I have completed a short study of aspects of advertising and I have presented my report.

☐ Date _____

I have participated in the planning and evaluating of a sales and marketing strategy in an enterprise and I have kept notes of our meetings.

☐ Date _____

I have presented a report on my role in the enterprise. (Where possible I have used ICT in the completion of one or more of the above assignments.)

☐ Date _____

■ Past Examination Questions

1. (a) Describe a mini-enterprise that was set up by your class. (5 marks)
   (b) What was your role in this mini-enterprise? (5 marks)
   (c) Write out the minutes of one of your mini-enterprise meetings. (10 marks)
   (d) Based on your experience, what advice would you give to students beginning a mini-enterprise? (10 marks)
2. Write a letter to your local credit union or bank requesting information on their financial packages for small industries and inviting their Enterprise Development Officer to visit your class. (15 marks)
3. (a) Describe a mini-enterprise that was set up by your class. (5 marks)
   (b) How was your mini-enterprise financed? (5 marks)
   (c) Outline how your mini-enterprise conducted its market research. (5 marks)
   (d) What was the role of the Health and Safety Officer in the mini-enterprise? (5 marks)
   (e) How did you benefit from working in the mini-enterprise? (10 marks)

4. (a) Explain any five of the following terms: entrepreneur, human resource manager, cash flow, invoice, wholesaler, agenda. (15 marks)
   (b) Describe one major source of employment in your locality. (5 marks)
   (c) Outline the career that you would like to pursue on leaving school. Give reasons for your answer. (10 marks)

5. Write out the speech you would make to a gathering of local business people on 'My experience of student enterprise/mini-company'.
   Your speech could include a description of the enterprise/mini-company, the importance of teamwork, the benefits of the experience for you, and any other information that you regard as relevant or important. (30 marks)

6. Your class has been involved in a group communication project or case study.
   (a) Briefly describe the project or case study. (5 marks)
   (b) What was your contribution to the project or case study? (5 marks)
   (c) How did the class conduct its research for the project or case study? (10 marks)
   (d) How did you benefit from your participation in the project or case study? (10 marks)

7. Read this profile of a student enterprise (mini-company) and then, in the light of your experience of enterprise, answer the questions that follow.

   The Leaving Certificate Applied class in school A is experiencing difficulties with its mini-company. The students decided to make Christmas decorations and borrowed 100 euro from the school bank to buy materials. Disagreement has arisen over design and production of the decorations and the managing director is concerned that they will fail to produce the decorations in time for the Christmas market. The students are also aware that they face competition from other mini-companies in the school.

   (a) Do you agree with the way this mini-company raised its capital? Give a reason for your answer. (5 marks)
   (b) How could the students have avoided disagreement about the design of the decorations? (5 marks)
   (c) What advice would you give the managing director of this company? (10 marks)
   (d) How did your mini-company organise the following?
      • Its market research (5 marks)
      • Its advertising and sales (5 marks)

8. You have been asked to make a speech at your school's open night for parents on the Communications Project undertaken by your class. Your speech should involve the following: a description of the project or study; how it was planned; your own involvement; its success; how the class evaluated the project or study; the benefits gained from involvement in the project or study. (30 marks)

9. (a) Briefly describe a mini-company which was set up by your Leaving Certificate Applied class. (5 marks)
   (b) Why did your class decide on this product or service? (5 marks)
   (c) Outline your role in the mini-company. (5 marks)
   (d) Name and explain one aspect of business that you have learned from your involvement in the mini-company. (5 marks)

(e) Describe any difficulties that you experienced as a group and explain how these difficulties were resolved. (10 marks)

10. Write a detailed report on a Communications Project or a visit that your English and Communications class was engaged in. You may include the following in your report: preparation and planning, your role in the project or visit, any surprising outcomes, benefits to you and/or your class. (30 marks)

 # Unit 1

Introduction to Mass Media

When we speak about the mass media, we are describing the way information is sent to large numbers of people. Media is the plural of medium, and a medium is a channel through which we can communicate. The mass media include newspapers, radio, television and film.

Strictly speaking, the mass media do not communicate with us in the true sense of the word. If we look again at the definition of communication, which we used in Module 1, we will see that communication is a *two-way process*; it involves both the sending of messages and the return of feedback.

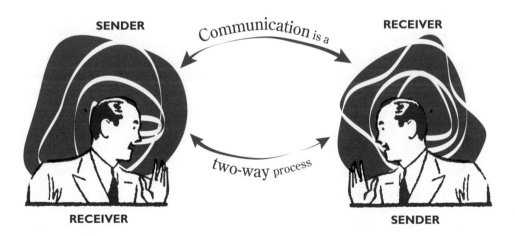

Meetings, verbal exchanges, telephone conversations, letters and e-mails all fit this definition of communication. Both parties have a chance to ask questions and make comments; both parties take an *active part* in the process. In contrast, when we examine the mass media we are looking at communication that is one-sided.

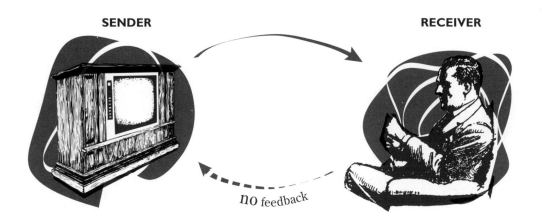

For example, if we are watching television we are *passive*; we are receiving messages but we are not sending anything back; we cannot ask for something to be explained; we cannot express our own point of view; we do not give feedback.

- It is important that we are aware of the huge influence that the media have on our lives.
- We need to know how the mass media work.
- We need to know who controls what we read, hear and see.
- We need to get into the habit of questioning the information and messages being 'fed' to us, instead of just accepting them as the true version of events.

In this module, we are going to critically examine newspapers, radio, television and film. The materials you use will largely be of your own choosing. It is important that you use material that is topical, i.e. it must be about events that are happening now. The materials used should also reflect your own interests. Each student should get into the habit of collecting items which they find interesting, e.g. articles from newspapers, recordings of radio and television programmes, films and film reviews. This can be a stimulating and rewarding module if it is approached in a practical way, and the issues are explored in a 'hands on' manner.

◼ Newspapers

The first newspaper was called *Acta Diurna*; it appeared in 59 BC in ancient Rome. It was a daily news-sheet and recorded the important events in the political and social life of the time.

In the fifteenth century, news-sheets circulated in Germany, and by the seventeenth century regularly published newspapers began to appear in many European countries. The first newspapers simply *informed* their readers about important events. As time went on, newspapers began to *interpret* and *explain* what was happening. Newspaper publishers also realised that their readers liked to be *entertained*, and the modern newspaper gradually took shape. The readership of these early newspapers was quite small, as generally only the upper classes were educated.

In England, one of the best-known newspaper publishers was Lord Northcliffe, who lived from 1865 to 1922. By the early years of the twentieth century, compulsory schooling had brought reading and writing to the ordinary people – the masses. It was he who first realised that there were now two different types of newspaper reader: the more serious reader who wanted *in-depth* news coverage, and the 'new' readers who wanted *brief* news reports, human interest stories and amusing features. Lord Northcliffe catered for both types of reader, publishing *The Times*, a serious 'quality' newspaper, and *The Daily Mirror*, a 'popular' newspaper aimed at a mass audience.

Before the advent of radio and television, people depended on the newspaper for information; the results of weekend football matches would not be known until the paper arrived on Monday; the results of elections might not be known for several weeks. Newspapers did provide the 'news' in a very real sense. Nowadays, we do not depend on the newspaper to 'break' the news. Indeed, thanks to satellite television we can see events unfolding before our eyes; we can watch football matches live that are being played thousands of miles away; we have access to twenty-four-hour news channels.

Why did newspapers survive? Why did they not just die out, like the medieval town crier?

Newspapers survived because they *adapted* and *changed* in order to appeal to a wide range of people; they have something for everybody. Newspapers do a lot more than inform us about recent events – they also
- give advice
- entertain and educate
- question the actions of politicians and businessmen
- help us find a job
- help us sell our car
- help us pick the winner of the 2.30 at Leopardstown
- tell us what our future holds
- help us choose which video to rent or which television programme to see
- keep us occupied on trains and buses with puzzles and crosswords

In Ireland, every day over half a million newspapers are sold. We have a wide range of titles to choose from, both Irish and foreign, and new titles continue to come on the market.

■ *Features of a Newspaper*

THE FRONT PAGE

1. Masthead
2. Banner headline
3. Subheadings
4. Photographs

THE MASTHEAD

The masthead appears at the top of the front page. It includes the title of the paper, the logo (if any), and the date. The title and logo will project a certain image; what image do you think words like 'examiner', 'independent' and 'mirror' are trying to convey?

BANNER HEADLINE

This is the headline that appears on the front page over the main story.

SUBHEADINGS

Subheadings break up a news report into small sections. This allows the reader to go directly to the part of the story that interests him or her.

COLUMNS

A newspaper page is usually divided into eight columns. This makes the paper much easier to read than if each page was a solid block of print. The amount of space given to a story is measured in column inches.

CAPTIONS

A caption is a line of print under a photograph or an illustration.

CONTENTS

Most newspapers will give their readers some idea of what is inside the newspaper.

Inside the newspaper, in addition to news items, you will usually find the following: editorial, feature articles, reviews, classifieds and obituaries.

EDITORIAL

The editor is the person who is in charge of the newspaper; he or she decides which items go in and which items are left out. He/she also writes an article called an editorial, setting out his/her own views on important issues. The editorial is sometimes called the leading article.

FEATURE ARTICLES

Feature articles are not news stories, but are related to news stories. For example, after a major earthquake we will usually get articles explaining why earthquakes happen, and how buildings can be designed to withstand them. Feature articles can also be seasonal; coming up to Hallowe'en we get articles on the dangers of fireworks; at Christmas we get advice on shopping and gifts; in June, exam students (and their parents!) get hints on how to cope with stress.

REVIEWS

Newspapers employ people to attend the opening nights of films, plays and concerts, to read books, or to try out new video games. These people are called CRITICS, and they will write a review giving their opinion on what they have seen or read. The success or failure of a book or play can hinge on the reviews it gets, as readers tend to be guided by the opinions of the critics.

CLASSIFIEDS

The classifieds are also known as the 'small ads'. They are a very important part of the paper as they bring in a lot of money; also, people will often buy a paper simply to look at the small ads. If you study the classifieds, you will see that the ads are divided into categories or *classes*, and each class is listed in alphabetical order, making it easy for the reader to find what he or she is looking for.

OBITUARIES

An obituary is a brief biography of someone who has died, usually paying tribute to his or her achievements.

Notice the different styles and sizes of print used. With modern technology, it is possible to vary the **typeface**; a page of print can be made to look more interesting and attractive.

✴ EXERCISES

1. Study the layout of a newspaper and find examples of the features outlined above.
2. Design your own front page for a newspaper, using the layout of the Dublin Daily on page 164. This could be done in IT class.

■ *Types of Newspaper*

We have already seen that from early in the twentieth century, newspapers were divided into two categories, i.e. the 'quality' newspaper and the 'tabloid'.

THE QUALITY NEWSPAPER

The quality newspapers devote a lot of space to in-depth news coverage. They analyse and interpret what is going on in the world, which gives a background to help the reader to understand the events better. As well as news stories, they will report on politics and business. These newspapers are regarded as 'serious' newspapers; they deal in facts rather than rumour or gossip. They are also known as broadsheets. The term broadsheet really refers to the size of the page, i.e. eight columns of twenty inches.

Name some quality daily newspapers.

1. _____

2. _____

3. _____

4. _____

Name some quality Sunday papers

1. _____

2. _____

3. _____

4. _____

THE TABLOID NEWSPAPER

The tabloid newspapers do not give in-depth treatment of news stories. Instead, they present the news in a way that is easy to understand. They tend to concentrate on 'human interest' aspects of important news stories; they will look at a story from the point of view of one person who was caught up in the event. They also print stories and gossip about the rich and famous.

They will tend to exaggerate stories in order to catch the reader's attention with a headline, but the article beneath the headline often has very little of interest in it.

The tabloids are also known as the 'popular press', and sometimes referred to as the 'gutter press'. The word 'tabloid' really refers to the size of the page, but we use the word now to describe the *style* of journalism we find in the popular press.
Name some daily tabloids.

1. _____

2. _____

3. _____

4. _____

Name some Sunday tabloids.

1. _____

2. _____

3. _____

4. _____

Not all newspapers fall neatly into these categories; some newspapers can be described as 'middle-of-the-road', a mixture of both quality and tabloid.
Identify one middle-of-the-road newspaper.

_____

The different types of newspaper will have different **target audiences**, i.e. they are aimed at particular groups of people. The staff of every newspaper know what appeals to their readers; huge amounts of money are invested in market research.
Who do you think is the target audience of a 'serious' daily paper and how do you know? Take into account age, education, job and interests.

_____

_____

_____

Who do you think is the target audience of the tabloid press and how do you know?

_____

_____

_____

_____

■ *Irish-Owned and Imported Papers*

If we look at the range of newspapers available, we can see that some of them are Irish owned and others are imported.

Irish-owned papers look at both Irish and world news from an Irish viewpoint; they reflect the values of Irish society.

Examine imported newspapers, particularly the ones which have 'Irish' or 'Irish edition' included in the title. You will notice that they are much cheaper than our native papers. The more copies that are printed, the more economical it is to produce the paper; the same amount of money and time go into producing a newspaper, regardless of whether you produce one million or four million copies – the only extra expense is the newsprint and the ink. There is a huge market in Britain, and it costs very little to print the extra numbers needed to satisfy the Irish demand.

The CIRCULATION of a paper refers to the number of copies of the paper which are sold.

The READERSHIP of a newspaper refers to the number of people who actually read the paper. The readership figures will be much higher than the circulation figures, as one paper might be read by several members of a family.

Newspapers usually tell us what their readership figures are. Where would you be likely to find this information?

★ EXERCISES

1. Compare a native Irish newspaper and an 'Irish edition' British newspaper. Approximately what proportion of the British newspaper is devoted to items of Irish interest? How does this compare to the native Irish paper?
2. Working in pairs, take two newspapers, a tabloid and a broadsheet, published on the same day. Compare them and answer the following questions:

	TABLOID	BROADSHEET
• What is the selling price?	_____	_____
• What size are the pages?	_____	_____
• How many pages are there?	_____	_____
• On average, how many graphics are there per page?	_____	_____
• Are the photos large or small?	_____	_____
• Where is the paper published?	_____	_____
• How many pages are devoted to sport?	_____	_____
• How many pages are devoted to business?	_____	_____
• Which uses the most colour?	_____	_____
• What percentage of the paper is taken up with advertising? Give an approximate figure.	_____	_____
• Can you identify the advertisers' target audience?	_____	_____
• How many stories are covered on the front page?	_____	_____
• Is there a list of contents on the front page?	_____	_____
• Are the following included:		
– horoscopes?	_____	_____
– comic strips?	_____	_____
– problem page?	_____	_____
– women's page?	_____	_____
• How long is the editorial?	_____	_____
• How many different typefaces are used?	_____	_____
• Which uses the largest print size?	_____	_____

OTHER DIFFERENCES

There are other differences between tabloid and broadsheet newspapers. For example, the style of writing will also differ.

The broadsheet will use more difficult and more formal language, while the language in the tabloid will be simpler and less 'correct', with more slang words; for example, a serious newspaper might use the word 'bombed', while the tabloid will tend to use 'nuked'.

The tabloids will use words that will cause an emotional response in the reader; for example, 'death crash' rather than 'fatal accident'. We can usually identify the 'slant' or 'angle' from which a story is reported.

The serious newspaper, on the other hand, will give us as much information as possible and allow us to form our own opinions. They will write the story in a more neutral way, remaining as *objective* as possible.

Descriptions of events in the tabloid press are usually very vivid, quite dramatic and often exaggerated. The tabloids engage in a lot of *speculation*, which is presented as fact, whereas the broadsheets tend to deal only in facts which can be proven. This dramatisation of events in the tabloid press is known as *sensationalism* – the journalist is deliberately trying to excite his/her readers.

★ EXERCISES

1. Find one story that is covered in both newspapers and compare them. Examine the following aspects:
   • position in the newspaper
   • size of headline
   • graphics used
   • amount of space given in column inches
   • approximate number of words used in the text
   • type of language used:
     – slang words
     – emotive language
     – exaggeration
2. Look again at the coverage of the story and identify a 'slant' or an 'angle' in the writing. Is the writer's attitude obvious from the language used?
3. Which newspaper uses words such as 'exclusive' and 'scoop' and what do these words mean?
4. Where do newspapers get their news?
5. Examine the news stories carefully and make a list of the different sources used.
6. The following headlines appeared in a tabloid newspaper. Rewrite them in the style of a serious paper:
   • Net Perv Jailed
   • Fans Gutted; Manager Axed

- Paedo 'Club' Sick Pics
- Thugs Terrify Tourists
- Burger Bar Brawl – 10 Arrested
- Holiday Giant Sacks 2,000
- Agony Of Irish Aid Worker
- Nuke Duo Held
- Cops Quiz Crime Boss
- Bubble Bursts For Sleazy Socialite

Headline writers try to come up with headlines that are clever and catchy. From studying the newspapers identify some ways in which they do this:

1. Alliteration, i.e. using words beginning with the same sounds.

2. _____

_____

3. _____

_____

4. _____

_____

5. _____

_____

■ *Local Newspapers*

When you examine an edition of your local newspaper, you will find that it concentrates almost entirely on the following local news items: social events such as weddings and retirements, meetings of the County Council or Corporation, parish fund-raising activities, sporting events at club and county level, District and Circuit Court cases.

Most of the advertising is also local.

A VISIT TO A LOCAL NEWSPAPER

Your local newspaper will usually be happy to organise a class visit – after all, you are an important section of both their present and future readership.

The working week in a local newspaper office goes through a cycle. For the few days before the paper is 'put to bed' everybody is working frantically to meet the deadline; once the paper is printed and distributed to the shops there will be a day or two of calm. It is during this calm period that you will have the chance to see what goes on behind the scenes.

SAMPLE REPORT

PREPARED BY: _____

Report on class visit to the *Meath Chronicle* office, Thursday 18 October 2001

PREPARATION FOR VISIT

In class we studied the quality and popular newspapers. We also looked at the differences between our local newspaper and the national newspapers.

We contacted the *Meath Chronicle* office and spoke to Mr. Pat Kean, Production Manager. He was very willing to show us around and answer our questions. Thursday was the most suitable day from his point of view, as the paper is in the shops from Wednesday. We confirmed that we would visit the office at 11.30 am on Thursday 18 October 2001.

Our next task was to put together a questionnaire. We had a brainstorming session in class and came up with the following list of questions:

• When was the *Meath Chronicle* established?
• Who owns the newspaper?
• How many people are employed?
• How many reporters are employed?
• Apart from reporters, where do they get news items?
• What is the circulation?
• How much does it cost to produce one copy of the newspaper?
• How much profit is made on each copy?
• How much money does the paper make from advertising?
• Why do people buy local newspapers?

On Thursday 18 October, we set off armed with questionnaires, pen, paper and camera.

THE VISIT

When we arrived at the office, Mr Kean was waiting to meet us in the reception area. This was a very busy area, with a steady stream of people coming in to place advertisements in the newspaper. Mr Kean brought us upstairs to the *newsroom* and *editor's office*. The newsroom was equipped with the latest in computer technology.

Members of staff were involved in various jobs. At one computer the cover page of their monthly magazine *Modern Woman* was being designed. At another computer, the classified advertising section was being laid out. As a lot of these ads are the same each week it is simply a matter of getting rid of the 'one-off' ads from the last edition, and replacing them with the new ones for the coming week. The sports editor was researching background information for a feature article on club football.

Mr Kean explained that once the layout is finalised, the paper goes to the 'dark room'. To get into this room we had to pass through a type of antechamber with revolving doors, which stops any light from getting in. Again, what struck me about this area was the modern technology; it is here that the paper is put on to *plates*, which are then sent to the printing press.

We were then taken to see the *printing press* in action. While the press was running, the noise level was unbelievable, and the speed at which the papers came off the press was amazing.

When the press stopped running, Mr Kean explained that one of the reasons the *Meath Chronicle* is doing so well is because the company runs a commercial printing business as well as a newspaper. Each week they print ninety different titles, including the *Leinster Leader* and the *Tallaght Echo*. A new printing press had recently been installed at a cost of more than €20 million.

The printing presses use 300 tonnes of paper each week at a cost of €570 per tonne. The paper comes in from the pulp mills of Sweden, through the port of Drogheda.

At the end of the tour we had a chance to ask questions.

We found out that the *Meath Chronicle* was established in 1897, and has been owned by the Davis family for most of that time. It is possible to look through the old editions of the paper which are kept in the archives.

Seventy people are employed by the paper, ten of whom are reporters.

The paper has a circulation of 20,000. When we asked Mr. Kean why local newspapers were still so popular, he said that it is simply because people get into the habit of buying the paper, and the younger members of the family keep up the tradition.

It costs 18 cent to produce one paper and it retails at €1.50. Allowing for the cost of distribution, profit to the newsagent, tax, etc., the company makes a profit of 38 cent on each paper.

We also asked Mr Kean about employment opportunities and training. A printer goes through a four-year apprenticeship, dividing his time between college and the newspaper.

Anyone interested in a job in the newsroom would need to be good at English, and be able to work under pressure. Two of the class expressed an interest in doing their work experience in the *Meath Chronicle* office, and Mr Kean said he would be happy to organise it for them.

BACK IN THE CLASSROOM

When we returned to school we wrote up our reports on the visit. When we got the pictures developed, we labelled them and used them in our reports. When we evaluated our visit, we all agreed that it was one of the more interesting visits we had taken part in. We learned a lot about the workings of a newspaper office and the technology used in the business.

■ *Survey of Reading Habits*

It might be interesting to examine the circulation figures of the various newspapers in your own area. One way of doing this is to approach one of the local newsagents and ask him to answer a few questions. Like all interviews, preparation is very important; explain to the newsagent what you are doing and arrange a suitable time for the interview; decide what information you need and have your questions ready in advance.

Add more questions to the sample questionnaire:

1. *How many different titles do you stock?*

2. *Which daily newspaper sells the most copies?*

3. *Which Sunday newspaper sells the most copies?*

4. _____

   _____

5. _____

   _____

6. _____

   _____

7. _____

   _____

8. _____

_____

9. _____

_____

10. _____

_____

After you have done the interview, write a short report on your findings. You may use the following headings in your report:

TITLE
AIM
PREPARATION
INTERVIEW
RESULTS
PREPARED BY

In your results section you could show the sales figures in the form of bar graphs. Your maths teacher will help you here.

Another way of getting information on the reading habits of the local population would be to conduct a vox pop. Make out a set of four or five suitable questions. Decide how many people you will interview and the locations you will use. When you have completed the vox pop write a short report on your findings.

★ EXERCISES

1. Your class has been asked to prepare and print a school newsletter. The newsletter will be distributed to parents and pupils at the Hallowe'en break, so you will be covering the events of September and October. As well as news and sports items, remember that you need to make your newsletter interesting and attractive.
2. Appoint an editor who will be responsible for all aspects of production.
3. Decide what jobs need to be done. Think about every stage of the process:

   (a) Gathering information

   (b) _____

(c) _____

(d) _____

(e) _____

The use of IT will be very important in the end product. This exercise would make a good Communications Project.

■ *Increase Your Word Power!*

Can you spell and use the following words correctly?
Kilogram, kilometre, kiosk, knack, knowledge, label, laboratory, labour, laminate, language, laser, lathe.

Unit 2

Radio

Radio has been with us since the beginning of the twentieth century. With the advent of television it was feared that its days were numbered. However, not only has radio survived: it has also gone from strength to strength, with more stations coming on air all the time.

Why is radio still so popular and how has it managed to survive?

Radio is *portable* – we can take it with us jogging, lying on the beach or driving in the car. The fact that radio is so accessible makes it a unique form of communication.

We can listen to radio while doing other things because it does not take our undivided attention as television does. In many workplaces, both indoor and outdoor, you will find a radio playing in the background. Can you suggest some reasons why this is common practice?

1. The work might be boring and repetitive.

2. _____

_____

3. _____

_____

178

4. _____

_____

5. _____

_____

Unlike television radio is cheap; it costs much less to produce an hour of radio than an hour of television.

Radio has survived because, like the newspaper industry, it changed and adapted. At first, radio was in competition with television because it was also broadcasting serials or 'soaps'. When these soaps transferred to television, radio found that it just could not compete. Instead, radio began to concentrate on two completely new and different types of programmes: wall-to-wall music and the radio talk show.

Most popular music stations use the same formula; the current hit songs are played over and over again by popular presenters. The target audience is largely the under-twenty age group.

Talkback radio has become very popular. People take an interest in the personal lives and tragedies of others. Listeners who phone in to radio chat shows seem to find it easy to talk about the most intimate aspects of their lives. The more controversial the subject-matter the better. The presenter will often make the situation even more dramatic and will encourage other listeners to phone in with similar stories or offers of advice and help. Very often those on air will become quite emotional; this of course is just what the presenter wants, as it makes the programme more interesting for the listener.

From the radio station's viewpoint, one major advantage of talkback radio is that it is very cheap to produce. Hours of broadcasting time can be filled by members of the public who are only too willing to talk; and who do not expect any money in return. The presenters of some of these shows have become household names, and have earned huge amounts of money. They have often been accused of taking advantage of people at a time when they are going through some dreadful tragedy and are at their most vulnerable.

FOR DISCUSSION

1. Can you name any talkback radio show?
2. Who presents it?
3. What radio station is it on?
4. What topics are being discussed on the show at the moment?
5. Have you ever phoned in to take part on the show? Why/Why not?
6. Why do you think people are willing to ring in to these shows?

7. Record a section of a talkback show and listen to it in class.
8. Do you feel that the presenter gives everybody a fair chance to get their views across?
9. Do you think the show serves a useful purpose?
10. Do you find your opinion on the topic changing as you listen to the discussion?
11. What topics would you like to hear discussed on the show?

In addition to pop music and talk shows, radio offers a wide variety of other programmes; like the newspapers, radio informs and educates as well as providing entertainment.

■ National Radio

On 1 January 1926 the first Irish national radio station began broadcasting from a small studio near Henry Street in Dublin. In the beginning it was on air for only a few hours a day. Today RTÉ Radio offers a range of stations and a wide variety of programmes. Radio One is the 'serious' radio station, and broadcasts around the clock, providing news and current affairs programmes as well as sports coverage, drama, music and religious programmes. In 1979 2FM came on air, in response to a strong demand for a popular music station.

RTÉ is run as a public service for the people of Ireland. It is funded by a mixture of licence fees and money from advertising. RTÉ is a semi-state body and is managed by a board known as the RTÉ Authority, which is appointed by the government.

★ EXERCISES

1. In addition to Radio One and 2FM what other stations are run by RTÉ?
2. Compare the types of programme broadcast by Radio One and 2FM. You will need a copy of the RTÉ Guide, or the TV/Radio magazine of a weekend newspaper. The RTÉ Guide is probably the best choice, as it gives more information about the programmes.

   Divide the class into seven groups, with each group working on the schedule for a different day; this will make it easier to look at the programmes broadcast over a week.

   Use the worksheet to guide your work. Fill in the number of hours given to each programme type. Try not to get bogged down counting minutes – you are looking for an overview.

RADIO

Day _____

TIME ALLOCATION

Radio 1   2FM

News, Current Affairs   _____   _____

Weather   _____   _____

Sport   _____   _____

Documentaries   _____   _____

Talkback radio   _____   _____

Music   _____   _____

Farming   _____   _____

Religion   _____   _____

Arts   _____   _____

Drama   _____   _____

Short Stories   _____   _____

Reviews   _____   _____

Other _____   _____   _____

When each group has completed a daily sheet the information can be filled in on the following grid to give weekly totals for the various types of programme.

TYPE OF PROGRAMME	WEEKLY TIME ALLOCATION	
	Radio I	2FM
News, Current Affairs	_____	_____
Weather	_____	_____
Sport	_____	_____
Documentaries	_____	_____
Talkback radio	_____	_____
Music	_____	_____
Farming	_____	_____
Religion	_____	_____
Arts	_____	_____
Drama	_____	_____
Short Stories	_____	_____
Reviews	_____	_____
Other _____	_____	_____

Write a short report on your findings under the following headings:
AIM: in four or five lines explain simply what you set out to do.
METHOD: describe how you carried out the work and the materials you used.
RESULTS: describe what you found out. It might be useful to present your findings in the form of bar graphs rather than in written form.
COMMENTS: give your own thoughts on your findings.

3. Do you feel we can use the terms 'quality' and 'popular' in relation to radio stations?
4. Look again at the Radio One schedule. Can you identify the target audiences for the following time slots?

7.00 am – 9.00 am _____

How do you know? _____

9.00 am – 1.00 pm _____

How do you know? _____

1.00 pm – 2.00 pm _____

How do you know? _____

2.00 pm – 5.00 pm _____

How do you know? _____

5.00 pm – 7.00 pm _____

How do you know? _____

7.00 pm – 11.00 pm _____

How do you know? _____

11.00 pm – 7.00 am _____

How do you know? _____

5. Radio is vitally important to certain groups of people. Can you name them and explain why they depend on radio?

(a) Fishermen   _____

_____

(b) _____   _____

_____

(c) _____   _____

_____

COMMUNICATION

(d) _____   _____

_____

(e) _____   _____

_____

6. RTÉ Radio sets out to *inform*, *educate* and *entertain*. Looking at the programme guide for Radio One, pick three items that inform:

(a) _____

(b) _____

(c) _____

Three items that educate:

(a) _____

(b) _____

(c) _____

Three items that entertain:

(a) _____

(b) _____

(c) _____

■ *Local Radio*

During the 1970s and 80s, there was a huge demand in Ireland for pop music stations. Many stations, known as 'pirates', were on the air illegally, operating without licences. In 1987 laws were passed that made it possible for radio stations to be set up, which were independent of the state. Licences were granted by a body called the Independent Radio and Television Commission. Many local radio stations grew out of these early 'pirate' stations.

Local radio in Ireland has been very successful. The mix of programmes broadcast on local radio is different from that on national radio. There is usually a great emphasis on what is going on in the local community.

Examine the programme listings for your local radio station. Make a list of the different types of programme and the time devoted to each.

NAME OF STATION _____

NUMBER OF HOURS ON AIR EVERY DAY _____

Type of programme	*Time given*
1. News	_____
2. Current affairs	_____
3. Music	_____
4. Talkback	_____
5. _____	_____
6. _____	_____
7. _____	_____
8. _____	_____
9. _____	_____
10. _____	_____

Your local radio station will try to accommodate you if you wish to visit the studio. However, many of these local radio studios are quite small and a visit would not be practical. If you ask somebody from the station to visit the classroom you will usually get a favourable response. As with any visit, it is important to prepare beforehand. As a class, decide what type of information you are looking for:
• You might want to know about the history of the station.
• Did it grow from a 'pirate' station?

- Who owns and runs it?
- How many people are employed?
- How did your visitor get into radio as a career?
- What is a typical day like for him or her?
- What does a producer do?

Remember that if everything goes well and you make a good impression on your visitor, he or she might consider involving you in a programme!

■ *News and Current Affairs*

Since its foundation in 1926, RTÉ Radio has regarded news and current affairs programmes as a very important part of its schedule. Radio does have an advantage over both newspapers and television when it comes to news reporting. Newspapers, as we have already seen, will always be several hours behind with the news because of the time involved in printing and distribution.

Television is a visual medium and camera crews and technicians have to be moved from place to place. The radio reporter simply needs a mobile phone and a tape-recorder; with this basic equipment he can phone in his story to the radio station from anywhere in the world.

RTÉ has to be impartial and objective in its reporting of the news, and in discussion programmes it must make sure that the different points of view are represented.

RTÉ Radio gathers news items in much the same way as a newspaper does. Reporters are employed who specialise in certain areas such as politics, business, law and sports.

The station also has correspondents based in different parts of the world. In the case of RTÉ the same reporters contribute to both radio and television news bulletins, and you will be familiar with some of the names and faces. Watch the main RTÉ news tonight and see if you can identify the reporters who work on the following:

TOPIC	*REPORTER*
Politics	_____
Business	_____
Legal affairs	_____
Sports	_____
Religious affairs	_____

It is impossible for RTÉ to keep correspondents in every part of the world, but some countries are considered to be important enough to have a permanent correspondent. Can you name the correspondents who report from the following places?

CITY   *REPORTER*

Belfast   _____

London   _____

Brussels   _____

Washington   _____

Discuss why these cities are considered by RTÉ to be important.

As well as their own reporters, RTÉ get news items from *News Agencies*. These large news organisations can afford to keep people all over the world, and they make their money by selling news items to national radio stations.

A news bulletin is put together by the editor and his staff in the newsroom. Because of the huge amount of information coming into newsrooms today, the editor has to decide which items are included and which ones are left out. The editor also decides the order in which the items are broadcast and the amount of time devoted to each item. Even in making these decisions the editor is showing a certain amount of bias – he has decided which items are important and which are not. The news bulletin is usually a mixture of:

- items written by the newsroom staff, based on what comes in from reporters and news agencies
- reports from journalists at the scene of some important event
- interviews with ' key players'
- analysis by 'experts'.

⭐ EXERCISES

I. Listen carefully to a news bulletin and comment on the following:
  (a) The style of language used – is it simple or complicated? Are sentences long or short? Are slang words used?
  (b) Are good descriptions given? Do you get a clear picture of the incident the reporter is describing – can you see the image or picture in your mind?
  (c) Are the reports balanced – do they give every side of the story?
  (d) Who is the target audience? How do you know?

2. Interviews have to be short and to the point because of the time constraints. A good interviewer has to try and keep the person talking. How does he do this?
   - He will avoid the 'closed' type of question, which can be answered with a 'yes' or 'no'.
   - The interviewer will use all his powers of non-verbal communication to keep his subject talking.
   Give some examples of non-verbal communication.

   (a) _____

   (b) _____

   (c) _____

   (d) _____

3. Work with a partner. One of you is a radio interviewer and the other is an eye-witness who has just witnessed a bridge collapsing at rush hour. The interviewer needs to get as much information as possible for his news programme, but his subject is not a very easy person to interview! Role-play the interview. When you have finished, change roles and do the interview again. At the end of this exercise discuss the following points:
   (a) When you played the role of the interviewer how did you feel while interviewing this witness? Did you stay calm or did you get annoyed?
   (b) What techniques did you use to try and get him to talk?
   (c) Were you successful?

   A three-minute interview will often be cut to just thirty seconds in the news bulletin. This edited version of an interview has become known as a SOUNDBITE.
   Politicians have become quite good at dealing with the media; they will always try to include one catchy phrase or comment in an interview, knowing that the news editor will probably use just that single phrase as a soundbite. In fact, many politicians employ teams of people whose job it is to create interesting soundbites that send the right message.
   Although news bulletins are an important part of the schedule on both national and local radio, a comparison of the two will show some interesting differences. Listen to the main morning news bulletin on both RTÉ Radio One and your local radio station. Compare the treatment of the news under the following headings:

	RADIO ONE	LOCAL RADIO
Total length of news bulletin	_____	_____
time given to international news	_____	_____
time given to national news	_____	_____
time given to local news	_____	_____
time given to interviews	_____	_____
time given to news analysis	_____	_____
style of language (formal/informal)	_____	_____

Some news and current affairs programmes are presented in a magazine-type format; such programmes usually last one or two hours and consist of news reports, analysis, interviews, discussions, reviews, traffic news and weather. Identify one such programme from the RTÉ Radio listings. Identify the target audience for this programme. How do you know?

■ *Drama On Radio*

Although radio drama is much cheaper to make than television drama, it is still more expensive than broadcasting wall-to-wall music. As a result, you will usually find drama only on national radio, as local radio stations would simply not have a large enough budget. A good radio play has to stimulate the imagination of the listener. Although the listener is using only one sense – the sense of hearing – the other senses must be brought into action as well.

- The listener must be able to *see* the scene or setting in his mind.
- The listener must be able to *smell* the foul waste in a Third World shantytown or the freshly cut grass in an Irish garden.
- The listener must be able to *taste* the food and drink served at an elaborate dinner party or the stale bread that makes up the prisoner's ration
- The listener must be able to *feel* the intense heat of the African jungle or the cold of the freezing wastes of Antarctica.

  If you listen to a radio play you will find that it is made up of the following ingredients:

- theme
- plot

- characters
- atmosphere
- sound effects
- music
- dialogue

The *theme* is what the play is about. We should be able to state the theme in a short, simple phrase, e.g. 'This play is about greed' or 'This play was written to show us what happens when . . .'

The *plot* is the order in which the story is told. A good plot will usually start off with some problem or difficulty that has to be resolved. For example, we might have the main character trapped in some impossible situation, or two characters who are in disagreement over something. We call this *conflict*, and without conflict we would not have a good story – we would only have a boring sequence of events that would not hold our interest. As the drama unfolds the *tension* increases and we get more involved in what is going on. Towards the end of the play the highpoint or *climax* is reached, when the conflict is resolved. The ending is very important; the listener must be satisfied that everything is sorted out in a satisfactory way. Endings that do not sort out or *resolve* everything leave us feeling cheated.

The *characters* are the people in the play to whom all these things happen. There is usually one *central character* who has to deal with problems and difficulties during the course of the action. As listeners we have to care about what happens to the central character – the playwright must bring the character to life; he must come across to us as a real person with real feelings, who is someone like ourselves, with hopes and dreams. If the playwright does not succeed in doing this the play will be a failure.

The *atmosphere* refers to the mood of the play. We can use words like sad, tragic, scary or happy to describe the mood. The writer does not have the benefit of lighting, costumes and scenery to create a mood; he has to do it with *sound effects, music* and *dialogue*.

Sound effects can be very useful in creating the setting for the play and giving the listener a sense of place. For example, the cry of a seagull and the noise of waves breaking on the beach will create the same scene for all listeners. Sound effects can also create an atmosphere; the creaky door and the heavy footsteps can conjure up an atmosphere of terror.

Music can also help to establish the mood or atmosphere. The introductory music will give us an idea of what is in store – a horror, a comedy or a romance. Music will also be used throughout the play, especially at times when the suspense or tension is building up.

The *dialogue* is the most important part of a radio drama; it has to set the scene and let us know when the scene is changing; it has to introduce us to the characters; it has to move the action along. The dialogue also has to create a mood by conveying to us the emotions being felt by the characters.

Some radio plays will have a *narrator*, who lets us know about changes in place and time.

On track number eleven of the CD you will find a dramatised story, first broadcast in America by NBC in 1950. This was a time when radio was hugely important as a source of entertainment for all the family. The weekly play or story was an 'event' that was eagerly looked forward to in many homes. You have to imagine children and adults gathered around the radio, anticipating the horrors and adventures that awaited them.

The story you are about to hear was part of a series called *Escape*. Each episode tried to capture the imagination of the listener by creating a 'spine-chilling', life-and-death situation, from which the hero or heroine had to escape. The story is called 'Three Skeleton Key' and is read by Vincent Price.

Listen to the story in its entirety first, to get an idea of the atmosphere or mood. When you listen to it a second time try and break it down into the different parts, such as voices, dialogue, music and sound effects. Think about how each part contributes to the overall effect. When you have listened to it a second time answer the following questions:

1. Who is the *narrator* of the story?
2. When the writer describes the setting, how many of our *senses* does he stimulate? Explain how he does this.
3. How does the writer 'show us' the inside of the lighthouse?
4. Who are the other two people who live in the lighthouse?
5. What do we learn about these two people? Think about their physical appearance and personality.
6. What is the theme of the play?
7. Describe the mood or the atmosphere. How did it make you feel?
8. Did you care about what happened to the main character? Why/Why not?
9. Did the playwright tell a good story? How did he build up the tension?
10. Did the music suit the action? Why/why not?
11. Which sound effects did you find most effective?
12. How would the play have come across without music or sound effects?
13. Did you think the ending was satisfactory? Why/Why not?
14. Would a modern audience be entertained by this drama? How have audiences changed since 1950?

★ EXERCISES

1. Record a modern radio drama and see how it compares to 'Three Skeleton Key'.
2. In your own time listen to a radio programme, (not a pop music programme), which you think might interest you. Write a short review of the programme under the following headings:
   (a) Title of programme.
   (b) Type of programme: did it inform, educate or entertain? What was the purpose of the programme?
   (c) Length of programme.
   (d) Your reaction to the programme: did it achieve what it set out to do? Were you informed, educated or entertained?
   (e) The strong and weak points in the programme.
   (f) Would you recommend this programme? Why/why not?

3. Make your own five-minute radio programme. Work in pairs or small groups.
   (a) Your first task is to decide on the type of radio programme that you are going to create, e.g. news, interview, discussion, play, short story, sport or an advertisement.
   (b) Appoint a producer with overall responsibility for the programme.
   (c) Identify the different jobs that need to be done and decide who is going to do them.
   (d) Write a suitable script, with sound effects if necessary. You will have to be creative when working on the SFX, and use whatever materials you have to hand.
   (e) After several rehearsals record your programme on tape. As you listen to the efforts of each group, make a note of the things that you found good, and suggest improvements that you think could be made.

FOR DISCUSSION

1. Do you think radio can be a good 'visual' medium?
2. What advantages has radio over other forms of communication?
3. If you had to choose between radio and television – if you could only have one – which would you choose? Why?

■ *Vox Pop on Radio Listening*

When you are conducting a vox pop on radio listening habits you need to find out what age your subjects are, to see if there is a relationship between age and listening habits. However, people may not like being asked the question, 'What age are you?' Can you think of some other way of getting this information?

Decide who you are going to target for your survey – are you going to confine it to school or are you going to take to the streets? What information do you need?

Find out how important radio is to the interviewee. Do they listen to the radio while driving or working? Which station do they listen to most often? Which type of programme do they prefer? Have they ever taken part in a radio chat show?

In pairs or small groups, work on suitable questions. Remember that it is best not to have questions that are open: try to have questions that can be answered with a simple 'yes' or 'no'.

When you have completed the interviews you need to share your information and present your findings in the form of a short report. This kind of information can be presented very effectively in graph form.

■ *Increase Your Word Power!*

Can you spell and use the following words correctly?
Launch, lawful, lawyer, league, legacy, leisure, lethal, liability, licence, likeable, lyrics.

Unit 3

Television

It might be interesting to start this unit by doing a quick survey of the class. Ask the following questions:

1. How many television channels do you receive at home?

Fewer than 10 ☐

10 – 100 ☐

Over 100 ☐

2. How many television sets are in your home?

None ☐

One ☐

Two ☐

More than two ☐

The results might not come as much of a surprise. After all, your generation has grown up with this medium and does not remember 'life before television'.

What if there was no television? Roald Dahl discussed this possibility in a poem.

Just Suppose There Was No TV

The most important thing we've learned
So far as children are concerned,
Is never, never, NEVER let
Them near your television set –
Or better still, just don't install
The idiotic thing at all.
In almost every house we've been,
We've watched them gaping at the screen,
They loll and slop and lounge about
And stare until their eyes pop out.
(Last week in someone's place we saw
a dozen eyeballs on the floor.)
They sit and stare and stare and sit
Until they're hypnotised by it.
Until they're absolutely drunk
With all that shocking ghastly junk.
Oh yes, we know it keeps them still
They don't climb on the windowsill
They never fight or kick or punch
They leave you free to cook the lunch
And wash the dishes in the sink
But did you ever stop to think.
To wonder just exactly what
This does to your beloved tot?
IT ROTS THE SENSES IN THE HEAD
IT KILLS IMAGINATION DEAD
IT CLOGS AND CLUTTERS UP THE MIND
IT MAKES A CHILD SO DULL AND BLIND
HE CAN NO LONGER UNDERSTAND
A FANTASY, A FAIRYLAND
HIS BRAIN BECOMES AS SOFT AS CHEESE
HIS POWERS OF THINKING RUST AND FREEZE!
HE CANNOT THINK – HE ONLY SEES.
'All right!' you'll cry, 'All right!' you'll say
'But if we take the set away,
What shall we do to entertain
Our darling children? Please explain.'
We'll answer this by asking you
'What used the darling ones once do?
How used they keep themselves contented
Before this monster was invented?
Have you forgotten? Don't you know? We'll say it very loud and slow
THEY...USED...TO...READ! They'd READ and READ,
And READ and READ, and then proceed
To READ some more. Great Scott! Gadzooks!

One half their lives was reading books!
The nursery shelves held books galore!
Books cluttered up the nursery floor!
And in the bedroom, by the bed,
More books were waiting to be read!
Such wondrous, fine, fantastic tales
Of dragons, gypsies, queens, and whales
And treasure isles, and distant shores
Where smugglers rowed with muffled oars,
And pirates wearing purple pants,
And sailing ships and elephants,
And cannibals crouching round the pot
Stirring away at something hot.
(It smells so good, what can it be?
Good gracious, it's Penelope.)
The younger ones had Beatrix Potter
With Mr Tod, the dirty rotter,
And Squirrel Nutkin, Pigling Bland,
And Mrs Tiggy-Winkle and –
Just How The Camel Got His Hump,
And How The Monkey Lost His Rump,
And Mr Toad, and bless my soul,
There's Mr Rat and Mr. Mole –
Oh, books, what books they used to know,
Those children living long ago!
So please, oh please, we beg, we pray,
Go throw your TV set away,
And in its place you can install
A lovely bookshelf on the wall.
Then fill the shelves with lots of books,
Ignoring all the dirty looks.
The screams and yells, the bites and kicks,
And children hitting you with sticks –
Fear not, because we promise you
That, in about a week or two
Of having nothing else to do,
They'll now begin to feel the need
Of having something good to read.
And once they start – oh boy, oh boy!
You watch the slowly growing joy
That fills their hearts. They'll grow so keen
They'll wonder what they'd ever seen
In that ridiculous machine,
That nauseating, foul, unclean,
Repulsive television screen!
And later, each and every kid
Will love you more for what you did.'

Roald Dahl paints a very negative picture of the effects of television. He maintains that children, in particular, can suffer both mental and physical damage because of television.

What physical effects are mentioned in the poem?

1. Bad posture.

2. _____

3. _____

Other physical effects that Dahl does not mention should also be considered. Doctors are becoming very worried about the level of *obesity* in the present generation of children. They feel sure that television has a huge part to play in this. Not only are children not getting enough exercise, they are soaking up the advertising messages for 'snack' foods which have a high sugar content; the only exercise they get is when they walk from the television to the kitchen to stock up on crisps, drinks and other junk food.

What mental effects does the poet mention?

1. Children are hypnotised by the television.

2. _____

3. _____

There is no doubt that television has an hypnotic effect; even the language we use shows how we think about it. We talk about viewing 'habits', or people becoming 'addicted' to soaps; we speak about television in the same way as we speak about drugs and there is no doubt that it can have the same effect as a sedative.

While it is very difficult to prove that there is a direct link between violence on television and anti-social behaviour, many psychologists are convinced that children who watch a lot of violent programmes do suffer long-term damage. Children can be DESENSITISED to the effects of violence – they simply become so used to seeing it that they take it for granted. As a result, they are not fully aware of the awful consequences of violence in the real world.

In his poem, Roald Dahl offers one alternative to television viewing, i.e. reading. As he was a writer, making a very good living from the sale of books aimed at children, we could accuse him of being biased! What arguments does he put forward in favour of reading?

1. _____

_____

2. _____

_____

3. _____

_____

Do you agree with his view? Why/why not?

Reading is not the only activity that is neglected. It is in the nature of young children to be *active*; they learn how to get on with others by playing and interacting with other children and adults; their imagination is developed through activities such as making things, exploring their surroundings and inventing games. When they are watching television they become *passive*; they are almost in a trance-like state unless, of course, somebody changes the channel!

Do you agree with Roald Dahl that television is used by parents simply to keep children (and teenagers) quiet?

Interview an older person who grew up at a time when television was not widely available and find out what they did for entertainment.

If television were suddenly removed from your world, how do you think you would react?

We must not forget that television has many positive aspects:
• It can be a great source of entertainment for people who are sick or lonely
• It can open up the world to us – we can all become armchair travellers.

- It can unlock the secrets of science and nature in a way that we can understand.
- Television technology allows doctors to put tiny cameras into the human body.
- CCTV can give us a sense of security.

Add some more benefits to this list:

1. _____

_____

2. _____

_____

3. _____

_____

Television has come a long way since John Logie Baird transmitted the first moving pictures in 1926. Ten years later, the BBC began transmitting television programmes to a very small audience. As the decades went on audiences grew. People living on the east coast of Ireland were able to receive pictures from the BBC.

On New Year's Eve, 1961, Ireland's own television station came on air. Like our national radio stations RTÉ television is looked on as a public service, and is under the control of the RTÉ Authority. During the early years of Irish television the number of hours of broadcasting was very limited, with the station opening at 6.00 pm and closing at 11.30 pm.

The pace of change during the last few decades has been very rapid; RTÉ now has three channels, RTÉ 1, Network 2 and TG 4. We also have TV3, which is an independent, commercial channel, not under the control of the RTÉ Authority.

With the advent of satellite TV we are no longer confined to terrestrial television; we also have access to a huge number of foreign channels, transmitting news, sport, music and entertainment twenty-four hours a day.

Television has become a hugely important medium of communication, as it has the ability to get into every household in the country. It affects the way politicians behave, it can shape world events by highlighting certain issues and, of course, it is responsible for the growth of a whole new generation of advertising techniques.

The power of television to influence voters was first recognised in 1960, in the US presidential election between John Fitzgerald Kennedy and Richard Nixon. This was the first election in which the candidates appeared together on television to debate important issues. JFK seemed more relaxed and 'at home' than Nixon; this ability to come across well on television tipped the balance in his favour, and he went on to win the election. The interesting thing about this is that the debates were broadcast on both radio and television; people who *heard* the debates on radio felt that Nixon was the better candidate, while those who *viewed* the debates felt that Kennedy came out on top. From then on politicians had to be conscious of the image they were projecting on television; they had to realise that they were being judged not only on what they said, but also on the way they said it. They had to learn how to come across well on television.

Television coverage of disasters, such as famines or earthquakes, can trigger action by governments or individuals. In the 1980s Bob Geldof raised over 50 million pounds for famine relief in Ethiopia; he had been moved to do something when he saw the powerful images of famine and death on his television screen.

Advertisers spend enormous amounts of money on television advertising, where time is sold in thirty-second segments. Because it is a visual as well as an audio medium, the impact of television advertising is much greater than that of the radio or print media.

★ EXERCISES

THERE'S NEVER ANYTHING ON!

Have a brainstorming session to identify as many different *types* of television programmes as you can. We hear the word GENRE a lot these days in the television and film world. Genre simply means type or style. For example, we can speak of soap operas as a *television genre*, or gothic horror as a *film genre*.

Your brainstorming session should produce fifteen to twenty different types of programmes. To have a closer look at the huge range of programmes on offer, we will examine the schedules for one day across a number of channels. Given the vast number of channels available, we will confine our investigation to the terrestrial channels based in Ireland and the UK.

Divide into groups. Each group will take one channel and fill in the worksheet below. Remember that we are looking for an overview, so try not to get too involved in counting minutes. The RTÉ Guide is probably the best publication to use, as it will tell you what the programme is about – it is not always possible to tell this from the title.

Fill in the *type* of programme being broadcast in each time slot.

CHANNEL: _____   DATE: _____

Time   Programme Type

12.00 midnight – 1.00 am   _____

1.00 am – 2.00 am   _____

2.00 am – 3.00 am   _____

3.00 am – 4.00 am   _____

4.00 am – 5.00 am   _____

5.00 am – 6.00 am   _____

6.00 am – 7.00 am   _____

7.00 am – 8.00 am   _____

8.00 am – 9.00 am   _____

9.00 am – 10.00 am   _____

10.00 am – 11.00 am   _____

11.00 am – 12.00 pm   _____

12.00 pm – 1.00 pm   _____

1.00 pm – 2.00 pm   _____

2.00 pm – 3.00 pm   _____

3.00 pm – 4.00 pm   _____

4.00 pm – 5.00 pm   _____

5.00 pm – 6.00 pm   _____

6.00 pm – 7.00 pm   _____

7.00 pm – 8.00 pm _____

8.00 pm – 9.00 pm _____

9.00 pm – 10.00 pm _____

10.00 pm – 11.00 pm _____

11.00 pm – 12.00 midnight _____

When you have completed the worksheet your next task is to calculate the total number of hours devoted to each type of programme. Share your findings with the class. Complete the following worksheet. Fill in the total number of hours devoted to each type of programme across the channels.

	RTÉ 1	NET2	TV3	TG4	BBC1	BBC2	ITV	C4
1. News/current affairs								
2. Sport								
3. Films								
4. Sitcoms								
5. Soaps								
6. _____								
7. _____								
8. _____								
9. _____								
10. _____								
11. _____								

	RTÉ I	NET2	TV3	TG4	BBCI	BBC2	ITV	C4
12. _____								
13. _____								
14. _____								
15. _____								
16. _____								
17. _____								
18. _____								
19. _____								
20. _____								

FOR DISCUSSION

1. Pick out the more 'serious' channels? How do you identify them?
2. Programme Classifications. RTÉ classify some of their programmes according to content and give the viewer some idea of the suitability of programmes for different age groups. An icon appears in the top right-hand corner of the screen for twenty seconds at the beginning of the programme. Identify the different classifications.

(a) GA _____

(b) CH _____

(c) YA _____

(d) PS _____

(e) MA _____

Do you think parents find this kind of information helpful?

3. The 9.00 pm watershed policy. To protect younger children, television companies have a policy of not broadcasting 'adult' material before 9.00 pm. From examining what is broadcast in the different time slots, do you think the companies stick to this policy? Do you think that 9.00 pm is a suitable time to start broadcasting adult programmes? Why/why not?

    Whose responsibility is it to make sure that children do not watch unsuitable programmes? The television companies? Parents? The Government?

4. Identify the target audiences for the following time-slots across the Irish channels.

	RTÉ1	NET2	TV3	TG4
10.00 am –1.00 pm				

How do you know? _____

3.00 pm – 6.00 pm				

How do you know? _____

6.00 pm – 7.00 pm				

How do you know? _____

7.00 pm – 9.00 pm				

How do you know? _____

9.00 pm – midnight				

How do you know? _____

midnight – 7.00 am				

How do you know? _____

5. What time of the day do you think attracts the biggest audiences? Why?

    We call this peak-viewing time *prime time*. What type of programmes are broadcast during prime time? Why?

6. Each week the RTÉ Guide publishes the Top Twenty ratings – the twenty most popular RTÉ programmes and the numbers who watched them. Study the list in the current RTÉ guide and list the five most popular *types* of programme:

(a) _____

(b) _____

(c) _____

(d) _____

(e) _____

7. Find out how these TAM Ratings are compiled. TAM stands for Target Audience Measurement. Ratings are a form of market research and are vitally important to people working in the advertising industry. Advertisers have to 'chase' consumers; they need to know what newspapers and magazines we read, which radio programmes we tune in to, which television programmes we watch; the Internet sites we are most likely to log on to.

8. Ratings are also important for the programme makers as they provide them with 'feedback'. Why do the managers of commercial television stations pay close attention to the ratings?

9. Find out how much it costs to advertise on television.

10. RTÉ is funded partly by advertising and partly by licence fees. Find out how much a television licence costs. Do you think it is value for money? Why/why not?

■ *Survey of Viewing Habits*

You can conduct a survey on television viewing habits in much the same way as you carried out the survey on radio listening habits. Before you start working on questions, you need to decide exactly what information you are interested in collecting.

• Who are you going to target? Do you want to do separate surveys for different age groups? Are you particularly interested in the viewing habits of young children? How many people will you survey?

• What information do you think would be useful?

• Are you going to ask for facts or do you also want opinions?

• How are you going to present your findings?

Note: Perhaps you could start off with a simple survey of the class to find out the number of hours per week spent watching television, and the types of programmes that are most popular.

■ *Television News*

Is there a danger that television is turning news into entertainment? News programmes have their own theme music and are introduced by people who have become celebrities. Everything is turned into a media event; we can witness terrorist attacks, wars and natural disasters unfolding before our eyes. Is there a danger that we can become immune to the horror of these events, in the same way as children become immune to the effects of violence?

The gathering of news items for television news is much the same as for radio, except that more equipment is required. We have seen that the same reporters contribute to both radio and television bulletins. However, when preparing a bulletin for television, the reporter does not have to create images for us through the use of vivid and descriptive language because the camera does that for him. If you watch the main evening news bulletin you will find that it is made up of several different parts:

- items read by the presenter
- live coverage of events
- interviews with the important people involved
- complicated facts and figures shown in the form of maps or charts
- experts brought in to explain events and to try and predict what will happen next.

Record two evening news bulletins on different channels, perhaps RTÉ 1 and TV3, on the same day and compare them under the following headings:

	RTÉ 1	*TV 3*
• *Length of news programme.*		
• *Main news item.*		
• *The order in which the items were dealt with.*		
• *The amount of time given to each item.*		
• *The style of presentation:*		
– *language used*		
– *dress and appearance of presenters*		
– *formal or casual atmosphere.*		
• *The amount of time given to interviews.*		

Analyse your findings.

■ *Soap Operas*

What exactly are soap operas and how did they get their name? A soap opera is a story or saga that continues week in, week out, year after year.

As we have seen, it is a television genre that can be traced back to radio; some would say that it can be traced back even further to the work of the nineteenth-century writer, Charles Dickens.

Dickens was one of the most popular writers ever, and he came up with the idea of publishing stories in *instalments*. One of his most famous works, *The Pickwick Papers*, was written in monthly instalments. Readers would queue up to get their hands on the next episode, impatient to see what happened next. Sales reached 40,000 copies each month. The fictional characters were looked on as real people living real lives – in much the same way as the public often look upon the characters in the soap operas of today. It is interesting too that the publishers of *The Pickwick Papers* made money from advertising!

It was during the 1930s that the first serialised dramas were broadcast on American radio. They were sponsored by a soap manufacturing company called Procter and Gamble. Since the 1880s Procter and Gamble had been aware of the power of advertising, and by 1939 they were spending over 9 million dollars a year on radio advertising, pushing their product brands. One of their techniques was to sponsor daytime serialised dramas, which became known as soap operas. The company has been very successful, and today it controls many leading brands such as Pampers, Head and Shoulders, Charmin, Crest, Bounce and Max Factor.

Television took over the soaps in the early 1950s and they soon became a very important part of daytime programming. Television has become the medium of the soap opera, and these programmes attract huge followings of loyal fans. One of the longest running soaps, *Coronation Street*, was first screened in 1960, and is as popular today as ever, with audiences of over twenty million. The early soaps often showed a perfect world, where the 'goodies' were rewarded and the wicked were punished. Gradually the style changed and today's soaps are seen as a more accurate reflection of real life.

WHAT MAKES A SOAP OPERA SUCCESSFUL?

Like any drama, if a soap is to succeed it must have two essential ingredients: great characters and great storylines. In this sense, today's soaps are no different from the instalments written by Dickens over 150 years ago. Dickens was able to create marvellous characters; he was also a master storyteller, building up the atmosphere and tension and leaving his readers with a 'cliffhanger' at the end of each episode. Writers of modern soap operas use exactly the same techniques. However, a soap opera is not written by just one person; this would be impossible given the amount of material that is needed. Scripts are written by a team of writers and editors, and members of the team are constantly changing.

Every four weeks or so the writing team will meet and put forward ideas for storylines. There will usually be a mixture of stories, some serious, some comic, so that the viewer experiences a mix of moods and emotions. It is essential that all the writers know and understand the characters, the kind of people they are, how they will react to events and, most importantly, what has gone on for them in the past. Someone has to keep track of important dates, such as wedding anniversaries and birthdays, so that they can figure in the story. Viewers must have strong feelings for the characters; it does not matter whether we love them or hate them as long as we respond to them in some way.

The writers still develop the same age-old themes, such as love, jealousy, hatred and rivalry. These are the same themes that Shakespeare wrote about in his plays and that Dickens dealt with in his novels. The writers have to translate these themes into believable stories.

At the writers' meeting new storylines are agreed on and each writer goes away to concentrate on one story and one set of characters. Writers also have to make sure that each episode has a 'good' ending – very often a cliffhanger. This will make sure that the viewers tune in to the next episode.

As with radio drama, good dialogue is essential. The dialogue has to carry the plot forward, and it also has to let us know what the character is thinking and feeling. A soap opera is different from a television drama; a drama is complete in that it has a beginning, middle and end. You will notice that most soap operas get their name from where they are set. The *setting* is what holds the story together; characters and storylines come and go but the setting remains the same.

Producers know that they have to make the soap appealing to younger viewers if they want to keep their audience figures healthy, so every now and again new characters will be introduced who will appeal to teenagers. Sometimes characters are written out of the show and if the ratings fall as a result, writers have to think up some imaginative way of bringing them back.

Soaps also deal with social issues. There is open discussion about matters such as abortion, HIV, domestic violence and drug abuse. The highlighting of certain issues can have very positive results. For example, a storyline relating to a character with cervical cancer led to a huge increase in the numbers of women coming forward for testing. It can also work the other way – in the week following the screening of an episode dealing with attempted suicide, hospitals reported a huge increase in the numbers of people who had overdosed on drugs.

How many hours per week did you find were devoted to soap operas across the six channels you studied? Were you surprised at this figure? Why/Why not?
• How many soap operas do you follow?
• Why do you think people get hooked on soaps?
• What would you say all soaps have in common?
• What, in your opinion, makes a soap opera successful?

 # FOR DISCUSSION

1. Can you think of a soap that is dealing with a social issue at the moment? Name the soap and the social issue and describe how it is being handled. Do you think it is important for soaps to look at social issues and problems? Why/Why not?
2. Can you find examples of stereotyping in any of the soaps you watch, e.g. the moody teenager or the interfering mother-in-law? Do you feel that this type of stereotyping is acceptable? Why/Why not?
3. Which would you say is the most serious soap? Why?
4. Which soaps would you say rely most on comedy? Can you pick out certain characters who are more comic than dramatic?
5. Which soap do you think gives us the most realistic portrayal of teenagers?
6. Which soap do you find the most credible? Why?

The soaps are a huge industry. Television channels compete with each other for audiences; magazines are published which deal solely with news and gossip surrounding soaps and soap stars; there are thousands of websites devoted to them.

 # EXERCISES

1. View a pre-recorded episode of a popular soap and discuss it under the following headings:
   • Setting – look at costumes and props
   • Characters – which ones are more important?
   • Number of scenes
   • Number of story lines
   • Type of story lines – serious, humorous, etc.
   • Dialogue
   • Social issues dealt with
   • Cliffhanger ending
   • Special effects
   • Stereotyping
   • Target audience
   • Your own response to the stories and characters
2. You are writing a short scene for your favourite soap in which a new character is being introduced. Your scene should include two well-known characters as well as the newcomer. You need to give the viewers as much information as possible about the newcomer: what kind of person they are, what they are doing here, any connections they have with the area, etc.

   Work in threes on this exercise and when you have finished the script perhaps you could act out the scene.
3. Name your favourite soap character and say why you like him/her. Be specific. Describe the character – both the physical appearance and personality. Describe the qualities that attract you to this character. Is he or she kind, caring, funny, etc? Give examples of how the character behaves in different situations.

FOR DISCUSSION

1. Soap operas are broadcast before the 9.00 pm watershed. Do you think this is appropriate? Why/why not?
2. Do you think the soaps reflect real life? Why/why not?
3. Do you think it is useful to deal with issues such as teenage pregnancy, drug abuse, etc in soaps? Give reasons for your answer.
4. Do you think Australian soap operas have any relevance for Irish teenagers?

■ *Situation Comedy (Sitcom)*

What do you understand by the term 'sitcom'? Identify some ways in which a sitcom differs from a soap:

1. Story lines are usually more light-hearted

2. _____

_____

3. _____

_____

4. _____

_____

5. _____

_____

Name your favourite sitcom and say why it appeals to you. Be specific. Describe the situation or setting, the characters, and the storylines.

■ *Reality Television*

1. What do you understand by the term 'Reality TV?
2. Can you name some programmes that are part of this genre?

Tens of millions of people worldwide tune into *Big Brother*, and versions of the programme

are now being made in almost twenty countries. The recipe is very simple:
- put ordinary people into an isolated environment
- cut them off from everything that is familiar to them
- take away their privacy by training cameras on them day and night
- make them compete with each other for a prize

All the producer has to do is sit back and wait for personality clashes and rivalries to develop, and he has the ingredients for an interesting programme.

The other secret is, of course, to involve the viewers by giving them a say in what happens to these people. Human nature being what it is, we seem to enjoy watching other people being humiliated. But where is it all going to end? As technology improves is reality television going to keep developing and changing into something more sophisticated and more sinister?

WORK TO DO

1. Find out why the show is called *Big Brother*.
2. Why, do you think, has reality TV become so popular?
3. If possible, watch the film *The Truman Show*, starring Jim Carrey and directed by Peter Weir.

In the film, Truman Burbank (Jim Carrey) gradually comes to realise that for the thirty years of his life he has been under surveillance, with 5,000 secret cameras recording every move he makes. His 'life' is transmitted live twenty-four hours a day as a soap opera *The Truman Show*. It is watched by millions of people around the world. His hometown of Seahaven is a huge, cleverly designed television set, which is so large it can be seen from space. Everyone in Seahaven is a professional actor, including Truman's wife Meryl. Like all soaps, *The Truman Show* is funded by advertising. Branded products are placed around the kitchen, people stop to talk to Truman in front of large advertising posters. The director of the twenty-four hour soap is a man called Christof. As his name suggests, he plays God with Truman's life. He tells us that he started the project because the viewing public were fed up with fake emotions and manufactured story lines – they wanted reality; in Truman he is giving the viewers the genuine article. We occasionally see shots of viewers watching the show in cafés and bars around the world. They never seem to question the morality of what is going on – they just accept it.

The film raises some interesting questions about the future of reality TV, consumerism, technology and, of course, human nature.

■ *Increase Your Word Power!*

Can you spell and use the following words correctly?
Machinery, magazine, maintain, maintenance, malfunction, malicious, management, manoeuvre, manual, manufacture, material, mechanics, mention, method, minimum, mortgage.

Unit 4

Film

Gabriel Byrne grew up in Dublin in the 1950s, and is one of Ireland's best-known screen actors. In the following extract from his autobiography *Pictures In My Head*, he describes his first visit to the cinema.

1   Looking back to an evening in the half-light of that room (at my grandmother's house), filled with the smell of lilac from her garden, among the faded photos and framed jigsaw puzzles, and stuffed owls, I know that memory has made all the evenings I spent there become as one. And I know that this was my first theatre, the beginning of my love for dark-ened rooms where words and image and music had power to move the soul in transports of delight, as the poet says. She loved talking and telling stories and books and music, but most of all my granny loved the pictures.

2   I remember crossing the park, my hand in her hand as she took me to the pictures for the first time. We stood for minutes watching the swans on Fairview Lake, but I was impatient to be away, for the thrill of the picture-house was greater than any swan. We waited for the doors to open, behind a sign on the pavement which said 'one shilling'. A man dressed in a red uniform came out and beckoned us and the other people to a glass box. Granny opened her purse and carefully counted out the coins, and received a ticket with a hole in it, which she gave to another man who stood like a soldier in front of two doors. He took the tickets and tore them and gave us back one half and kept the other and looped it onto a piece of string.

3   From inside the door I could hear loud voices, but not like the voices of real people, and I started to feel afraid and she looked at me and smiled and took my hand tightly and said, 'There's nothing to be afraid of. It's only the pictures.'

4   All around the foyer there were painted photographs of men with thin black moustaches and women with bright red lipstick like my mother. Then the sentry pulled back the door and we were in darkness with the noise of those strange voices all around us. We edged our way along by a wall like blind people, me holding on to her coat for fear, till suddenly, in an explosion of blinding colour, I saw before me the bluest sea I could ever imagine, and on it two huge boats with sails, sailing under a vast blueness of sky. I turned my head in terror into her body, and for an eternity of moments I dared not look again. When I opened my eyes I saw a light beam in the darkness and a voice asked for our tickets, as it came toward us. And with her arm around me, we followed the dancing light as it lit our way along the steps, 'til we found our seats and I sat down overwhelmed by the fear and the mystery and the magic of it all. But as the wonder grew, the terror died. And so I came to know the lovely dark womb of the picture-house for the first time.

5   Now the lights came slowly on from the red stars of glass set high above us in the blue roof and around the walls from flickering lamps. And a snowy curtain that folded into silver trees as it slowly fell, covered the sea and the boat and the white writing and the voices.

    'Was that a picture, granny?'

    'No, that was only an old trailer,' she said. Then she gave me a marshmallow mouse and a Trigger bar which I broke in two over my knee. And she hoped I wouldn't be afraid of the next picture because the banshee was in it. But so was Jimmy O'Dea and he was great gas.

6   A girl in a yellow coat came up the steps between the seats with a tray of sweets. And we bought two Toblerones, and she kept one for after and we split the other between us.

7   And now the curtain of trees was going up to the roof again, and the lights faded 'til I could see only the outline of things. And then nothing at all. Then it began. The first picture I ever saw – *Darby O'Gill and the Little People*.

8   Time has dimmed the memory of the plot, but I remember the fairies and Jimmy O'Dea and the banshee, charging white and terrifying over the hill. And somebody throwing a lantern at the dreaded thing and as it burst into flames the gasps and screams of the few people who were in the audience. But above all I remember a smiling man and a girl sitting on the edge of a swaying hay cart, talking as the music played. Nothing more. But the memory of those scenes has stayed with me always.

9   When we came out it was raining and the lights from the shops shone in the wet pavements but now I looked at everything as if for the first time. For I knew that something had been born within me. And that the world outside the picture-house would never be the same again. That evening she played the accordion as usual but the tune she played from under her fingers was the music from the picture. And as she sang,

    Oh for the days of the Kerry dancing,
    Oh for the call of the piper's tune,

FILM

I made of my winged chair a swaying hay cart, and that night I slept dreaming of lanterns and silver stars and Jimmy O'Dea sailing the biggest of ships on the bluest of seas.

FOR DISCUSSION

1. Gabriel Byrne remembers his first visit to the cinema in the 1950s in vivid detail. What age do you think he was at the time? Can you remember the first time you were brought to the cinema as a young child? What film did you see? Which cinema did you go to? What was your impression of the experience? How did you feel?
2. How do you think your experience might have been different from Gabriel Byrne's? Were you 'overwhelmed by the fear and the mystery and the magic of it all'?
3. In paragraph 1, Byrne says that he developed a love of 'darkened rooms where words and image and music had power to move the soul in transports of delight'. What do you think he means by this? Would you agree with his description of the world of film? Why/why not?
4. How do we know from paragraph 9 that his visit to the cinema made such a huge impression on him?
5. Can you describe the relationship between the young Gabriel Byrne and his grandmother? Would you agree that she was an important influence in his life? Do you think she would have encouraged him to become an actor?
6. In paragraph 4, Byrne describes the cinema as a 'lovely dark womb'. He conjures up an image of being apart from the real world, totally caught up in the make-believe world of the film. Do you think we can get the same strong sense of being present if we look at the film on video? Why/why not? Compare the experience of watching a movie in the cinema and watching it on video.
7. List some ways in which film-making techniques have changed and developed since the 1950s:

1. _____

_____

2. _____

_____

3. _____

_____

213

4. _____

_____

5. _____

_____

■ *Making Motion Pictures*

Before you attempt to study a particular film and write a film review, it would be helpful to learn a little about the making of a film and the jobs of the different people involved. Very often on television, the first screening of a successful film will be accompanied by a programme showing how the film was made. It would be useful to record a programme of this type and use it as a basis for the work in this section.

THE SCREENWRITER

The screenwriter writes the script or the screenplay. The screenplay includes the 'dialogue' or words which the actors will speak, as well as instructions relating to the actions. The screenwriter will usually include suggestions regarding camera angles and settings.

THE DIRECTOR

The most important person on a film set is the director. It is the director who transforms the story into a film. The director is an artist – he makes all the creative decisions. He has a vision of how the finished product will look; he will select the actors, settings, costumes and props; he will 'direct' the actors to play their parts in a particular way. He will decide on the music, effects and camera angles. He decides on the final 'cut' of the film, i.e. what is left in and what is edited out.

THE PRODUCER

While the director is the creative genius, the producer is like a general manager in the business world. He makes sure that the director has everything he needs when he needs it. He organises locations and travel arrangements. He is in charge of the money and his main task is to finish the film in the agreed time without going over budget. He is also responsible for marketing and distributing the film.

THE CAMERA CREW

When we are watching a film we tend to take the work of the camera crew for granted; however, they have huge demands made on them and camera operators are both artists

FILM

Long Shot

Medium Long Shot

Mid Shot

Medium Close-up

Close-up

Big Close-up

Very Long Shot

and technicians. As well as understanding the complicated technology, they also have to have an eye for a 'good' *shot*. A shot is a continuous piece of film and can last for a few seconds or for several minutes. A *scene* is made up of a series of shots with the same background, and a number of scenes make up a *sequence*.

When describing a particular shot we need to ask the following questions:

1. What is the *distance* between the camera and the subject? Is it a long, medium or close-up shot? A director might use a long shot at the beginning of a scene to give us a lot of information about the setting; he will use a close-up to show the expression on the face of a character.
2. What type of camera *angle* is being used: low, high or neutral? If a low angle is used the character will appear strong and powerful; a high-angle shot will make the character appear weak and vulnerable.
3. Is the camera *moving*? If the camera is following a character we are looking at a *tracking shot*. To avoid any shaking the camera will be moved on tracks. In the early days of the motion picture the camera was mounted on a small hand-propelled vehicle called a *dolly*. If the camera is moved from left to right, or right to left, to sweep a large area we call it *panning*. A *boom* shot is taken from a height, with the camera fixed to a crane.

THE EDITOR

Directors usually shoot far more film than is needed; it is the job of the editor to 'cut' the movie down to size. In the early days of film, this literally meant cutting a piece out of the reel of film and splicing or joining the two ends together again. Techniques today are much more sophisticated as all the images can be changed into computer format, and an editor can cut and paste pictures in much the same way as a word processor can cut and paste text. Editing is also part of the creative process. The editor has to make the cuts in the right place for maximum impact; if it is done properly the audience will not be aware of it. When the picture editor is satisfied with the finished product, the sound editor adds the dialogue, background noises and music.

FILM MUSIC

Music has always been considered an essential part of film. Even in the days of the silent pictures, a musical score was written and played live in the cinema while the film was being shown. The *pace* of the music usually reflected the speed of the action on screen.

Film music has progressed a lot since the 1920s. In the early days music was looked on as a sort of background for what was happening on screen; today it is considered to be just as important as the action.

The movie soundtrack has become a huge part of the marketing when a new film is released. Sometimes the director will use the music of the time in which the film is set. For example, in *Stand by Me*, based on a short story by Stephen King, the director used the rock 'n' roll music of the 1950s to give the viewer a feel for the time in which the action took place.

However, most musical scores are written especially for the film, and are the result of co-operation between the director and the composer. One of the most successful partnerships was that between Alfred Hitchcock and Bernard Herrmann. Herrmann wrote the music for many Hitchcock films, including *Vertigo, North by Northwest* and *Psycho*; his music successfully reflected the psychological or emotional states of the characters. The music helped to build up the atmosphere of mystery and excitement that Hitchcock was so good at creating.

On track number twelve of the CD you will hear part of the soundtrack from the film *Psycho*. This is probably one of the best-known pieces of film music, and certainly seemed to suit the stark images on the screen. You may need to listen to the track a couple of times in order to recognise the different sequences.

In the film the character, Marion Crane, is fed up with the way her life is working out. She is in love with Sam, but they cannot afford to get married because Sam is supporting his ex-wife. One day Marion is given 40,000 dollars to bank for her employer, and she sees this as her chance to start a new life. She takes the money and sets out for California and Sam; she gets caught in a storm and decides to pull off the highway and seek refuge in The Bates Motel. There she meets a quiet young man called Norman . . .

On the CD you will first hear the opening music to the film. This opening sequence lasts for one minute and fifty-five seconds, and creates an atmosphere of unease and panic. Listen for the five musical 'stabbings' in this piece. Herrmann uses this music again later in the film to build up the tension as the climax of the film approaches.

The second sequence you will hear lasts for just over one minute and represents Marion leaving the hot, humid city, having made her decision to start a new life in California with Sam.

The storm sequence is next, lasting one minute and twenty seconds. Here the opening music is repeated, evoking the same atmosphere of unease and panic.

The shower scene is represented by thirty seconds of violent stabbing movements, which are screeched by the violins. Even in the absence of the shocking visual images, the music makes a powerful impact.

The final thirty seconds portrays the final, trembling moments of Marion's life as she bleeds to death.

★ EXERCISE

The soundtrack you have listened to is from the horror genre. Listen to extracts from soundtracks of other genres and examine how effective they are in reflecting the atmosphere of the film.

COMMUNICATION

■ *Film Genre*

We have already come across the word genre in relation to television. We also use genre to distinguish between different types of film.

Identify as many different types of film as you can and give an example of each genre.

GENRE	*TITLE*
1. Thriller	_____
2. _____	_____
3. _____	_____
4. _____	_____
5. _____	_____
6. _____	_____
7. _____	_____
8. _____	_____
9. _____	_____
10. _____	_____

Using a copy of the latest magazine from your local video shop, put the top ten films into categories according to genre:

TITLE	*GENRE*
1. _____	_____
2. _____	_____
3. _____	_____

4. _____   _____

5. _____   _____

6. _____   _____

7. _____   _____

8. _____   _____

9. _____   _____

10. _____   _____

With your teacher, you will decide on a film for detailed study. Before watching the film make sure that you know a little bit about the background to it: the genre it belongs to; where and when it is set; the theme or themes that it deals with. You should first look at the entire film in order to get an overall impression. At the end of this first viewing you should be able to give your own *response* to the film. How would you describe the atmosphere or mood of the film? What emotions did you feel as you watched the film? Were you impressed by the camera work? What did you think of the quality of the acting? Was the music suitable?

When you look at the film for a second time, pick out two or three scenes that you found particularly striking or dramatic. What was it about these scenes that you particularly liked? Why did they work so well? In your discussion you should refer to settings, camera work, special effects, costumes, acting and music.

■ *Writing a Film Review*

Collect a number of film reviews from newspapers, magazines, radio or television. Look at them carefully. You will find that certain aspects of the film will be dealt with in a review.
1. We will usually be told the genre of the film and the age group that it is suitable for.
2. The reviewer will give us some idea of the storyline – just enough to get us interested but not enough to give away the whole story.
3. We will be introduced to the main characters, and the reviewer will give his opinion on the way the actors played the parts of these characters. We will be told if any of the actors got Oscars for their performances, or if they were nominated for an Oscar.
4. The music, make-up, special effects and camera work will all be commented on.
5. The review will usually end with a recommendation – either positive or negative.

✦ EXERCISES

1. Write a review of a film that you have seen recently, either in the cinema or in class.
2. Write a short report on a film actor of your choice. In your report you should give a brief outline of his career, and say what you particularly like about his work.
3. Find out why the Academy Awards have become known as 'The Oscars'.

■ *Increase Your Word Power!*

Can you spell and use the following words correctly?
Naturally, necessary, neglect, neighbour, nervous, neutral, nonsense, notify.

■ Key Assignments

I have studied the coverage of a particular event or news story in two newspapers and I have written a short report on the differences and similarities between them.

☐ Date _____

OR

I have written an account of an event or news item to be included in a newspaper and I have given my article an appropriate headline.

☐ Date _____

I have visited my local radio station or newspaper office, or I have participated in a visitor exercise with a representative from either of these and I have presented a report on this experience.

☐ Date _____

OR

I have participated in a survey on radio listening or TV viewing and I have presented my findings.

☐ Date _____

I have completed a review of a TV programme, film or documentary.

☐ Date _____

OR

I have planned a TV programme schedule for an evening, taking account of time slots, audience and a range of programme types. I have presented a report explaining my choices.

☐ Date _____

I have completed a short study of aspects of film and I have presented my report.

☐ Date _____

(I have used IT in the presentation of at least one of the above).

Past Examination Questions

1. (a) Name your favourite radio station and say why it appeals to you. (5 marks)
   (b) Describe how news is covered on that particular station. (10 marks)
   (c) Your Leaving Certificate Applied class has been asked to present a short programme on your local radio station. Outline the contents you would use and explain your choice of material. (15 marks)
2. (a) What are the main differences between tabloid newspapers and broadsheet newspapers? You may refer to specific newspapers in your answer. (10 marks)
   (b) You have been appointed editor of a teenage entertainment page in your local newspaper.
   (i) Make a list of five items you would include on the page. (5 marks)
   (ii) Write a brief article on one of these items for inclusion on the page. (15 marks)
3. (a) Name and describe your favourite television advertisement. (5 marks)
   (b) Describe two techniques used in this advertisement which made it effective. (5 marks)
   (c) Would this advertisement influence you in any way? Explain your answer. (5 marks)
   (d) State the differences between television advertising and newspaper/magazine advertising. (15 marks)
4. (a) You have an opportunity to interview a film actor or film producer of your choice. List five questions you would ask and give reasons for your choice. (15 marks)

   Name of film actor or film producer _____

   (b) Outline how this person's work has impressed you. You should refer to specific examples of his/her performance or productions. (15 marks)
5. Examine this CERT advertisement for training in the Tourism Industry and then answer the questions which follow.
   (a) Name three of the courses available. (3 marks)
   (b) What are the requirements for the Hotel Receptionist course? (3 marks)
   (c) Where can you get information on the courses available? (4 marks)
   (d) What is the target audience for this advertisement? Give a reason for your answer. (5 marks)
   (e) What effect does the following caption have? 'The Tourism Industry is growing fast – be part of it!' (7 marks)
   (f) Identify and describe two effective advertising techniques used in this advertisement. Do not include the caption in your answer. (8 marks)

6. Read the review of Steven Spielberg's film *Saving Private Ryan* printed below and then answer the questions that follow it.

HOPE AND GORY

Could Saving Private Ryan *be the movie that saves Steven Spielberg and reinvents the WW2 genre? An obsessed Tom Hanks and a troop of weeping veterans think it can and will.*

After a summer of less-than-inspiring blockbusters you'd imagine the latest human conflict epic from Steven Spielberg is unlikely to break the run of deserving flops. But he's come up with probably the most important film of the year in *Saving Private Ryan*, a near three-hour-long WW2 assault on the senses that's already being hailed as the greatest war movie ever made.

It's a simple story: a mother is to be told of the death of three of her four sons in battle. So army officials send a team of soldiers led by Tom Hanks behind enemy lines to bring home the surviving brother, one Private James Ryan (Matt Damon).

The eight-man squad comprises the usual war movie staples. There's the boorish, tobacco-chewing Sergeant (Tom Hanks), the sharp-shooting good ol' boy (Barry Pepper) and the bookish wimp (Jeremy Davis). *Brothers McMullen* writer/director Ed Burns also stars alongside Adam Goldberg and Giovanni Ribisi, and the whole cast pump life into characters that rise above the stereotypes.

But it's the opening scenes that will remain imprinted on the mind, long after the film's end – 25 minutes of the most brutal conflict ever committed to film. Recreating the Normandy beach landings, it's shot from the soldiers' point of view. Non-stop machine-gun fire, the occasional silence implying loss of hearing following a nearby shell explosion, and relentless, intense bloodshed that turns the sea red, all add up to a representation of the horrific realities of war that most movies avoid. 'Every day on the beach with *Private Ryan*,' explains Spielberg, 'I had to pinch myself to say, "Make it the way it was, not the way we've been making movies about it."'

Spielberg consulted historians and made the actors endure a real training camp with ex-Marines for authenticity. This resulted in all except Tom Hanks threatening to walk. Hank admits to taking on the leadership aspect of his character, telling his fellow actors, 'Listen, you jerks, this is the only chance we're going to have to prepare for what we have to do.' The rest of the cast agree, mostly because, as Ed Burns says, 'Tom was like a man possessed.'

Hanks' fervour came from the belief that the actors had to respect the real pain and suffering of those who died in, and those who survived, the war. Amongst those were Spielberg's father. His stories were different to what Spielberg had previously seen on screen and it was only recently he realized that, 'My dad had been telling the truth all along and Hollywood had been fibbing.' Anxious to maintain the integrity of his film, Spielberg screened it to many WW2 veterans, moving several to tears.

Saving Private Ryan couldn't have come at a better time for Spielberg. The critical acclaim after *Schindler's List* was shortlived, and *Amistad*, though a return to form, was marred by a lawsuit.

But it appears a career – and a genre – is about to be resurrected. Inevitably, the normal schmaltzy Spielberg touches are present, but are actually welcome amongst the sheer horror of the violence. And at a time when the best Hollywood has to offer is a giant lizard or an even bigger asteroid, here's an extremely powerful and moving tale which places the extreme brutality of war in a believable context of courage and human frailty. Those Oscar nominations forms are being written as we speak.
LUCY BARRICK

(a) How long is the film? (3 marks)

(b) Why, according to the review, will the opening scenes of the film remain 'imprinted on the mind'? (6 marks)

(c) How did Spielberg ensure that the acting in the film was as realistic as possible? (7 marks)

(d) Why was the film so important to Spielberg (i) in his personal life and (ii) in his career? (7 marks)

(e) From your reading of this review say why you would or would not like to see this film. (7 marks)

7. Examine the radio schedules for Radio 1 and 2FM and then answer the following questions.

RADIO 1

6.00am The Weekend on One
with Padraig O'Rourke

6.00   News

6.02   Sea Area Forecast

7.00   News

7.55   Weather Forecast

8.00   News followed by **It Says In The Papers** with Valerie Cox

8.10   Mo Cheol Thú
le Ciarán Mac Mathúna

8.55   Weather Forecast

9.00   News
Followed by **It Says In The Papers** with Valerie Cox

9.10   Sunday Miscellany
Producer: Martha McCarron
FM1 only:
See Medium Wave box below

10.00 News

10.02 The V.I.P. Suite
Gloria Hunniford invites her guest to spend an hour in the V.I.P Suite
This week: Alexander Walker, Film Critic of the London Evening Standard. Producer: Aonghus McAnally

11.00 News

11.02 O' Brien on Song
Jack O'Brien selects some of his favourite recordings.

11.30 News

11.31 The Sunday Show
Presented by Andy O'Mahony

12.00 News
Producer Michael Kealy

12.53 Weather & Sea Area Forecast

1.00   This week
Presented by Gerald Barry with David McCullagh and Kevin Rafter Editor: Gerald Barry

2.00   Mooney Goes Wild on One
Presented and produced by Derek Mooney

2.30   Weekend Sport
Presented by Con Murphy Gaelic Games: Munster and Ulster Football Championships Athletics: Cork City Games
Racing: Gowran Park

3.00   News

MEDIUM WAVE

10.00 Mass
from St. Patrick's Church, Fermoy, Co. Cork.
Celebrant: Fr Gerard Coleman

10.45 Holy Communion Service
from St. Swithin's Parish Church, Magherafelt, Co. Derry Conducted by the Rev Terry Scott and the Rev John Anderson
Organist: Lynn Fullerton

page ten of twenty five

4.00   News

5.00   News

5.55   Nuacht

6.00   The Angelus

6.01   News

6.06   Oireachtas Report

6.30   News

6.34   Weather and Sea Area Forecast

6.37   Weekend Sport
With Con Murphy

7.00   News

7.02   Theatre Nights
Live from the Great Southern Hotel, Killarney. Featuring the finalists at the AIMS Awards
Presented and produced by Kevin Hough
email-houghk@rte.ie

7.45   Scéalta San Aer
Anocht: Micheál O Laoghaire
Léiritheoir: Cathal Póirtéir

8.00   News

8.02   Sounds Classical
Presented and produced by Fionn O'Leary

9.00   Journey's End
A tribute to Nelson Mandela
Presented by Emer Woodful
Repeat

9.30   From the Mist
A series about the landscape of Ireland
3: Lasair's Well
Presented and produced by Pat Feeley

10.00 News

10.02 The Godline
Teri Garvey and guests discuss questions about religious matters
Producer: Michael Campion
Phone No 1850 715 900
NI/UK 0345 85 7777

11.00 News

11.02 GAA Sports Results

11.10 Balfe's Sunday Best
Superior Sounds for Sunday evening with Brendan Balfe

11.55 Weather

12.00 News

12.04 Sports News

12.05 Late Date
Presented by Lilian Smith

1.00   Late News Summary

2.00   News

2.02   The Irish Collection
From the RTE Studios in Cork
Presented by Daragh Murphy
2.00   News and Sport this Week/News Sports Bulletins)

3.00   News

3.02   The V.I.P. Suite

4.00   News

4.02   From The Mist

4.30   Cogar

5.00   News

5.02   Sunday Miscellany

2FM

SUNDAY

2.00 Gerry Wilson
Producer: Maggie Stapleton

7.00 Ruth Scott
Producer: Maggie Stapleton

10.00 Moloney at the Weekend
Producer: Pat Dunne

12.00 Ireland's Biggest Jukebox
with Simon Young

3.00 Shane O'Donoghue
Producer: Maggie Stapleton

6.00 Classic Rock
With John Kenny
Producer: Ian Wilson

8.00 Fanning on Sunday
Producer: Ian Wilson

11.00 The Album Show
with John Clarke
Producer: John Clarke

2FM Live -Red Hot Chilli Peppers, Sunday, 10pm

(a) List three different types of programme broadcast on Radio One. (6 marks)

(b) What type of programme does 2FM mainly broadcast? Refer to the schedule in support of your answer. (4 marks)

(c) Comment on the difference between the Radio One schedule and the 2FM schedule under the following headings: (12 marks)

    (i) Variety of programming

    (ii) News coverage

    (iii) Target audience

    (iv) Imagine you are an announcer on either Radio One or 2FM. Write out the introduction you would make to any one of the programmes on the schedules. (8 marks)

8. The editor of the school magazine has asked you to write a detailed review of a film you have studied. Your review should include the following: film's title, a brief comment on what the film is about, comments on setting and actors' performances, use of cinematic effects, audience suitability, your judgement of the film. (30 marks)

9. The following article has been adapted from a piece that appeared in the *Travel* supplement of the *Sunday Times* on 7 November 1999. Read carefully and then answer the questions that follow.

WANTED

Potent, poised, the deadly jungle dweller – everyone wants a piece of the tiger. Sandy Gall travels to India and Nepal to earn his stripes.

It was a cool autumn morning in Ranthambhor National Park in Rajasthan, northern India. Dappled sunlight lay across the forest fringe. 'There,' the guide said, and we all stared across the lake. On the far side, filling the lenses of my binoculars, a full-grown tigress crouched at the water's edge, drinking, watching. The binoculars brought us to within a few feet of one another and, as I looked straight into her huge, yellow-green eyes, *I felt a shock of pure fear.*

After several seconds, the tigress rose and stalked through the trees along the far side of the lake – unhurriedly. But tigers have no fear; only when they are killing, or attacked, do they move with the speed of light.

We reversed the little 4WD, called a Gypsy, and drove along the near side of the lake to a point on the road that the tigress was likely to pass. She came towards us at the same easy, measured pace, the black stripes against the golden-orange fur making her surprisingly well camouflaged, almost invisible against the sere blanket of dead grass. As she passed us, regally indifferent to the vehicles and their camera-wielding occupants, she paused midstride, raised her head and sniffed the air for a second or two, and then dropped back into the silent, padding stride.

We sat transfixed by her beauty and latent power, conscious that we were watching the largest and most majestic of all the great cats . . .

According to Valimik Thapar, India's Mr Tiger, the country is now losing a tiger a day. Bushy-bearded, articulate and impassioned, Valimik overflows with statistics. 'In round figures,' he says, 'India is losing 350 tigers a year – that's one a day – to poaching, poisoning and natural causes. The annual growth of the tiger population is about 150, so there is a net loss each year of about 200. Remember, if you kill a tigress with three cubs, four tigers will die.'

   (a) Describe the weather conditions when the author first saw the tigress. (4 marks)
   (b) What caused the author to feel 'a shock of pure fear'? (4 marks)
   (c) Do you think the style of writing conveys the beauty of the tigress? Give reasons for your answer. (8 marks)
   (d) Describe the impact of:
      (i) The photograph of the tigress. (3 marks)
      (ii) The word WANTED above the photograph. (3 marks)
   (e) Do you think the article makes a powerful plea to save tigers in the wild? Give reasons for your answer. (8 marks)
10. Examine the extract from *Xtra*, the entertainment magazine from Xtra-Vision video rental shops, and then answer the questions that follow.
   (a) Would you be influenced by the picture on a cover of a video when choosing a film to rent? Give a reason for your answer. (5 marks)
   (b) What do you think is meant by the term 'thriller' in many of the descriptions of the films in this extract? (5 marks)
   (c) Choose one film from the list in the extract that you would like to see and explain how the review of this film has influenced your choice. (10 marks)
   (d) Write a brief review of any film that you have studied or seen recently, to be included in *Xtra's* next publication. You should not review a film already listed in the accompanying extract. (10 marks)

TOP 10 MOVIES TO RENT

1 THE GREEN MILE
IRL 18, NI 18, Drama, 180 mins

Tom Hanks stars as a humane prison guard whose territory covers Death Row. Based on a novel by Stephen King it is a powerful and moving tale that features compelling performances from a strong ensemble cast.

2 THE BONE COLLECTOR
IRL 15, NI 15, Thriller, 133 mins

Starring Oscar winners Denzel Washington and Angelina Jolie, The Bone Collector is an effective moody murder mystery that will pull you into its game of thrills and have you suitably perched on the edge of your seat.

3 THE TALENTED MR. RIPLEY
IRL 15, NI 15, Thriller, 134 mins

Leading man Matt Damon impersonates other people to such an extent that he can inhabit their everyday lives. The fun really begins when the person in question is millionaire playboy Jude Law who lives the high life in Italy with glamorous girlfriend Gwyneth Paltrow.

4 THE BEACH
IRL 15, NI 15, Dramatic Thriller, 115 mins

Leonardo DiCaprio stars in this exciting dramatic thriller that chronicles the travels of a hedonistic backpacker drifting through Thailand. Adapted from the best-seller by Alex Garland and from the director of Trainspotting this is a definite tale for Leo fans and a cautionary tale for those who feel that paradise is easily achieved.

5 AMERICAN BEAUTY
IRL 18, NI 18, Thriller, 121 mins

American Beauty is one of the most celebrated and successful films of recent years winning five Oscars at this years ceremony. Starring Kevin Spacey and Annette Bening it delivers a unique and memorable experience which will linger.

6 THE END OF THE AFFAIR
IRL 18, NI 18, Drama, 97 mins

Irish director Neil Jordan has adapted the semi-autobiographical novel by Graham Greene to create a movie that is perfect for those who want to see a good old-fashioned melodrama with a sting.

7 SLEEPY HOLLOW
IRL 18, NI 15, Gothic Thriller, 106 mins

Based on the chilling Washington Irving tale this is a classic Tim Burton fare. Johnny Depp plays a New York detective called to the village of Sleepy Hollow to investigate a series of murders which might be linked to the Headless Horseman.

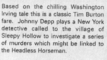

8 ANGELA'S ASHES
IRL 15, NI 15, Drama, 105 mins

Based on the novel by Frank McCourt the movie brings the oft humorous, oft depressing tale to life as it chronicles the struggle of a family in Limerick in the 1940's. Directed by Alan Parker it's a powerful and emotional piece of work that will appeal to a wide spectrum of audience.

9 STIGMATA
IRL 15, NI 18, Thriller, 98 mins

Starring Gabriel Byrne and Patricia Arquette, Stigmata combines the elements of a great thriller and a classic supernatural horror tale. This is a well made movie that will appeal greatly to fans of the genre. Just don't watch it on your own.

10 SUMMER OF SAM
IRL 18, NI 18, Thriller, 142 mins

Summer of Sam traces the events of the summer of 1977 where tempers are short and apprehension is high as New York lives in the shadow of a menacing psychopathic killer called 'Son of Sam'. A gripping film this will make an impression on all movie watchers.

⌨ closed caption symbol

All film certificates in the top ten chart are correct at time of going to press and are subject to change.

11. The following article is adapted from a piece by Gavin McEldowney that appeared in the *Education and Living* supplement of the *Irish Times*. Read it carefully and then answer the questions that follow.

THE RAIL THING
Gavin McEldowney has some good advice for inter-railers.

Each year, thousands of students pick up their phrase books and rucksacks and travel around Europe on trains. For €330, a global inter-rail pass can be purchased from USIT in Dublin which allows free and unlimited travel, for one month, on most European railway systems.

Before setting out there are some important things to do. First, get a sturdy rucksack with well-padded shoulder straps. These can be bought in any camping shop. Second, make sure to get your insurance documents. These can be obtained when purchasing your ticket, and your E111, which you can get from any of the local health boards. The Thomas Cook timetable book, which has all the European train times and which can also be obtained at the USIT office, is a must. It is also advisable to make a list of those you know who are staying or living in Europe – in desperation, remember they can come in handy for free food and accommodation.

When packing your rucksack it is very important to keep in mind the countries which you intend to visit. For example, while it could be freezing in Amsterdam, it might be scorching in Barcelona. It is also a good idea to pack plenty of deodorants, socks and underwear as hours of walking in hot countries will inevitably lead to horrid stenches which, while very useful in clearing out train carriages and guarding against thieves, will cause problems when conversing with the opposite sex.

The most important thing, however, is to ensure that you have plenty of money. Travelling around Europe is extremely expensive, with accommodation, food and sightseeing tours all being costly. Never bring cash, as you can never tell when Mr Robber is lurking around the corner. It is a good idea to get a money belt, which you wear at all times and where you can keep your money, passport and other valuables.

Although people will have different preferences as to where they want to visit, there are some places not to be missed.

Prague, with its picturesque layout of fairytale buildings and cobblestone streets, is one such place. The cost of living is also extremely low with accommodation for as little as €6 a night and Big Mac meals for around €2.50. It is also a very lively place at night with numerous discos and nightbars.

Munich is another place deserving of a visit. While a little expensive, it is very beautiful and has lots to offer in the way of museums and art galleries. I would recommend a visit to the BMW factory. There is also a large Irish community in Munich and a wide variety of Irish pubs.

The average price for a night's accommodation in a German hostel is around €13 with breakfast included. It is worth noting that breakfast will not be included in every European hostel. It is also cheaper to stay in the dormitories but, be wary, as you may find yourself in the same room as some very rowdy and drunken louts and find it difficult to get a good night's sleep.

One final tip. It is important to find out if you are required to pay a reservation supplement before you board a train, as failure to do so may result in you being thrown off in the middle of nowhere. Inter-railing is a great experience and a cheap way to see Europe.

Happy backpacking!!!

(a) What are you entitled to when you pay €330 for a global inter-rail pass? (3 marks)
(b) Name three important things you should do before setting out. (10 marks)
(c) Name two cities recommended by Gavin McEldowney for a visit. Why does he recommend these cities? (10 marks)
(d) Would this article encourage you to go inter-railing? Give a reason for your answer. (5 marks)

229

Unit 1

The Poetry of Popular Song

Find a CD with the song 'I Am A Rock', written by Paul Simon and sung by Paul Simon and Art Garfunkel. Listen carefully to the lyrics (words) of the song.

I Am a Rock

A winter's day in a deep and dark December I am alone,
Gazing from my window
To the streets below
On a freshly fallen silent shroud of snow.
I am a rock;
I am an island.

I built walls
A fortress deep and mighty
That none may penetrate.
I have no need of friendship,
Friendship causes pain.
It's laughter and it's loving I disdain.
I am a rock;
I am an island.

Don't talk of love;
I've heard the word before,
It's sleeping in my memory;
I won't disturb the slumber
Of feelings that have died.
If I never loved, I never would have cried,
I am a rock,
I am an island.

I have my books,
And my poetry to protect me;
I am shielded in my armour;
Hiding in my room,
Safe within my womb
I touch no one,
No one touches me.
I am a rock,
I am an island.
And a rock can feel no pain…
And an island never cries…

FOR DISCUSSION

1. What kind of *mood* do you think the writer was in when he wrote this song? What was he *feeling*? We get an idea of his mood in the very first line.
2. What kind of experience do you think the writer has had?
3. What is the *message* or *theme* of the song? What is the writer telling us?
4. There are several *comparisons* in the song. For example, the poet compares himself to a rock. A rock is something strong and hard that can withstand a lot of punishment before it collapses; the poet is telling us that he can be just as strong and tough as a rock. He does not say that he is *like* a rock, he says he *is* a rock. This kind of comparison is called a *metaphor*. Can you pick out other comparisons which the poet uses? Do you think they are effective? Why/Why not?
5. Why do you think the writer repeats the last two lines of each verse?
6. The writer uses *images* to describe things and to help us to see these things in our mind. For example, in verse two he says

'I built walls,
A fortress deep and mighty
That none may penetrate.'

In these lines he is telling us that he does not want anyone getting close to him again; he has done everything he can to cut himself off from other people. He uses the image or picture of a fortress with strong walls that cannot be broken down; he is trying to get across to us that he wants to be on his own, away from people who might hurt him.

Find other images used by the poet. Pick one that you like and say why you like it.

7. Look again at lines one and five in the first verse. Does anything strike you about them? Do you think they are particularly musical? Say the lines aloud and listen to the sounds.
8. Can you pick out any other 'sound effects' in the poem?
9. How did you *feel* when you heard the song? Do you agree with the poet's view of life? Why/Why not?

Here are the lyrics to a second Paul Simon song, 'Bridge Over Troubled Water'.

Bridge Over Troubled Water

When you're weary, feeling small,
When tears are in your eyes, I'll dry them all.
I'm on your side, oh, when times get rough,
And friends just can't be found,
Like a bridge over troubled water,
I will lay me down,
Like a bridge over troubled water,
I will lay me down.

When you're down and out, when you're on the street,
When evening falls so hard, I will comfort you.
I'll take your part, oh, when darkness comes,
And pain is all around,
Like a bridge over troubled water,
I will lay me down,
Like a bridge over troubled water,
I will lay me down.

Sail on silver girl, sail on by,
Your time has come to shine, all your dreams are on their way.
See how they shine, oh, if you need a friend,
I'm sailing right behind,
Like a bridge over troubled water,
I will ease your mind,
Like a bridge over troubled water,
I will ease your mind.

 # FOR DISCUSSION

1. How does this song make you feel? Can you explain why you respond to the song in this way?
2. What is this song about? What is the theme of the song?

3. Who is the poet talking to in the song? How do you know?
4. Choose some images or pictures that you like and explain why you like them.
5. This song is sometimes sung at Leaving Certificate graduation evenings. Choose some lines that make the song particularly suitable for this type of occasion.
6. In this song Paul Simon compares himself to a 'bridge over troubled water'. He does not say he *is* a bridge – he says he is *like* a bridge. This kind of comparison is called a *simile*.
7. What do you think he means by the words 'troubled water'?

OVER TO YOU!

1 We all have our favourite singers and songwriters. Bring in some of your own favourites to be listened to in class. Explain to the class why particular songs are important to you. (It is important that you bring in a copy of the lyrics so that they can be photocopied and given out.)
2. Write your own lyrics. Think about some event that affected you deeply – perhaps something very personal to you or something that happened on a global level. Try and remember how you felt at the time and try and put those feelings into words.

■ *Increase Your Word Power!*

Can you spell and use the following words correctly?
Objection, obligatory, observe, obstruct, occupation, occasion, occupy, official, operative, operate, option, ordinary, otherwise.

 # Unit 2

Poetry

Most People Ignore Most Poetry

Most people ignore most poetry
  Because
Most poetry ignores most people

Adrian Mitchell

This short verse captures quite well how many of us feel about poetry – we feel it has no relevance for us. However, if we think about it, poetry does play a part in our lives:

Poetry becomes very popular around St. Valentine's Day, when people express their feelings for each other through verse.

At funerals, a family member or close friend might read a poem expressing their feelings at the loss of someone they love.

In both of these situations powerful *emotions* or *feelings* are at work, feelings of love and feelings of loss. The person writing the poem is expressing an emotion or feeling, and he is trying to communicate this emotion to us. A poem may make us laugh or cry; it might bring out feelings of sadness or pity or happiness.

■ *Poems Are Used to Communicate Feelings*

Identify other situations or places where poetry is used in everyday life, and describe the feeling that is being communicated in the poetry.

POETRY

SITUATION	FEELING
1. Songs sung by football fans	_____
_____	_____
2. _____	_____
_____	_____
3. _____	_____
_____	_____
4. _____	_____
_____	_____
5. _____	_____
_____	_____

A poem is different from a story because it presents things to us in a *concentrated* way; the poet has to think very carefully about each word that he uses and he leaves out anything that is not absolutely necessary.

Some of the earliest poems were riddles; the most famous riddle is probably the riddle of the Sphinx:
'What walks on four legs in the morning,
On two legs at noon,
And on three legs in the evening?'

Like modern poetry this riddle uses *symbols* to get a message across; morning stands for the beginning of life or childhood, evening stands for old age. Have you worked out the answer to the riddle? When you are reading poetry try and figure out what symbols the poet is using.

A poem also differs from a story because poetry is musical – a poet will be very careful to choose words that sound well.

Read the following poem 'Mother to Son' out loud. It is important that it is read aloud so that you can hear the sounds made by the words.

Mother To Son

Well, son, I'll tell you:
Life for me ain't been no crystal stair.
It's had tacks in it.
And splinters.
And boards torn up,
And places with no carpet on the floor –
Bare.
But all the time
I'se been a-climbing' on.
And reachin' landin's
And turning corners,
And sometimes goin' in the dark
Where ther ain't been no light.
So boy, don't you turn back.
Don't you set down on the steps
'Cause you finds it's kinder hard.
Don't you fall now –
Sor I'se still goin', honey.
I'se still climbin'.
And life for me ain't been no crystal stair.

Langston Hughes

 FOR DISCUSSION

1. We know from the title of the poem that a mother is speaking to her son. What do we know about the mother from the poem?
2. What message is the mother giving to her son?
   The poet uses symbols in the poem. Identify the symbols and say what they stand for?
3. Did you find the poem musical when you read it aloud? What was musical about it?

■ *Limericks*

A limerick is a comic or nonsense poem.

There was an old person from Crewe
Who found a dead mouse in his stew
Said the waiter 'Don't shout
And wave it about,
Or the rest will be wanting one too.'

Collect some examples of limericks. A limerick has a particular pattern of repeating rhyme sounds and rhythms. When you have listened to a few limericks see if you can identify the pattern; tap out the rhythm and find the rhyming pattern.

Now, compose your own limerick! They usually start 'There was a ...'

When you are reading a poem in class you need to be able to do the following:

1. Say what the poem is about.
2. Describe the mood or atmosphere of the poem. Describe how you felt when you read it.
3. Explain any symbols used in the poem.
4. Pick out images that you particularly like and say why you like them.
5. Find examples of similes or metaphors.
6. Describe the musical qualities of the poem.

■ *Increase Your Word Power!*

Can you spell and use the following words correctly?

Package, pallet, panel, parallel, participate, pattern, passport, patrol, pension, percentage, personally, phrase, physical, policy, possess, possible, present, promising.

Unit 3

Short Story

You are already familiar with the terms we use when talking about a short story, novel, drama or film. Look at these terms again and write a short definition of each one:
Setting
Theme
Character
Narrator
Plot
Conflict
Climax
Flashback

■ What Makes a Good Story?

The most important parts of a story are the characters, the setting and the plot; you must have interesting people in interesting situations.

■ *Characters*

A short story will usually deal with only one character. The writer has to help us to form a picture of the person in our minds; the character has to 'come alive' on the page. The writer will want us to feel a certain way about the character – we must care about what happens to him. When we are reading a story (or watching a film) how do we make up our minds about a character? How do we decide what kind of person he is? How do we decide whether or not we like him?

1. *We learn about him from what he says.*

2. _____

_____

3. _____

_____

4. _____

_____

5. _____

_____

When describing characters we are describing *characteristics*. Add to this list of characteristics:

1. *gentle*

2. *clever*

3. *loyal*

4. *snobbish*

5. _____

6. _____

7. _____

8. _____

9. _____

10. _____

Some of these characteristics are positive and some are negative.

✴ EXERCISES

1. Working in pairs, write a short character sketch of your partner. Describe at least three characteristics. For each characteristic that you give, describe a time when your partner acted in this way.

2. Think of your favourite soap or drama. Choose a character who displays positive characteristics:

   Name of soap: _____

   Character: _____

   Characteristics: _____

   How you feel towards him/her: _____

   _____

   _____

   _____

3. Now pick a character with negative characteristics:

   Name of soap: _____

   Character: _____

   Characteristics: _____

   How you feel towards him/her: _____

   _____

   _____

   _____

■ *Plot*

When we talk about the plot we are talking about the storyline and how all the different events are connected.

In a short story the plot has to be kept fairly simple, and usually deals with just one event. We have already seen that a good story usually describes some sort of conflict. For example, conflict is present when two characters are looking for different things. From your reading of short stories or novels, give some examples of conflict.

1. _____

_____

2. _____

_____

3. _____

_____

4. _____

_____

5. _____

_____

As the story is told, the writer will try to build up the suspense and excitement until the high point of the story is reached and the conflict is resolved or sorted out.

Some short stories have unexpected or surprise endings – a 'twist in the tail'.

■ *Increase Your Word Power!*

Can you spell and use the following words correctly?
Qualify, qualification, quality, radiator, random, ratify, recession, regarding, register, relevant, release.

Unit 4

Novel

Below is an extract from the novel *Old Money, New Money* written by Peter Sheridan.
Redser and Pancho are two teenagers from Dublin's North Wall. Redser is top of the class, especially good at maths. Pancho's knack is for finding money, not adding or subtracting it. Redser's parents run the local credit union. Pancho's dad runs riot in the city pubs on pay day. The boys' worlds could not be further apart. Yet the pair are the best of friends.

Old Money, New Money

Redser de Barra and Pancho Nolan became friends on their first day in the big school. They had known each other in the little school but they sat in different rows. It was only when they went over to the Christian Brothers that things happened. They were put standing in a line against the wall. Their new teacher, Brother Armstrong, looked like a cheetah prowling before them. He had green, flashing eyes. He looked like a cat about to pounce on its prey. He called out a name and the boy put his hand up like a frightened mouse. He pointed to a desk and the mouse sat down. He consulted the roll book and picked out another name. That was how Redser and Pancho ended up sitting together like paired mice.

At eleven o'clock, Brother Armstrong let his charges out into the playground. 'I'm glad I'm sitting beside you, Redser,' Pancho said, 'you've got brains.' Redser was chuffed at the compliment. 'You've got brains, too, Pancho,' he told him. Pancho shook his head: 'I'm a dunce, Redser, you're sitting beside a dunce.'

Redser thought Pancho was joking. It was their first day in the big school and he was nervous. All the boys were nervous. Five more years ahead of them. Thousands of days with Brother Armstrong. It was too long to think about.

'My Da was no good at school and neither am I,' Pancho confided, 'it runs in the family.' Redser had never met anyone like Pancho. All the other boys lied about how good they were at things. Dominic Foley claimed he was a genius at maths. Tom Bradley said he could run a mile in under three minutes. Myles Plummer was going to be the President of America when he got out of school. Pancho Nolan, on the other hand, admitted to being a dunce. From that day, he became Redser's best friend. They adopted each other like long-lost twins. They had very little in common for best friends. In fact, according to most things, they should have been enemies.

For a start, they were from opposite sides of the parish. Redser lived in a house and Pancho lived in the flats. The two sides were like water and oil. They didn't mix. The men drank in different pubs and the women bought their messages in different shops. In the chapel, they knelt on opposite sides even though they prayed to the one God. There was a line dividing the parish in two. It was invisible but more real than if it had been painted by the Corporation.

Redser and Pancho didn't recognise the invisible line. Pancho played in Redser's house and Redser played in Pancho's flat. Redser loved the view of Dublin from the balcony of the flats. More than that, he loved getting up on the roof and inspecting the pigeon lofts. Nobody from the houses raced pigeons. Budgies in cages were all you'd see in the houses. The roofs of the flats were dotted with lofts. Pigeons flew down to the river and picked up grain in their beaks. After they'd stuffed themselves, they flew back in formation to their lofts. It was a great thrill to watch them.

Pancho preferred Redser's house. He didn't care that much for pigeons. He loved the half-sized snooker table in Redser's front room. He had a great eye for potting balls. He knew how to play a screw shot and he could stun the ball, too. No one had taught him to do it, it came naturally to him. He glided around the table and stroked the balls into the pockets. It was like poetry. Everyone loved to watch him but hated playing him. He was so good he didn't need to boast about it. 'It doesn't take brains to pot a few balls,' he'd say, 'it only takes a good eye'.

The only thing Pancho admitted to being good at was finding money. He was a genius at it. Walking along the street with him, he'd suddenly jump down. He'd come up with anything from a penny to fifty pence. It was like a sixth sense. It seemed he could smell money. On the footpath, in gardens, down shores, there was nowhere safe for money to hide when Pancho was around. If he wasn't finding it, he was making it. Collecting empty jam jars, Guinness bottles, Harp bottles, cider bottles, he'd get a penny on each of them at the off-licence. His best moneymaking scheme was carrying cases.

One day he showed Redser the ropes. It was during the summer holidays. They hadn't the price of an icepop between them. The sun was melting the tar on the streets. How they'd love to be going to Tara Street baths. Or getting a bus out to Dollymount Strand for the day. At Amiens Street railway station, Pancho placed Redser at one side of the steps. He stood at the opposite side. Together they waited for passengers. Passengers with cases. 'Remember, Redser, pick up a case and start to walk,' Pancho advised him, 'don't wait for them to say no'.

A woman with four cases struggled into view. She was pumping sweat. No wonder, considering the Aran sweater she was wearing. She had two small cases tucked under her arms and two larger ones in her hands. Pancho pounced straight away. Redser followed his example. 'Can I carry your case, Miss?' Pancho said as he took one from her. In seconds, the two boys were heading up Talbot Street with the woman chasing behind. 'I'm going to the Gresham Hotel,' she shouted after them. 'Just follow us so,' Pancho replied. 'Yeah, just follow us,' Redser echoed the command.

At the Gresham Hotel, the woman gave them a ten-shilling note. Pancho, for once, was speechless. Redser couldn't believe his eyes. A beautiful, crisp ten-shilling note. Bright orange, like the setting sun. They could do whatever they wanted now. The baths, the beach, the pictures – anything was possible. They went down to Mattie's, their favourite sweet shop, and stared in the window. The coconut bars looked appealing. So did the gobstoppers. In the end, they couldn't resist the lucky lumps. The chance of finding a thrupenny bit was too hard to resist.

They came outside to divide them up. 'One for you and one for me,' Pancho started off. Redser put a hand out and stopped him. 'It's twenty each,' Redser said, 'twenty for you and twenty for me.' Pancho looked at him and squinted. He was brutal at sums. Redser explained it to him but it was no good. Pancho put one in his mouth and started to suck. 'I'd love to have your brains, Redser,' he said. Redser knew it was useless to answer. Pancho had taught him more than any school could. Without Pancho there would be no lucky lumps to start with. There was no point in telling him. If he said anything, Pancho would just find a way of putting himself down. So he said nothing and divided them up. Redser put one in his mouth and started to suck. He looked across at Pancho and saw that he was biting into his. It was against the rules to bite lucky lumps. Pancho just couldn't wait to see what he'd find inside his. He had one in his mouth and nineteen more to go. He couldn't suck them all. It was torture. He had to find out as fast as he could what lay in store for him.

Pancho's luck didn't last. That night his father caught him in his bedroom sucking the lucky lumps. At first, he accused Pancho of stealing them. Pancho said that he found them on the street. When his father took off his docker's belt, he told him the truth. 'You made ten shillings carrying cases and you didn't bring it home here,' his father said in a rage. Pancho said he was sorry but it was too late. He got four lashes of the belt for being a selfish bastard. Four lashes for the lucky lumps that turned out to be unlucky after all.

 # FOR DISCUSSION

1. From whose *point of view* is the story written? How do you know?
2. We meet teenagers 'Redser' de Barra and 'Pancho' Nolan, who become best friends. Redser is surprised that they become good friends as he feels they have very little in common.

   Describe the *characters* of Redser and Pancho, highlighting the differences between them. What did Redser like about Pancho? How was Pancho different from the other boys in school?

Do you think it is possible to form a lasting friendship with someone who is quite different from you? Why/Why not?

3. Can you describe the *setting* for the novel? What clues does the writer give us about the setting? Remember that setting refers to *time* as well as *place*.

4. What does the writer mean when he says that there was an invisible line dividing the parish in two? What does this tell us about the social setting?

5. Towards the end of the extract we meet Pancho's father. What kind of person do you think he is?

6. Pancho seemed to have a knack for making money. Can you describe one example of his entrepreneurial skills?

7. 'Pancho had taught him (Redser) more than any school could.' What does the writer mean by this? Do you think that we put too much emphasis on school-based learning and not enough on the skills we pick up outside of school? Who do you think was the more intelligent of the two?

8. The boys were from different backgrounds and had different talents and abilities. Which one, do you think, will get on better in life? Why?

9. The writer has some lovely descriptions in this piece. For example, when he describes Pancho playing pool he says:

'He *glided* around the table and *stroked* the balls into the pockets.'

Why does he use the verbs 'glided' and 'stroked'? What do they suggest? Choose some descriptions or images in the extract that you liked and say why you liked them.

10. Do you like the way the writer is telling the story? What do you like about his *style* of writing? Having read the extract would you like to read the whole book?

11. What do you think is the *theme* of the novel?

■ *Reviewing a Novel*

When you are reviewing a novel you should concentrate on your own personal response to it.

Begin by giving the title of the novel and the name of the author.

Start your review by giving some idea of what the novel is about, where it is set and who the main characters are. Give enough of the storyline to make the reader interested but do not give away the ending. Go on to say what you liked or disliked about it.

• How did the novel make you feel when you read it? Why?
• Did you think the story was good? Why?
• Did the writer bring the settings and characters alive for you? How did he do this?
• Which characters did you like and why?
• Did you like the ending? Why/Why not?
• Can you pick out certain sections which you particularly liked? Can you describe them briefly and say why you liked them?

At the end of your review you might recommend the book. You might also say what age group you think it is aimed at.

■ *Adapting a Novel for Stage or Screen*

At the beginning of Module I you read an extract from *My Left Foot* by Christy Brown. This extract is quite dramatic, as it describes an event that was to change Christy's life. Read the extract again; this time try and imagine this episode being staged in a theatre, with you as director. You might like to work in pairs for this exercise.

1. Describe how you would prepare the stage. You need to give detailed instructions about the background, doors, furniture, etc.
2. What props would you need?
3. What SFX would you use?
4. How many characters would be involved? Name them.
5. Where will they be positioned on the stage as the action starts?
6. Describe the costumes worn by the actors.
7. What instructions would you give about the lighting?
8. Write the dialogue for this scene. Include instructions regarding movement, body language, etc.
9. How would you build up the tension in the scene?

   If possible watch the film *My Left Foot* and examine how this scene was treated by the director. Look in particular at the following:
   • How did the actors play the roles? Are the characters how you imagined them to be?
   • Describe the atmosphere. How does the director create this atmosphere?
   • Is the setting how you imagined it? What is the same? What is different?
   • Is the event the same as it is described in the novel? What does the director change? Why do you think he made these changes?
   • Do you think Christy Brown would have approved of the way the scene was done? Why/why not?

■ *Increase Your Word Power!*

Can you spell and use the following words correctly?
Satisfaction, scheme, secondary, section, serious, separated, settlement, smooth, solemn, special, storage, submit, supervise, surround, tactic, tariff, through, trailer, transfer.

Unit 5

Drama

A play is meant to be seen on a stage rather than read. The atmosphere of the theatre, the costumes, lighting and scenery all help to bring the play to life.

The following extract is from *Forty-Four Sycamore*, a play by Bernard Farrell. In the extract we meet a young married couple, Vinny and Joan. They have just moved to a new, up-market housing estate. They have invited their neighbours, Derek and Hilary, for drinks. When the play opens, Vinny and Joan are waiting for their guests to arrive.

Forty-Four Sycamore

ACT 1

Vinny and Joan's lounge in their new detached house on Sycamore Estate. It is evening. Door from hall is S/L. Door to the kitchen is upstage right. A large window at the back with a venetian blind, slats open, showing a green glow outside. The furniture includes a console which houses an electronic unit with many lights and switches. Also a stereo unit and a drinks cabinet.

We notice the amount of electric gadgetry in the room: speakers, spots, security lights, telephones (olde-world, decorative models) and a security TV monitor in the back wall. (Ideally, this monitor should be concealed behind a wall-panel and only revealed as required.) All gadgetry neatly installed. Vinny is 23, dressed in a suit – the jacket now off. He seems assured. He is busily (and proudly) blending his elaborate lighting system, using a remote control that he points at the console. Lights change tastefully across the room. Then all the phones tinkle – indicating that someone is dialling out somewhere in the house. Vinny notices this with irritation.

Pause. Then Joan comes from the kitchen with bowls of crisps. She is 21, glamorous, in a rather short, attractive party dress. She will nervously nibble at the crisps as she adjusts the furniture for the umpteenth time.

Vinny: *(Easily)* Were you phoning your mother again?

Joan: When now?

Vinny: Thought I heard the phones tinkling.

Joan: Oh yes. She was engaged. Just wanted to tell her how all the preparations is going.

Vinny: *(Corrects)* Are going. *(Of the lights)* So what do you think?

Joan: Don't make it too comfortable – they're only coming for 'drinks'.

Vinny: I'll make the garden blue.

(The garden light changes to blue.)

Joan: *(Anxiously)* You did say drinks, didn't you?

Vinny: Did indeed.

Joan: They better not think they're coming for a sit-down meal...

Vinny: No – 'drinks' was the word. 'Come over for drinks – bring the wife and meet the wife'.

Joan: Well I only hope they don't come in carrying a bottle of Blue Nun and thinking I've prepared...

Vinny: *(Laughs)* Blue Nun? Derek and Hilary would be more likely to come in carrying a bottle of Dom Perignon or...

Joan: *(Angrily)* They shouldn't come in carrying a bottle of anything if they're only coming for drinks!

Vinny: *(Reacts)* I know that Joan! I'm only saying that if they weren't coming for drinks, that's what they would be carrying but, as they are, they won't. *(More calm)* You'll like Derek – a great guy, life and soul of the squash club. And a doctor. And big in the Residents' Association. Very influential is our Derek.

Joan: Well I don't know him.

Vinny: Joan, you have to show interest, get out of the house, contribute. Otherwise we'll be another six months in the estate before we know anyone.

Joan: I know Mr. Prentice.

Vinny: He's not in the estate.

Joan: He is.

Vinny: He's up in that big house, on his own and he's not liked! And you should have told me before inviting him. Supposing he doesn't get on with Derek and Hilary?

Joan: He gets on with me.

Vinny: But why?

Joan: My ma says it's because he's lonely...

Vinny: Which is a great reason for not inviting him. We're trying to make important contacts here, Joan, not set up a branch of the Samaritans. *(Looks)* And I'd go easy on the crisps.

(Joan angrily pushes the crisps away.)

Joan: What did you tell this Derek you were when he said he was a doctor?

Vinny: He didn't actually say he was a doctor. In the club, the word just gets around.

Joan: Well you should make sure that the word gets around that you're a security engineer. It sounds better. And my ma thinks so too.

Vinny: *(Ignores this. Hopefully)* Yes, tonight should be very impressive indeed.

Joan: As long as we don't have any of them big long silences.

Vinny: *(Annoyed)* Joan!

Joan: Well we could have!

Vinny: *(Corrects)* Those big long silences.

Joan: What?

Vinny: It's 'pardon' not 'what' – and you said 'any of them big long silences'.

Joan: Them or those, I won't be able to stick it if there is one.

Vinny: There won't be one if everyone contributes. Contributing is the art of conversation. And now you've eaten a whole bowl of crisps!

Joan: *(Picks it up)* All right!

Vinny: No sense in serving crisps and then having none for our guests.

Joan: I said 'all right'!

(Joan takes the empty bowl into the kitchen. Vinny adjusts his lights. Then the phones tinkle again. Vinny notices this with annoyance – but then, a sudden 'bleep' is heard and a red light flashes on the wall. He quickly pulls on his jacket as he goes to the intercom on the wall and presses the 'kitchen' button. A buzzer is heard.)

Vinny: Joan, are you receiving me?

Joan: *(V/O)* What?

Vinny: *(Corrects)* Pardon! I'm getting a red flash here.

Joan: *(V/O)* It's not them already, is it?

Vinny: I'll check the monitor...

Joan: *(V/O)* Okay – and Vinny...?

Vinny: And I'll activate the outside security lights...

Joan: *(V/O)* Okay – and Vinny...?

Vinny: ...and Joan, there's no time now for ringing your mother. Over and out.

(Vinny rushes to the red light/bleep and turns it off. Takes the remote control and presses a series of buttons. The blue light outside changes to a dazzling white. Presses another button – and the TV monitor is automatically revealed from behind the wall panel. In black and white, we see a car come up to the house. This as Joan anxiously comes in, carrying a bowl of crisps.)

Joan: Vinny? Listen Vinny...

Vinny: Hold on!

Joan: I meant to tell you...

Vinny: That's them – that's Derek's Volvo...

(He presses a button. A wall panel automatically conceals the monitor again.)

Joan: Vinny, listen...

Vinny: *(Checking)* Drinks over there ... glasses in place...

Joan: I meant to tell you before – but one of them ornamental elephants in the hall is broke and...

Vinny: *(Sudden anger)* Joan, for Christ's sake, one of those elephants is broken!

Joan: *(Sudden anger)* There's no need to correct me if you know what I mean!

(The door-bell chimes melodiously.)

Vinny: There they are – are you all set?

Joan: Did you hear what I said about...?

Vinny: Yes, I'll move the bloody thing – are you all set?

Joan: Why are you snapping at me?

Vinny: Right, if you're ready, I'll let them in. Soon as you hear the door close, turn the light back to blue and put the stereo on with...

Joan: You know I'm no good at them things...

(Vinny furiously presses the remote control.)

Vinny: For God's sake; this switch is 'off' – the light colours are numbered – could anything be easier...?

(The outside light goes from white to blue.)

            Now all you have to do is press these two together and the music comes on – and don't tell me you can't do that!

Joan: *(Suddenly in tears)* It's not my fault if I'm no good at this...

Vinny: *(Stops. Suddenly calm, patient. Holds Joan.)* It's all right, love – I know, I know – I'm sorry I snapped at you. Please don't get upset...

Joan: *(Sobbing)* This is going to be awful...

Vinny: No it's not...

(The door-bell rings again.)

Joan: *(Crying)* I hate living here and I'm going to let you down and ruin your business chances...

Vinny: No, you're not...

Joan: I can't do anything ... I can't contribute...

Vinny: You can – you can contribute with Mr Prentice...

Joan: *(Indicates)* But them!

Vinny: If you can't contribute with them, just be agreeable – until someone else contributes – being agreeable is the secret of conversation.

(The door-bell rings again.)

Joan: *(Calmer)* All right – I'll do my best.

Vinny: That's it. And anyway, I know how to handle these people – leave it all to me. They don't call me Mr. Fix-It for nothing.

(Anxious to go)

Joan: *(Gently)* We were right to move here, Vinny, weren't we?

Vinny: *(Patiently)* Course we were.

Joan: Like they were friendlier where we were – near my ma and all.

Vinny: But we've moved up in the world, Joan – and aren't we the envy of them all, living here in Sycamore Estate?

Joan: I suppose so.

Vinny: Course we are. Now, those two buttons when you hear the door closing...

(The door-bell rings vigorously. Vinny going)

Joan: All right – and you won't forget the elephant that's broke. *(Vinny stops but decides not to correct her.)*

Vinny: I won't.

(Vinny goes. Joan presses the two buttons on the remote control. Wrong combination. The outside window light goes rapidly from blue to red to white to blue. She panics. Voices are heard outside as she presses more buttons. The lights in the room dance. Panic as she presses more buttons. The lights dim low, the music comes on at high speed, an alarm bell begins to ring and a dazzling white light hits the door as Derek and Hilary enter, ahead of Vinny.

Both are 27, both very assured. Hilary in tasteful casuals. Derek looks very professional in a suit. Both now blinded by the spotlight.)
Hilary: *(Blinded)* Oh my God...
Vinny: Sorry – just a slight adjustment...
Joan: I couldn't manage...
Vinny: *(Angrily)* It's all right...
Derek: *(Still blinded. Merrily)* Anyone out there?
(Vinny presses the buttons. The room-lights become normal, the alarm stops, the music is soft and gentle.)
Hilary: Oh that's better...
Vinny: It's a burglar device actually...
Derek: *(Getting his vision back)* And a good one – a blind burglar can't do much harm.
Vinny: Exactly – and we have the dogs as well.
Hilary: We didn't see any dogs.
Vinny: You'll meet them later. But now, I'd like you to meet my wife, Joan. Joan, Derek and Hilary from Sycamore Grove – the big houses at the top with the double garages.
Joan: Oh yes. *(Hand out)* Hello Hilary.
Hilary: Lovely to meet you Joan. *(Kisses her)*
Derek: *(Kisses Joan)* Great to meet you Joan.
Joan: Hello Derek. Hope you had no trouble finding us?
Derek: Not with your address.
Hilary: We think forty-four Sycamore sounds so wonderful.
Joan: Oh thank you.
Hilary: And your house is really lovely... *(Looks)* with your lovely olde-world telephones...
Joan: We got them especially...
Vinny: Our policy is to mix the old style with the new...
Derek: Absolutely – and that picture out in your hall is very stylish indeed.
Hilary: Of the horses – it's really fabulous.
Joan: *(Trying)* The one of them all galloping?
Derek: Yes – a very stylish painting.
Joan: We have another, nearly the same, in our master bedroom.
Derek: Have you really?
Vinny: *(Trying)* Except, in that one, the horses are all galloping in the other direction...
Joan: And there's more of them...
Vinny: That's right – and some of them are jumping. *(To Derek)* You see, both of us just love collecting pictures of horses.
Joan: I think they look so wild and, at the same time, they have such lovely faces and real sad eyes.
Hilary: You don't actually own any, do you?
Joan: Oh yes, we have three.
Hilary: Do you really?
Joan: Yes.
Hilary: And where do you keep them?
Joan: Well, there's one hanging in the hall and there's another in the master bedroom and we have a little one out in the kitchen.

Hilary: No, no, real horses.

Joan: Real horses? Oh no, we've no real horses.

Vinny: *(Laughing it off)* And certainly not in our master bedroom.

Derek: *(Laughing it off)* Nor hanging in the hall.

Hilary: *(Laughing it off)* Or in the kitchen.

Vinny: No. Very good. Yes. *(An awkward moment)*

Hilary: *(Prompting)* Derek...?

Derek: *(Aroused)* Oh yes of course. *(Goes towards the door)* Left it outside – the shock of seeing Vinny holding two elephants. *(Derek goes outside)*

Hilary: *(To Joan)* Vinny had a handful of elephants when he opened the door.

Joan: *(Merrily)* Had he really?

Derek: *(Coming in)* Now Joan. Hope I got it right. It's red.

(He gives Joan a bottle of wine.)

Hilary: Don't worry Joan – if it should be white, if you're serving fish tonight, just keep it for another time.

Derek: *(Laughs)* It's only vinegar anyhow.

Vinny: *(Bravely)* Not if I know you, Derek, not if I know you. Many thanks indeed. Now, what are we all drinking?

(Joan holds the wine, aghast.)

Derek: *(Laughs)* I can see I got it wrong, Joan.

Vinny: No no...

Derek: But you can blame me – Hilary said bring white because it's Friday and it could be fish but I must confess I'm a meat man myself.

Hilary: Derek, you like fish.

Derek: Oh anything on a plate for Derek.

Vinny: Talking of which, Derek – well of glasses not plates – I think I saw you drinking Bushmills at the club?

Derek: *(Sitting)* Well observed, Vinny.

Vinny: Thank you, Derek – and coming up. *(Goes to the drinks.)*

(Joan would follow Vinny for protection.)

Hilary: *(Sits)* Your kitchen is out there, is it, Joan?

Joan: What? *(Corrects)* Pardon?

Hilary: In our houses – and in Sycamore Downs and Sycamore Lawns – the kitchen is over there. *(Opposite)*

Joan: *(Stunned)* Is it?

Vinny: *(Covering up)* Oh yes, remember we looked at that showhouse – beautiful houses, magnificent layout.

Hilary We like them. But Amanda and Tony have one of these, haven't they, Derek?

Derek: Amanda and Tony, yes – in forty-eight Sycamore.

Vinny: *(Trying hard)* Oh yes a lovely couple.

Hilary And you have the walk-in cloakroom, have you?

Vinny: No, we have the king-size sunken bath en suite in the master bedroom with the mahogany surround and the porcelain taps.

Hilary: That's funny – Amanda and Tony have the walk-in cloakroom.

Derek: I'd say they put that in darling.

Hilary: Very likely. Not coming tonight, are they?

Vinny: Amanda and Tommy? No, they said they couldn't make it.

Derek: No, Amanda and Tony in forty-eight.

Vinny: Oh, Amanda and Tony! No, they couldn't make it either. Now a Bushmills
— and Hilary, I haven't forgotten you.

FOR DISCUSSION

1. At the opening of the play we are introduced to Vinny and Joan. Which of these two characters, do you think, is the dominant one? How do you know?
2. What kind of person is Vinny? What words can you use to describe his characteristics? Do you like him? Why/Why not?
3. Describe the character of Joan? How do you feel towards her? Why do you feel like this?
4. Imagine you are directing this scene. What directions would you give to Joan regarding her body language?
5. If you were putting on a production of this play would you find it difficult to organise all the changes in lighting? Give your ideas on how you might go about this.
6. Do you think Joan is happy in the new house? How do you know what she is feeling?
7. Why is it important to Vinny that the evening is a success? What is he trying to achieve?
8. What is the nature of the conflict in the play?
9. How, do you think, does Joan feel about entertaining Derek and Hilary?
10. Hilary and Derek are meeting Joan for the first time. What kind of impression do you think they get?
11. How do you see the plot developing from here?
12. Do you think this play is a comedy? Why/Why not?

WORK TO DO

If possible, go to see a play. Write a review of the performance. Give the name of the play and the name of the writer. Comment on the plot, characters, setting, scenery, costumes; talk about the quality of the acting. Say who directed the production.

◼ *Increase Your Word Power!*

Can you spell and use the following words correctly?
Undertake, vacancy, versatile, verdict, victim, view, wasteful, weigh.

Unit 6

Film

■ Report on a Visit to the Cinema
14 January 2002

For our film study we decided to go to the cinema to see *The Lord of the Rings*. This film had been given a great deal of publicity and we wanted to see if it lived up to its reputation.

■ *Preparation for Visit*

- Some people in the class had read *The Hobbit* and knew something about the world created by Tolkien.
- We watched a television programme called *Quest for the Ring* which described this imaginary world of Middle-earth in great detail.
- We read extracts from *The Lord of the Rings Official Movie Guide* by Brian Sibley, which explained the techniques used in the making of the film.
- We collected reviews which were published in the newspapers and on the Internet.

BACKGROUND INFORMATION
J.R.R. TOLKIEN

John Ronald Reuel Tolkien was Professor of English at Oxford University during the 1930s. His first book, *The Hobbit*, was written as a serial to be read to his three sons on winter evenings. The main character was Mr Bilbo Baggins who lived in Hobbiton, a village in the Shire. The Hobbits are a race of small people who have a childlike innocence. They are peace-loving and live a simple life. In the book, Bilbo Baggins sets out on a journey full of adventures in lands peopled by strange and terrifying beings. By chance, he finds a magic ring with strange powers.

The Hobbit was so popular that the publishers asked Tolkien to write more stories. It took Tolkien fourteen years to write the story of Bilbo's nephew, Frodo. Frodo inherited the magic ring from his uncle and set out on a dangerous journey to the Land of Mordor to destroy it – it could only be destroyed in the volcanic fires where it had been made.

Tolkien was very critical of his own writing and kept editing and rewriting the stories, but they were eventually published in the three volumes that make up *The Lord of the Rings: The Fellowship of the Ring*, *The Two Towers* and *The Return of The King*.

The Setting

Tolkien's story is set in an imaginary world called Middle-earth, which is really Europe as Tolkien imagined it to be in the dim distant past, before the dawn of history.

Middle-earth is divided into many distinct realms or countries, each inhabited by unique creatures. In his books, Tolkien included maps and drawings which showed the landscape and the inhabitants in great detail: the towns and cities populated by men, the woodland kingdoms of the elves, the underground cave dwellings of the dwarfs and the fiery, volcanic peaks of the land of Mordor.

Tolkien also created a complete language and a history for each of his realms.

The Plot

The Lord of the Rings is the story of a journey through the many lands of Middle-earth. The journey begins at Hobbiton in the Shire where Frodo Baggins and his uncle, Bilbo, live. Bilbo

gives Frodo a ring; it is the most powerful ring in Middle-earth – the One Ring, belonging to the Dark Lord, Sauron, the Lord of the Rings. It is an instrument of absolute evil and must be destroyed before it destroys the people of Middle-earth. Anyone who holds the ring finds it almost impossible to resist its force. Frodo's task is to destroy the ring by throwing it into the fires of Mount Doom in the land of Mordor.

Frodo sets off with three companions, Sam, Pippin and Merry. These three-foot high Hobbits seem to be no match for the evil forces they will meet as they journey through Middle-earth. On their journey they are joined by the Wizard Gandalf, Legolas the Elf, Gimli the Dwarf and humans Aragorn and Boromir. Together, this group form the Fellowship of the Ring.

The film tells the story of their journey and the many obstacles they meet. It is a story of exciting chases and pitched battles with the enemy, and all the time the ring's power to tempt the members of the Fellowship becomes greater.

THE DIRECTOR

The Lord of the Rings was directed by Peter Jackson. Jackson was born in 1961 in New Zealand. As a child he had a very lively imagination and was always reading comics and fantasy books. It was when he was watching the 1933 film *King Kong* that he realised that he wanted more than anything to be a film director. His first movies were shock-horror movies, featuring vampires and monsters. He directed *Braindead*, *Heavenly Creatures* and *The Frighteners* before starting work on *The Lord of the Rings*.

Most people believed that Tolkien's book could not be made into a live-action movie because with over a thousand pages it just seemed to be too long and complicated. Jackson solved this problem by making three films. Although trilogies have been made before, this one is different. Usually each film in a trilogy is complete in itself and tells a story from start to finish; the three films which make up *The Lord of the Rings* are like the instalments of a serial – you need to see all three to get the whole story. Jackson also made all three movies at the same time. He approached it as if he was just making one long movie and the entire process took over two years.

Jackson was aware that *The Lord of the Rings* was one of the best-loved books of the twentieth century. It is estimated that it has been read by over 100 million people. People who loved the book would have very strong ideas about how it should be filmed, and would be very critical if it was not true to the book. At the same time Jackson also wanted his audience to understand and enjoy the film even if they had never read the book. He is quite happy that he has stayed true to 'the heart and spirit' of Tolkien's vision. Advances in technology made it possible for him to bring Middle-earth and its people alive in a way that would not have been possible even ten years ago.

■ *Making The Film*

THE STORYBOARD

Before shooting the films Peter Jackson made a 'storyboard' of all three movies. A storyboard consists of thousands of tiny sketches or frames showing all the scenes in the film. When the storyboard was complete, Jackson made the entire picture as an 'animatic', i.e. a filmed version of all the still pictures. He added a soundtrack to the animatic, which included the dialogue, the music and the sound effects. He found this a great help in planning the filming of the actual movie.

FINDING LOCATIONS

Jackson felt that his native New Zealand would be the ideal location for the films as it contained all the different landscapes that were needed – snow-capped mountains, forests, marshes, deserts and volcanoes. Two years before filming began, seventy suitable locations were found and carefully prepared as Jackson wanted them to be as realistic as possible. For example, a year before filming started, flowers and vegetables were planted in the gardens of Hobbiton.

PROPS

Hundreds of thousands of props (short for properties) were used, and each one had to be either found or made. Props include everything from the characters' personal belongings, such as swords, to the various objects seen on the sets, such as tables, books, cups and saucers.

The most important prop was the ring itself, because it is such a significant image in the film great care went into its design. Although it is just a normal-sized ring, every time it is shown a close-up shot is used, so that it seems much bigger. Jackson also added sound effects to give the impression that the ring is a living, breathing entity – it had to be more than just a piece of metal.

Some of the props had to be made in two scales, as they had to look normal when used by men but over-large when used by the Hobbits.

The swords and other weapons used by the main characters are very elaborate, beautifully inscribed and decorated. In making the swords, the same techniques as hundreds of years ago were used. The thousands of 'extras' used in the huge battle scenes had swords made out of semi-rigid rubber, painted the colour of steel so that they looked realistic. This meant that these scenes could be filmed without anyone getting hurt.

COSTUMES

Costumes had to be designed for twenty main characters in the three films, dozens of minor characters and thousands of extras. Also, because *The Lord of the Rings* is the story of a journey, costumes had to be made which showed signs of wear and tear. This meant that each of the Hobbits, for example, had at least five different costumes during the course of the filming. Only natural materials were used in the making of the clothes worn by the Hobbits, and the overall effect was a kind of 'home-made' look.

Each group of characters in the film was given an individual look; the elves, for example, were dressed in layers of fine, delicate fabrics, while the dwarfs had costumes of leather.

■ *Film Review*

Having done our background research we set out to see the film on 14 January 2002 in Dublin's Savoy Cinema.

GENRE

The *Lord of the Rings* belongs to the fantasy genre, although Peter Jackson feels that it is perhaps more action-adventure than fantasy.

THEME

At first sight the main theme would seem to be the fight between Good, in the form of the Fellowship, and Evil, in the form of the Dark Lord, Sauron. However, it is not quite that simple and the film explores many themes such as friendship, loyalty, love, fellowship and courage. It also deals with some difficult decisions, which have to be made by some of the characters, such as giving up personal power and ambition for the greater good. It also explores the question of Nature versus the Machine. Sauron has mines and factories at his disposal to create armies and weapons, while the Fellowship have only their courage and their faith in what they are doing.

VISUAL QUALITIES

We choose the Savoy Cinema as the film was advertised as being of great visual quality and we wanted to experience the maximum effect on the big screen.

We were not disappointed. Visually, the film was spectacular. The settings were realistic and constructed with great attention to detail. The most magnificent setting was the Argonath, two mighty statues hundreds of feet tall, standing at either side of the River Anduin, marking the boundary of an ancient kingdom.

The natural, unspoilt beauty of New Zealand is a strong feature of this movie – some locations were totally isolated and had never been settled.

The attention to detail seen in the costumes and props adds greatly to the visual impact.

ACTING

The acting was brilliant. We felt that the casting was excellent as the actors seemed to suit their parts very well. Jackson used a mixture of well-known Hollywood actors such as Sean Bean and Cate Blanchett, newcomers such as Orlando Bloom, and the English Shakespearean actor, Ian McKellen.

We all agreed that Sean Bean's portrayal of Boromir was particularly powerful, as it showed a character developing and changing as the film progresses. Bean had to portray a complex and tortured character – a man trying to cope with the burden of despair because of the plight of his people, a man trying to resist the temptation to use the ring for his own ends, his own pride and ambition. His character is further complicated by the bonds of friendship which grow between the members of the Fellowship; Boromir starts off as arrogant and aloof, but as the adventures unfold he is drawn closer to his companions as bonds of love and loyalty develop.

Christopher Lee was cast as Saruman, the head of the Order of Wizards. Lee is famous for his many portrayals of Dracula. In *The Lord of the Rings* his screen presence is such that he seems to tower over the others. He brilliantly plays the part of a great man who has succumbed to temptation.

DIALOGUE

Some of the characters speak an old form of English, and this gives the film a feeling of being real or genuine. Tolkien was a student of languages and created separate languages for the many races and cultures of Middle-earth. Throughout the film these are used and add greatly to the overall impact.

SPECIAL EFFECTS

In a world of magic, wizards and elves, special effects will feature strongly. Although we knew that scale models and computer graphics had been used for some of the more elaborate sets in the film, it was impossible to say where the special effects ended and reality began. Not only are the effects technically excellent and convincing, they have been constructed with great artistry and add greatly to the impact of the story.

Several of the monsters faced by the Fellowship, such as the Watcher in the Water and the Balrog, are computer generated, but come across as genuinely fearsome and terrifying.

MUSIC

An orchestral soundtrack was written specially for the film. While there is one recurring theme, in each scene the music changes to reflect the mood and the events which are taking place. We felt that the music was very well suited to the film.

When we came out of the cinema we could not believe that three hours had passed. We had been spellbound by the film and would highly recommend it. It has a PG 12 rating, which we felt was correct as younger children would find parts of it terrifying.

The second and third instalments are due in December 2002 and December 2003. It will be difficult to wait that long to see how the story ends, but we can always find a copy of Tolkien's book and see for ourselves what happens.

■ Key Assignments

I have made a close study of a number of texts from each
of the following:

The work of a songwriter, singer or group.

☐ Date _____

A range of contemporary poetry or the work of a contemporary poet.

☐ Date _____

A short story writer or anthology.

☐ Date _____

A novel or extracts from a novel.

☐ Date _____

A play.

☐ Date _____

A film.

☐ Date _____

And I have kept evidence of my work. I have kept one or more samples of my own creative
writing and where possible I have used IT.

☐ Date _____

■ Past Examination Questions

The song, 'Ironic', is taken from Alanis Morissette's CD *Jagged Little Pill*. Read the words of
the song carefully and then answer the questions which follow it.

Ironic

An old man turned ninety-eight
He won the lottery and died the next day
It's a black fly in your Chardonnay
It's a death row pardon two minutes too late
Isn't it ironic...don't you think

Chorus

It's like rain on your wedding day
It's a free ride when you've already paid
It's the good advice that you just don't take
Who would've thought...it figures

Mr Play It Safe was afraid to fly
He packed his suitcase and kissed his kids good-bye
He waited his whole damn life to take that flight
And as the plane crashed down he thought
'Well isn't this nice...'
And isn't it ironic...don't you think

Repeat Chorus

Well life has a funny way of sneaking up on you
When you think everything's okay and everything's going right
And life has a funny way of helping you out when
You think everything's gone wrong and everything blows up
In your face

A traffic jam when you're already late
A no-smoking sign on your cigarette break
It's like ten thousand spoons when all you need is a knife
It's meeting the man of my dreams
And then meeting his beautiful wife
And isn't it ironic...don't you think
A little too ironic...and yeah I really do think

Repeat Chorus

Life has a funny way of sneaking up on you
Life has a funny, funny way of helping you out
Helping you out

1. (a) What do you think the word 'ironic' means in the song? (5 marks)
   (b) Select a line or lines from the song which had particular meaning for you. Explain
       your choice. (10 marks)
   (c) 'Modern song writers are the poets of young people'. Discuss this statement. (15
       marks)
2. Name a novel or short story you have studied.
   (a) Briefly summarise its plot. (6 marks)
   (b) Describe its setting. (6 marks)
   (c) Give a profile of the central character. (6 marks)
   (d) Discuss the theme. (6 marks)
   (e) Give an assessment of the work. (6 marks)

3. Read this extract adapted from *Angela's Ashes*, a childhood memoir by Frank McCourt, and then answer the questions which follow it.

Angela's Ashes

My father and mother should have stayed in New York where they met and married, and where I was born. Instead, they returned to Ireland when I was four, my brother, Malachy, three, the twins, Oliver and Eugene, barely one, and my sister, Margaret dead and gone.

When I look back on my childhood I wonder how I survived it at all. It was, of course, a miserable childhood; the happy childhood is hardly worth your while.

Above all – we were wet.

Out in the Atlantic Ocean great sheets of rain gathered to drift slowly up the river Shannon and settle forever in Limerick. The rain dampened the city from the feast of the Circumcision to New Year's Eve. It created a cacophony of hacking coughs, bronchial rattles, asthmatic wheezes, consumptive croaks. It turned noses into fountains, lungs into bacterial sponges. It provoked cures galore; to ease the catarrah you boiled onions in milk blackened with pepper; for the congested passages you made a paste of boiled flour and nettles, wrapped it in a rag, and slapped it, sizzling, on the chest.

From October to April the walls of Limerick glistened with the damp. Clothes never dried: tweed and woollen coats housed living things, sometimes sprouted mysterious vegetations. In pubs, steam rose from damp bodies and garments, to be inhaled with cigarette and pipe smoke laced with the stale fumes of spilled stout and whiskey.

The rain drove us into the church – our refuge, our strength, our only dry place. At Mass, Benediction, novenas, we huddled in great damp clumps, dozing through priest drone, while steam rose again from our clothes to mingle with the sweetness of incense, flowers and candles.

Limerick gained a reputation for piety, but we knew it was only the rain.

(a) What age was the writer when he returned to Ireland? (3 marks)
(b) What was the effect of the constant rain and dampness on people's health? (6 marks)
(c) What was the cure for the congested passages? (3 marks)
(d) 'Limerick gained a reputation for piety, but we knew it was only the rain.' Why did the writer come to this conclusion? (6 marks)
(e) Select one example of effective writing from the extract and account for your choice. (6 marks)
(f) Were you depressed or amused by this extract? Account for your answer. (6 marks)
4. Name a poem or popular song that you have studied.

_____

(a) Give the name of its writer or performer. (2 marks)
(b) What are the main ideas in the poem or song? (8 marks)

(c) Select a line or phrase which you regard as central to the poem or song. Account for your choice. (5 marks)

(d) I like this poem or song because . . . (10 marks)

(e) Mention one point of comparison between this poem or song and another poem or song that you have studied. (5 marks)

5. Read this extract from *The Field*, a play by John B. Keane, and then answer the questions which follow.

The Field

ACT ONE

Action takes place in the bar of a public house in Carrigthomond, a small village in the south-west of Ireland.

Time: *The present – noon.*

Leamy Flanagan *sweeping.*

Enter The 'Bird' O'Donnell.

Bird: Give us a half of whiskey for God's sake, Leamy, to know would anything put a bit of heat in me.

Leamy: 'Tis freezing!

Bird: 'Tis weather for snowmen and Eskimos. Where's your father?

Leamy: He's gone down to O'Connor's for the paper... That'll be half a dollar.

Bird: Take your time, will you? Why aren't you at school?

Leamy: Still on my Easter holidays. How's trade?

Bird: Same as it always is...lousy!

Enter Mick Flanagan.

Mick: I thought I told you to sweep out the shop.

Leamy: It's nearly finished.

Mick: You've been long enough about it. Good morning, Bird.

Bird: How're you, Mick?

Mick: Did you clean out the store?

Leamy: I've done the half of it.

Mick: The half of it! – I told you to do the whole of it.

Leamy: I had to look after the kids while my mother was feeding the baby.

Mick: 'Tis too fond you are of hanging around with women and children. 'Tis a daughter you should have been, not a son. Go and ask your mother will the dinner be ready soon.

Leamy: Yes, Da.

Mick: And finish off that store or you'll hear all about it from me.

Exit Leamy. Bird whistles.

Mick: In the name of goodness, will you cut out that bloody whistling! One would swear you were a canary.

The whistler, whose name is 'Bird' O'Donnell, looks at Mick in surprise.

Bird: *(Throwing a ring at a ring-board)* I thought you liked whistling?

Mick: Whistling, yes. I like whistling. But that bloody noise you're making isn't whistling.

Bird comes to the counter. He has thrown two rings and leaves the other four on the counter.

Bird: Give me another half-one. It might improve my pipes.

Mick: Have you the price of it?

Bird draws some change from his pocket and places it on the counter.

Mick: *(<u>Counts money first, gets off stool, fills whiskey</u>)* Who did you take down now?

Bird: Take down! That's illegal. That is! I could get you put in jail for that. A pity I hadn't a witness. 'Twould pay me better than calf-buying.

Mick places whiskey on counter and takes price of it which he deposits in cash register. Bird scoops up the rest of the money.

Mick: There must be great money in calf-buying.

Bird: Not as much as there is in auctioneering.

Mick: *(Goes to stove, to poke and put fuel on fire).* Very funny! Very funny! Don't forget I have to use my head all the time.

Bird: *(Leftish along counter)* Not half as much as I do. Did you ever try to take down a small farmer?

Bird sits in the angle of bar watching what is going on. Enter a small dumpy woman wearing a black-coloured coat. She is piled with parcels. She is Maggie Butler, a widow.

Mick: Good morning, ma'am. Ah! Is it Mrs. Butler? I didn't see you in a dog's age.

Maggie: Good morning to you, Mr Flanagan. I'm afraid I don't be in the village very often.

Mick: What will I get for you?

Maggie: *(Laughs at the idea)* 'Tisn't a drink I'm looking for, Mr. Flanagan. 'Tis other business entirely that brought me. I've been thinking of paying you a call for some time.

Mick: You wouldn't be selling property now, by any chance? The bit of land or the house or maybe both?

Maggie: No, not the house! Lord save us, do you want me on the side of the road or stuck in a room in some back lane in Carrigthomond? 'Tis the field I came to see you about. I'm a poor widow woman and I want the best price I can get. They say you're an honest man to get the last halfpenny for a person.

Mick: *(Suddenly expansive, comes from behind counter)* Sit down here, Maggie girl. I can guarantee you, you won't be wronged in this house. You came to the right spot. Am I right, Bird?

Bird: No better man. As straight as a telephone pole.

(a) How do you think an audience would react to Mick Flanagan's treatment of his son, Leamy? Give a reason for your answer. (6 marks)

(b) What does the stage direction underlined in the extract tell the audience about the character of Mick Flanagan? (6 marks)

(c) How does Mick Flanagan's behaviour change as a result of the entry of Maggie Butler? Refer to the extract in your answer. (6 marks)

(d) You have been asked to design the set (stage) for this scene. Describe what your set would look like. You could include reference to furniture, lighting or any other items that an audience would see on stage. (12 marks)

6. Name a short story or novel which you have studied.

(a) Briefly describe (i) the setting and (ii) the plot of the short story or novel. (10 marks)
(c) Select three adjectives (descriptive words, e.g. *honest, brave*) which would describe the main character in the novel or short story. Give reasons for your choice of adjectives. (10 marks)
(c) If you had an opportunity to interview the author of the short story or novel, what two questions would you ask him/her about his/her work? Why would you ask these questions? (10 marks)
7. The poem *The Choosing* by Liz Lochhead, printed below, deals with the relationship between two girls.
Read the words of the poem carefully and then answer the questions which follow it.

The Choosing

We were first equal Mary and I
with the same coloured ribbons in mouse-coloured hair,
and with equal shyness
we curtseyed to the lady councillor
for copies of Collins' Children's Classics.
First equal, equally proud.

Best friends too Mary and I
a common bond in being cleverest (equal)
in our small school's small class.
I remember
the competition for top desk
or to read aloud the lesson
at school service.
And my terrible fear
of her superiority at sums.

I remember the housing scheme
Where we both stayed.
The same house, different homes.
where the choices were made.

I don't know exactly why they moved,
but anyway they went.
Something about a three-apartment
and a cheaper rent.
But from the top deck of the high-school bus
I'd glimpse among the others on the corner
Mary's father, mufflered, contrasting strangely
with the elegant greyhounds by his side.

He didn't believe in high-school education,

especially for girls,
or in forking out for uniforms.

Ten years later on a Saturday –
I am coming home from the library –
sitting near me on the bus,
Mary
with a husband who is tall,
curly haired, has eyes
for no one else but Mary.
His arms are round the full-shaped vase
that is her body.
Oh, you can see where the attraction lies
in Mary's life –
not that I envy her, really.

And I am coming from the library
with my arms full of books.
I think of the prizes that were ours for the taking
and wonder when the choices got made
we don't remember making.

(a) Describe the relationship between the girls while they were at school. (5 marks)
(b) How has life changed for both girls since Mary moved house? (5 marks)
(c) 'Not that I envy her, really.'
   How do you think the speaker in the poem feels about Mary's life now? Give a reason for your answer. (5 marks)
(d) What, in your view, is the theme (main idea) of this poem? Give a reason for your answer. (5 marks)
(e) Compare this poem with another poem or song that you have studied. You may discuss how they are similar or how they differ. (10 marks)

8. Read this extract from *Lies Of Silence* by Brian Moore, and then answer the questions that follow it. In the extract the IRA break into a house owned by Michael Dillon and his wife Moira.

Lies Of Silence

'Put that down', a voice said. 'Stay where you are.'
A blinding light shone in his face. 'Where's the switch?' a second voice said. They were young voices, flat, male, Ulster accents. The blinding light came closer.
   The hall light came on.
   Facing him, a flashlight in one hand and a revolver in the other, was a hooded figure, its head masked in a woollen balaclava helmet, the eyeholes cut wide showing the cheekbones. The intruder wore woollen gloves, a cheap blue Western-style shirt with metal-

clip buttons, faded jeans and running shoes. Behind him, standing by the light switch, was another, similarly dressed figure, also pointing a revolver.

He had seen them on the evening television news and in newspaper photographs, theatrical figures, firing revolver volleys over paramilitary graves, marching in parades with banners and flags. But like most people he kept well away from the events themselves so that now, for the first time in his life, he was looking at them, here in his house, real revolvers, faceless, staring eyes, scruffy boys in woollen masks. Who are they? Are they Protestants or Catholics – UDA or IRA? Is this one of those mistakes where they come in and shoot the wrong person?

'What do you want?' He heard the fear in his voice.

'IRA. Where's your wife?'

'She's upstairs, asleep.'

As he spoke, there was a sound of footsteps in the kitchen. Two more masked intruders came through the kitchen into the hall. One of them was very tall and carried a walkie-talkie. Both were armed. They went into the darkened sitting-room, then came out again. The tall one shut off his walkie-talkie, which had been making a crackling sound.

'Go up and bring her down,' the one with the flashlight told Dillon, then turned and pointed to the smallest member of the group. 'Volunteer, you go with him.'

The small one kept his revolver pointed at Dillon's back as they went upstairs. When they reached the landing, Dillon said to him, 'Wait here, would you, I don't want to frighten her.'

Blue eyes white-circled by the holes of the balaclava studied him for a moment. 'Is there a phone in there?'

'Yes.'

'Then I have to come in with you.'

Dillon switched on the landing light which permitted him to see into the bedroom. She was still asleep. He went into the bedroom and, as he did, she sat up.

'Oh!' she called in a half-shriek as though wakened from a frightening dream. At once he ran to the bed and caught hold of her. 'It's all right, Moira, it's all right. It's me.'

Oh, Christ,' she said. 'What are you doing up at this hour?'

Suddenly, the bedroom light came on. Standing by the switch was the small masked intruder, pointing his revolver at them. 'Ohh!' Moira gasped, but Dillon held her, pressing her tightly to him.

'Shsh! It's all right.'

She stared over his shoulder at the masked man, and then, surprisingly, eased herself out of Dillon's embrace. 'Who's he? What's he doing here?' she said in an aggrieved voice.

'Get up,' said the masked man.

'What do you want from us?' she said. She did not sound afraid.

(a) How many IRA men entered the house in all? (2 marks)

(b) List the equipment brought on the raid by the IRA. (5 marks)

(c) In your opinion which of the IRA men is the leader? Explain your answer. (5 marks)

(d) Who do you think is more afraid of the IRA men, Michael Dillon or Moira? Explain your answer. (5 marks)

(e) Show how dialogue plays an important role in this extract. (5 marks)

(f) This novel has been described as a thriller. What qualities of a thriller do you see in this extract? Account for your answer. (8 marks)

9. The song *Fast Car* by Tracy Chapman tells the story of a girl who wants to begin a new life. Read the words of the song carefully and then answer the questions that follow it.

Fast Car

You got a fast car
I want a ticket to anywhere
Maybe we can make a deal
Maybe together we can get somewhere

Anyplace is better
Starting from zero got nothing to lose
Maybe we'll make something
But me myself I got nothing to prove

You got a fast car
And I got a plan to get us out of here
I been working at the convenience store
Managed to save just a little bit of money
We won't have to drive too far
Just cross the border and into the city
You and I can both get jobs
And finally see what it means to be living

You see my old man's got a problem
He lives with the bottle that's the way it is
He says body's too old for working
I say his body's too young to look like his
My mama went off and left him
She wanted more from life than he could give
I said somebody's got to take care of him
So I quit school and that's what I did

You got a fast car
But is it fast enough so we can fly away
We gotta make a decision
We leave tonight or live and die this way

268

I remember we were driving
driving in your car
The speed so fast
I felt like I was drunk
City lights lay out before us
And your arm felt nice
wrapped round my shoulder
And I had the feeling that I belonged
And I had a feeling I could be someone
be someone, be someone

You got a fast car
And we go cruising entertain ourselves,
You still ain't got a job
And I work in a market as a checkout girl
I know things will get better
You'll find work and I'll get promoted
We'll move out of the shelter
Buy a big house and live in the suburbs

You got a fast car
And I got a job that pays all our bills
You stay out drinking late at the bar
see more of your friends that you do of your kids
I'd always hoped for better
Thought maybe together you and me would find it
I got no plans
I ain't going nowhere
So take your fast car and keep on driving

You got a fast car
But is it fast enough so you can fly away
You gotta make a decision
You leave tonight or live and die this way.

(a) What in her life does the singer in the song wish to leave behind? (5 marks)
(b) Were her plans for a new life successful? Give reasons for your answer. (5 marks)
(c) In songs and poetry repetition is often used. What, in your opinion, is the effect of
    repeating the phrase 'You got a fast car'? (5 marks)
(d) What is ironic about the ending of the song? (5 marks)
(e) Songs and poems often express feelings or tell a story. Choose a song or poem that
    you have studied and discuss it under the following headings: (10 marks)
    (i) The story it tells or the feelings it expresses.
    (ii) The way it tells the story or the way it expresses feelings.

10. Read these poems and then answer the questions that follow.

A Time To Talk

When a friend calls to me from the road
And slows his horse to a meaning walk
I don't stand still and look around
On all the hills I haven't hoed
And shout from where I am, 'What is it?'
No, not as there is a time to talk.
I thrust my hoe in the mellow ground,
Blade-end up and five feet tall,
And plod: I go up to the stone wall
For a friendly visit

Robert Frost

In The Cafe

People stare
At people staring
At other people
Staring
And all will go on staring
Until
All the lonely tea-leaves
Of all their tea-cups
Show

Liam Ó Muirthile, translated from the Irish 'Sa Chaifé' by Eoghan Ó hAnluain

(a) Which poem do you prefer? Give a reason for your answer. (5 marks)
(b) Select a line from one of the poems that you particularly liked. Say why you chose this line. (5 marks)
(c) Describe in your own words the differences in the scenes suggested in each poem. (10 marks)
(d) Compare any **one** of the poems with a poem or a song that you have studied. (10 marks)

11. Read this extract from *Fawlty Towers* by John Cleese and Connie Booth and then answer the questions which follow.

Fawlty Towers

In this excerpt from the script of 'The Germans' episode of *Fawlty Towers*, Basil is suffering from the effects of having been knocked on the head in a hotel fire-drill. Unaware of his condition, he is waiting for some German guests to arrive.

BASIL:	*(Masterfully)* Manuel!
MISS TIBBS:	Oh Mr Fawlty!
BASIL:	Ah, good evening.
MISS TIBBS:	Are you all right now?
BASIL:	Perfectly, thank you. (To MANUEL) Take this to the room please, dear.

(MANUEL takes the case, somewhat taken aback)

MISS GATSBY:	Are you sure you're all right?
BASIL:	Perfectly, thank you. Right as rain. *(He makes his way a little unsteadily towards the desk, but misses. He reappears and goes correctly to his position behind the desk. MANUEL rushes up.)*
MANUEL:	You OK?
BASIL:	Fine, thank you, dear. You go and have a lie-down.
MANUEL:	Qué?
BASIL:	Ah, there you are. Would you take my case . . . How did you get that?
MANUEL:	What?
BASIL:	Oh never mind . . . take . . . take it upstairs!
MANUEL:	Qué?
BASIL:	Take it . . . take it . . .
MANUEL:	*(Staring)* I go get Polly.
BASIL:	I've already had one. Take it!
MANUEL:	What?
BASIL:	Take it, take it now . . . *(MANUEL hurries off)* Tch! The people I have to deal with . . . *(He looks up to see a couple approaching the desk. He beams at them.)*
ELDERLY GERMAN:	Sprechen Sie Deutsch?
BASIL:	. . . Beg your pardon?
ELDERLY GERMAN:	Entschuldigen Sie, bitte, konnen Sie Deutsch sprechen?
BASIL:	. . . I'm sorry, could you say that again?
GERMAN LADY:	You speak German?
BASIL:	Oh German! I'm sorry, I thought there was something wrong with you. Of course, the Germans!
GERMAN LADY:	You speak German?
BASIL:	Well . . . er . . . a little . . . I get by.
GERMAN LADY:	Ein Bisschen.
ELDERLY GERMAN:	Ah – wir wollen ein Auto mieten.

271

BASIL:	*(Nodding helpfully)* Well, why not?
ELDERLY GERMAN:	Bitte.
BASIL:	Yes, a little bit tricky . . . Would you mind saying it again?
GERMAN LADY:	Please?
BASIL:	Could you repeat . . . amplify . . . you know, reiterate? Come on! Yes?
ELDERLY GERMAN:	Wir . . .
BASIL:	Wir? . . . Yes, well, we'll come back to that.
ELDERLY GERMAN:	. . . Wollen . . .
BASIL:	*(To himself)* Vollen . . . Voluntary?
ELDERLY GERMAN:	Ein Auto mieten.
BASIL:	Owtoe . . . out to . . . Oh I see! You're volunteering to go out and get some meat. Not necessary! We have meat here!
(Pause; the couple are puzzled)	
BASIL:	*(Shouting very loudly)* Vee haf meat hier . . . in ze buildink! *(He mimes a cow's horns)*
BASIL:	Moo. *(POLLY comes in)*
BASIL:	Ah, Polly, just explaining about the meat.
POLLY:	Oh! We weren't expecting you.
BASIL:	Oh, weren't you? *(Hissing through his teeth)* They're Germans. Don't mention the war

(a) How is it shown in the extract that Basil is suffering from the effects of having been knocked on the head? (5 marks)

(b) Basil Fawlty is frequently used as an example of someone lacking good communication skills. Do you agree? Refer to the extract in your answer. (5 marks)

(c) *Fawlty Towers* is considered to be a very humorous drama. Do you agree? Refer to the extract in your answer. (5 marks)

(d) Write a brief report on your favourite television comedy programme. Say what the programme is about and why you particularly like it. You may **not** use *Fawlty Towers* as your favourite television comedy programme.

12. You have been asked to write a short review for your school magazine of a novel **or** a short story **or** a play you have studied. (30 marks)

Name the novel **or** short story **or** play.

Your review should deal with the following:

• What the novel **or** the short story **or** the play is about.

• The most interesting character in the novel **or** short story **or** play.

• Why you would recommend others to read the novel **or** short story **or** play.